AGAINST NEW MATERIALISMS

Also Available from Bloomsbury

New Realism and Contemporary Philosophy, ed. Gregor Kroupa
and Jure Simoniti
Romanticism and Speculative Realism, ed. Chris Washington
and Anne C. McCarthy
Is There an Object Oriented Architecture: Engaging Graham Harman, ed.
Joseph Bedford

AGAINST NEW MATERIALISMS

Edited by Benjamin Boysen & Jesper Lundsfryd Rasmussen

BLOOMSBURY ACADEMIC
LONDON • NEW YORK • OXFORD • NEW DELHI • SYDNEY

BLOOMSBURY ACADEMIC
Bloomsbury Publishing Plc
50 Bedford Square, London, WC1B 3DP, UK
1385 Broadway, New York, NY 10018, USA
29 Earlsfort Terrace, Dublin 2, Ireland

BLOOMSBURY, BLOOMSBURY ACADEMIC and the Diana logo are
trademarks of Bloomsbury Publishing Plc

First published in Great Britain 2023
This paperback edition printed in 2025

Copyright © Benjamin Boysen, Jesper Lundsfryd Rasmussen and Contributors, 2023

Benjamin Boysen, Jesper Lundsfryd Rasmussen have asserted their right under the
Copyright, Designs and Patents Act, 1988, to be identified as Editors of this work.

Series design by Charlotte Daniels
Cover image: Abstract Marble Waves Acrylic Background. Gray Orange
Marbling Texture. Agate Ripple Pattern. (© oxygen / Getty Images)

All rights reserved. No part of this publication may be reproduced or transmitted
in any form or by any means, electronic or mechanical, including photocopying,
recording, or any information storage or retrieval system, without prior
permission in writing from the publishers.

Bloomsbury Publishing Plc does not have any control over, or responsibility for,
any third-party websites referred to or in this book. All internet addresses given in this
book were correct at the time of going to press. The author and publisher regret any
inconvenience caused if addresses have changed or sites have ceased
to exist, but can accept no responsibility for any such changes.

A catalogue record for this book is available from the British Library.

A catalog record for this book is available from the Library of Congress.

ISBN: HB: 978-1-3501-7287-6
       PB: 978-1-3503-3108-2
       ePDF: 978-1-3501-7288-3
       eBook: 978-1-3501-7289-0

Typeset by Integra Software Services Pvt. Ltd.

To find out more about our authors and books visit www.bloomsbury.com
and sign up for our newsletters.

CONTENTS

Preface   vii

INTRODUCTION: LEAVING MODERNITY FOR THE WORLD OF THE TEACUP
    Benjamin Boysen & Jesper Lundsfryd Rasmussen   1

OBJECT-ORIENTED ONTOLOGY AND THE PASSION FOR THE REAL
    Zahi Zalloua   43

CORRELATIONIST STERILITY: A CRITIQUE OF THE ABSOLUTIZATION OF CONTINGENCY IN MEILLASSOUX
    Diana Khamis   59

FACTS, NOT FOSSILS: NEW VS SPECULATIVE REALISM
    Markus Gabriel   73

PRODUCTION OF REAL PRESENCE: WHAT PRESENCE CANNOT CONVEY
    Benjamin Boysen   91

INTERPRETING THE FACTS: NIETZSCHE AND THE NEW REALISTS
    Hans Ruin   109

MODERN THROUGH AND THROUGH: LATOUR'S QUASI-OBJECT AS A MODERN MIX-UP
    Jesper Lundsfryd Rasmussen   125

ACKNOWLEDGING MATERIALITY WITHOUT FETISHIZING IT: SOME PITFALLS IN SPEAKING FOR MATTER
    Alf Hornborg   143

THE KANTIAN CATASTROPHE? ANTI-CORRELATIONISM AND THE ABSOLUTE
    Lars Lodberg and Jacob Lautrup   161

NEW MATERIALISMS, NATURAL HISTORY, AND HUMAN HISTORY
  Interview with Dipesh Chakrabarty by Benjamin Boysen &
  Jesper Lundsfryd Rasmussen   177

THE REAL KANT & HEGEL: A POSTSCRIPT ON THE CRITIQUE OF
SPECULATIVE REALISM AND OBJECT-ORIENTED ONTOLOGY
  Andrew Cole   187

List of Contributors   211
Index   213

PREFACE

The Emergence of the new materialisms (e.g., speculative realism, new materialism, object-oriented ontology, dark ecology, agential realism, and actor-network theory) has been one of the most influential trends in the humanities, social sciences, and the art world in the last decades. Cutting across the richly variegated theories that sometimes follow quite divergent trajectories, the new materialisms share a radical realist commitment critical of all sorts of "correlationisms," accentuating instead the need to put human subjectivity under erasure.

The ardent calls of the new materialisms for a reconnection with immediate reality have left a deep impact and sparked widespread enthusiasm and hope for a renewal of the humanities and the political imagination. As has the critique of modernity for having endowed us with a fatal misconception of human exceptionality, which, many argue, has led us into our current predicaments – which above all means the climate crisis. With the promise to regain immediate reality and to teach us ontological humility by reorientating our place in the cosmos, the new materialisms embody a pledge to revolutionize our understanding of the universe, allowing us to join forces with new politico-ethical communities stretching across human and nonhuman realms.

However, discarding modernity and human subjectivity comes with a heavy price.

For the theories advanced by the the new materialisms entail serious theoretical and practical problems. It is these problems that are at the center of *Against New Materialisms*. The present anthology provides a comprehensive scrutiny of this popular theory complex from the angle of ontology (Markus Gabriel), historical materialism and political theory (Alf Hornborg), culture, aesthetics, and intellectual history (Benjamin Boysen), theory and psychoanalysis (Zahi Zalloua), phenomenology and hermeneutics (Hans Ruin), metaphysics and philosophy of modernity (Jesper Rasmussen), philosophy of nature (Diana Khamis), epistemology (Lars Lodberg and Jacob Lautrup), and ecological history (Dipesh Chakrabarty).

The anthology, with its interdisciplinary approach, attempts to achieve a more nuanced understanding of one of the most towering trends in the academies and our culture today, thus enabling us to take an important step toward apprehending our time in thoughts.

An age whose clarification we still need to achieve.

INTRODUCTION: LEAVING MODERNITY FOR THE WORLD OF THE TEACUP

Benjamin Boysen & Jesper Lundsfryd Rasmussen

In her Nobel Lecture in Literature, "The Tender Narrator," delivered on Saturday December 7, 2019 at the Swedish Academy in Stockholm, Olga Tokarczuk paints a dark picture of our contemporary global situation stressing "the painful impression […] that there is something wrong with the world."[1] She draws attention to the current "climate emergency and the political crisis" as the end result of a disenchanted modernity in which "[g]reed, failure to respect nature, selfishness, lack of imagination, endless rivalry and lack of responsibility have reduced the world to the status of an object that can be cut into pieces, used up and destroyed." Unlike Jean-François Lyotard, who claimed that we cannot sustain our needs for great, universalizing narratives, Tokarczuk finds that the collapse of *les grand récits* following in the wake of postmodernity has left us with a crestfallen and atomized mechanical world. Therefore, she believes that the essential task for the writer today is to recreate a holistic sense of belonging to a living, vibrant world: "*That is why I believe I must tell stories as if the world were a living, single entity, constantly forming before our eyes, and as if we were a small and at the same time powerful part of it.*"[2]

Tokarczuk recollects how fairytales read to her by her mother achieved just that. She recalls how "I listened to these fairy tales with flushed cheeks and tears in my eyes, because I believed deeply that objects have their own problems and emotions, as well as a sort of social life, entirely comparable to our human one."[3] Indeed, in her childhood universe of fairytales, everything "was alive […] the entire visible and invisible world."

However, as she grew up and became an adult, "everything became different, less nuanced, simpler."[4] The subtle and immediate perception of the world that she experienced as a child gave way to the crude, compartmentalized, and abstract notions of the adult world. Moreover, the leveling perception of the mediated categorial thinking of adulthood went hand in hand with a harsh disenchantment. So, as she grew older, she began to have doubts, and the deep feeling that all things constituting the universe (animate as inanimate) "were living beings that mapped our space and built a sense of belonging"[5] was thus "replaced by the din of the city, the murmur of computers, the thunder of airplanes flying past overhead, and the exhausting white noise of oceans of information." In other words, for Tokarczuk, becoming an adult meant being introduced to a relentless modernity in which "[t]he world's whisper fell silent." Instead of the *sense of belonging* that characterized her childhood perception of the universe, the adulthood of modernity reared her to a world of chill atomization and radical *unbelonging*: "Everything is separate from everything else, everything lives apart, without any connection."[6] Zooming out from her personal story of growing up, Tokarczuk makes her own tale exemplary of the modern world and the dire situation now:

> The world is dying, and we are failing to notice. We fail to see that the world is becoming a collection of things and incidents, a lifeless expanse in which we move around lost and lonely, tossed here and there by somebody else's decisions, constrained by an incomprehensible fate, a sense of being the plaything of the major forces of history or chance. Our spirituality is either vanishing or becoming superficial and ritualistic. Or else we are just becoming the followers of simple forces—physical, social, and economic—that move us around as if we were zombies. And in such a world we really are zombies.[7]

Today's world of fatally accelerating climate crisis, apparent political impotence and fatalism, socioeconomic insecurity, specialization, and secularization means that we moderns are consigned to living the numb and mindless life of a zombie. Hence, with reference to Hans Christian Andersen's fairytale, "The Teapot," which her mother read to her when she was a child, Tokarczuk concludes her recollection of her childhood memories by expressing a yearning for the world before the fall of adulthood and modernity: "This is why I long for that other world, the world of the teapot."[8]

Entering "That Other World, the World of the Teapot"

Tokarczuk's declared longing is shared by many others today. Her sentiments and arguments resonate emphatically with a strong cultural current in the last decades that can, perhaps, best be characterized by a shared feeling within modernity of having lost, and needing to recapture, reality. In other words, Tokarczuk's Nobel Lecture is representative of a dominant *Zeitgeist* in which "reality" serves as a mantra, a means to exorcise the "unreality" of ontological and political alienation and invoke a dream of a more direct and therefore more authentic feeling of immediacy and presence, unsoiled by modernity.[9]

In *My Struggle* (2009–11), which is itself an uncompromising autobiographical quest to "reintroduce a presence,"[10] Karl Ove Knausgård offers an apt description of this present-day feeling of alienation: "The sense of the untrue world becoming increasingly dominant in our lives, to the extent of almost of becoming the world we live in, is what brings about the forceful craving for reality that has begun to emerge around us."[11] Arguably, this *forceful craving for reality* embodies the impetus behind much art and thinking in the last decades, which really constitute a cultural movement, perhaps most famously formulated in David Shields's *Reality Hunger: A Manifesto* (2010).[12]

Similarly, from the perspective of cultural and literary theory, Hans Ulrich Gumbrecht has problematized the cultural-theoretical priority of semiotics, meaning, and interpretation in the modern epoch in *The Production of Presence: What Meaning Cannot Convey* (2004), a book that remains highly influential in the humanities (especially in the art world and in cultural and literary studies). Gumbrecht makes a passionate plea for a return to a notion of "presence" in the humanities that would satisfy "the desire for […] immediacy."[13] Responding to a longing for unmediated reality, the concept of "presence" not only points to the way cultural phenomena and cultural events become tangible and impact the senses and the body, but also embodies a "desire to be in sync with the things of the world."[14] "Presence" therefore also mediates a dream about what Gumbrecht labels a "redemption" that carries "the hope of achieving a union—or, even better, a presence-in-the-world […] an unmediated state of being-in-the-world."[15] Professing the "(famous) wish to be a tree," Gumbrecht's presence project takes its point of departure from the "intensity of wanting to be and of being there, unpermeated by effects of distance."[16]

Except for his rationalist peers, many academics welcomed Meillassoux's deep frustration with modern finitude (and what he conceived as its overemphasis on human subjectivity) and were fascinated with the promise of transcending the human world (*correlationism*) and re-connecting with the entirely other (*the great outdoors*).

Graham Harman, one of the founding figures of the philosophical trend named *speculative realism*, explicitly formulates his own position in opposition to "*anti-object-oriented standpoints*,"[17] which are all—but especially correlationism—characterized by their effort to eliminate objects in one way or the other.

In his book *The Quadruple Object* (2010), Harman makes it clear that he shares Meillassoux's conviction that correlationism is the main adversary to be superseded by a new ontology.[18] Therefore, the fundamental grounding of Harman's object-oriented ontology is an outspoken antihumanism: "However interesting we humans may be to ourselves, we are apparently in no way central to the cosmic drama, marooned as we are on an average-sized planet near a mediocre sun, and confined to a tiny portion of the history of the universe."[19] According to Harman, these "facts [of antihumanism] are sacrificed […] by Kant's Copernican philosophy and its successors."[20] In other words, the time has come to drive "a stake in the heart of Modernism."[21] Modernity's notion of human finitude following in the wake of Kant's critical philosophy, which stipulates that the mind is bounded within itself and is limited by its finite capacity for understanding, precludes access to and knowledge of the other of the human being, i.e., the thing-in it-self, and concludes in a loss of reality.[22] To save reality, Harman insists, it is necessary to discard human exceptionality: "We ourselves are things-in-themselves while inhabiting this very world, and so too are tables, hyenas, and coffee cups."[23] This stance brings about a *polypsychism*, according to which perception is inherent in all of reality. In short, objects "perceive insofar as they *relate*."[24] Since every relation between objects consists in mere adumbrations of relations, there can be no direct contact between objects.[25] This viewpoint applies to all kinds of relations, be they human or nonhuman, and therefore philosophy can never *stricto sensu* result in knowledge, but can at most *allude* to objects and their being.[26] Harman's realism thus amounts to a rejection of the "sober moderation" of the metaphysical claims of modern philosophy and its insistence on knowledge,[27] arguing instead that "philosophy's sole mission is *weird realism* […] it [philosophy] must be weird because reality is weird."[28]

Theorizing a "nonorganic life" and ecological "force" of things, politologist Jane Bennett—borrowing a concept inherited from the vocabulary of religion and idealism—defines things as the *absolute*.[29] According to Bennett's new materialism,[30] things are totally disconnected from a human conceptual and sensuous field (not unlike Harman's objects), and the *absolute* of things therefore designates this "moment of independence (from subjectivity) possessed by things."[31] In addition, Bennett and her fellow new materialists conceive of "matter as possessing its own modes of self-transformation, self-organization, and directedness," as Coole and Frost have it.[32] Things are endowed not only with a kind of self, but also with ethical and political agency.

Appreciating "vibrant matter," "thing-power," and the way human and nonhuman, organic and inorganic, living and lifeless matter are not in fact distinct from humans, but united in a material network of worldwide intercorrelation, will help us understand that we, too, are part of a bigger picture as one agent among others, Bennett, argues: "The moral of the story is that we are also nonhuman and that things, too, are vital players in the world."[33]

Discussing a power blackout that affected 50 million people in North America in 2003, Bennett argues that

> a case can be made for including nonhumans in the demos. The prevention of future blackouts, for example, will depend on a host of cooperative efforts: Congress will have to summon the courage to fight industry demands at odds with a more common good, but reactive power will also have to do its part, on condition that it is not asked to travel too far.[34]

In other words, electrons and magnetic fields must also be "summoned" and "sworn in" when political decisions are taken. This may sound extravagant, but what must be kept in mind here is that "everything is, in a sense, alive."[35]

It therefore becomes untenable and irresponsible to uphold the reflexive human self as the primary source of ethically and politically responsible agency. Furthermore, seeing that agency is situated in bodies and material assemblages rather than in conscious, spontaneous, and reflexive human subjects, we need to upscale the role and importance played by things and downscale the subjectivist and humanistic "fantasies of human uniqueness."[36] Inasmuch as the dominant self-understanding of the West has advanced a view of the human "as synonymous with (self-)consciousness, cognition or rationality,"[37] the ethical, moral, and political subject has been too self-absorbed and thus oblivious to the ways humans are, in fact, embedded within material contexts from which they neither can nor should entirely distinguish themselves.

In like manner, posthumanist Karen Barad, another crucial figure in close relation to the new materialisms, has, against a background in theoretical physics, advanced a theory of "agential realism," according to which "questions of ethics and of justice are always already threaded through the very fabric of the world."[38] As a consequence, she argues, for example,[39] that human ethics must be founded on the *in*human, subatomic reality characterized by infinite potentiality, as quantum physics allows for the emergence of pairs of particles and antiparticles out of empty space. This might look like a simple category-mistake, but when we recall that there is no principal ontological difference between the subjective and the objective pole, between animate and inanimate matter, the human self and the inorganic passivity of inert matter, and the systematic behavior of structures in the micro-quantum register and the social macrolevel, it becomes perfectly consistent to claim, as Barad does, that "feeling, desiring and experiencing are not singular characteristics or capacities of human consciousness. Matter feels, converses, suffers, desires, yearns, and remembers."[40]

Although she defines the absolute of things as what, in principle, we "cannot *know*" and stresses that the absolute points to an "epistemological limit," that is to say, "the limits of *intelligibility*," Bennett declares that we need to "shift from the language of epistemology to that of ontology," i.e., to a language that perceives things as "an active, earthy, not-quite-human capaciousness." In other words, though the project of uttering the absolute reality of things beyond human perception is deemed "impossibl[e],"[41] Bennett nevertheless endeavors to "give voice to a vitality intrinsic to materiality"[42] and thus recommends that we "cultivate a bit of anthropomorphism" in order to allow for the emergence of the absolute, i.e., the reality of things-in-themselves. The traditional concept of objects installs a false sense of difference, which is why we need to follow through "the idea that human agency has some echoes in nonhuman nature." For Bennett, this means that the deployment of anthropomorphism can serve as a strategic "attempt to counter the narcissistic reflex of human language and thought."[43] In a seemingly paradoxical gesture, Bennett explains how employing anthropomorphism is well-suited both to render the otherness of things, their absolute difference from us, *and* to sharpen our awareness of how things mirror us and our world.

It is noteworthy, furthermore, that Bennett cloaks her theory in a religious guise in a manner that Slavoj Žižek finds "in no way wholly ironic."[44] Bennett thus presents her materialist position as a "Nicene Creed for would-be materialists"—the Nicene Creed being the profession of faith widely used in Christian liturgy (originally adopted in the city of Nicaea by the First Council of Nicaea in 325). The litany or prayer of Bennett's new materialism thus runs:

> I believe in one matter-energy, the maker of things seen and unseen, I believe that this pluriverse is traversed by heterogeneities that are continually doing things. I believe it is wrong to deny vitality to nonhuman bodies, forces, and

forms, and that a careful course of anthropomorphization can help reveal that vitality, even though it resists full translation and exceeds my comprehensive grasp.[45]

Therefore, as Alan R. van Wyk writes, in an enthusiastic review of *Vibrant Matter*, Bennett's "post-secular ontology" is very much in keeping with her earlier book *The Enchantment of Modern Life* from 2001,[46] which, in Bennett's own words, advocates for a "quasi-pagan" and "neo-pagan" ontology of re-enchantment.[47] In this book, she criticizes the modern tale of disenchantment that has, regrettably, emptied the universe of any religious, moral, or metaphysical support. Bennett's post-secular project with *Vibrant Matter* is therefore, as Wyk notes, another attempt "to hear matter speak by repeating religion."[48]

Applying Harman's object-oriented ontology to ecology, Timothy Morton gives special attention to the climate crisis as a logical culmination of modernity. Since his book *Ecology without Nature* (2007), Morton has, in an environmental context, criticized what he finds to be a dominant anthropocentric outlook and instead stressed the overarching importance of the nonhuman. The discomfort with humanism expressed in Morton's writings is also nourished by his conviction that language deforms and occludes reality. Language distorts reality simply by thematizing it, because "when you mention environment, you bring it into the foreground. […] It stops being That Thing Over There that surrounds and sustains us." As the title of his book (*Ecology without Nature*) indicates, we should strive to do without the concept of nature in discussions of ecology altogether: "[T]he very idea of 'nature' […] will have to wither away in an 'ecological' state of human society."[49] Trying to grasp the other by means of language is doomed to failure. Consequently, we will have to give up "the idea of constant presence: the myth that something is real insofar as it is consistently, constantly 'there.' The concept space was always a constant-presencing machine for making things appear consistent and solid, to make them easier to colonize, enslave, and plunder."[50] It is time to pursue a new kind of thinking that embraces a *dark ecology*, insisting that humans only play a very limited role and that the ecological system itself contains an active knowledge that infinitely surpasses that of humans. The only adequate means to get in touch with reality is the eco-system itself, not the human *ego*, but a so-called *ecognosis*.

> What thinks dark ecology? Ecognosis, a riddle. Ecognosis is like knowing, but more like letting be known. It is something like coexisting. It is like becoming accustomed to something strange, yet it is also becoming accustomed to strangeness that doesn't become less strange through acclimation. Ecognosis is like a knowing that knows itself. Knowing in a loop—a weird knowing.[51]

When confronted with such strangeness, we find that we, in fact, cannot meaningfully distinguish ourselves from the rest of the world.

In *Hyperobjects* (2013), Morton radicalizes this idea, introducing the notion of *hyperobjects* as "things that are massively distributed in time and space relative to humans." They are *"viscous," "nonlocal,"* and "they exhibit their effects *interobjectively*,"[52] which to Morton implicates that hyperobjects "are all over me. They are me."[53] In a quasi-physical manner, the human being thus regains a sense of the real (of presence) by joyfully embracing the weirdness of the world emanating from *ecognosis*.[54] Accordingly, well-established categories of modern philosophy (from Descartes and onwards) take on a new significance. Immediacy, for example, does not imply obviousness or simplicity,[55] as it contrarily shows how "appearance is always strange" and the *"local is in fact the uncanny."*[56]

This inescapable strangeness dictates that the human being must recognize itself as an (insignificant) part of these *hyperobjects*. Morton understands this process as a submergence, labeling it a so-called *subscending*, and argues that this must be effectuated by means of aesthetics. However, it is *not* the aesthetics from the tradition of Kant and onwards that highlights the autonomy of art and human freedom that Morton has in mind. Discussing Friedrich Schiller's humanistic and educational emphasis upon play in the *Letters upon the Aesthetic Education of Man*, Morton castigates the German for emphasizing free play as an expression of a specifically *human* cognitive power. For play is not a sovereign display of human agency; rather, human agency is nothing but a passive plaything for the capricious workings of objects beyond our control: "The trouble resides in Schiller's sense of 'fullness' […] To be 'fully human'—what a drag. We seem to have been trying that for twelve thousand years. Playing as a broken toy among other broken toys sounds more like it."[57] Playing is far from an exclusively human phenomenon, for things actually play amongst themselves, and the only possibility for humans of truly engaging in play consists in their yielding and *subscending* into the play of objects.[58]

In continuation of Harman's object-oriented ontology,[59] Morton gives expression to a longing for reality in the guise of an aestheticized ontology, in which, simply put, "causality is aesthetic."[60] The ontological play between objects seems to conclude with an animistic re-enchantment that, taking the cue from Franz Anton Mesmer's vitalism and concept of "animal magnetism," advances the idea of a vital force pervading the entire universe, affecting humans and nonhumans alike: "Animal magnetism is to all intents and purposes identical with the Force of *Star Wars* fame; it is, as Obi Wan Kenobi observes, an 'energy field' that 'surrounds' and 'penetrates' us, and we can interact with it, with healing and destructive consequences."[61]

The craving for reality and the quest for immediacy are difficult to untangle from a religious impetus—which is also tangible in Gumbrecht, Bennett (and fellow new materialists), and to a lesser extent Harman—that may be seen as a compensatory reaction against the disenchantment and alienation of the contemporary, modern world. In other words, Morton is representative of the new materialisms in his desire to reanimate the inanimate and nonhuman world—a desire driven by a fantasy to undo the claustrophobic consequences of a modernity that insists on human finitude, secularization, and a dreary autonomy that harshly places responsibility solely upon weak human shoulders.

The yearning—which is more or less a shared feature of these theories—to undo or compensate for modernity by formulating what, in effect, constitutes an *Ersatzreligion*, is probably nowhere more clearly formulated than by one of the "founding fathers" of the new materialisms, namely Bruno Latour. Latour, whose work has been met with general approval amongst adherents of the new materialisms, has arguably provided the most elaborate critique of modernity in the frequently cited book *We Have Never Been Modern* (1993), whose influence in shaping the new materialisms' discussions and analysis of the modern project can hardly be overstated.[62]

To be modern, according to Latour, equals a belief in a pure dualism between "two entirely distinct ontological zones: that of the human beings on the one hand; that of nonhumans on the other."[63] Culture and Nature, object and subject, were strictly segregated in modernity, which thus constituted itself "by leaving out what was in the middle."[64] However, by doing so, modernity misconstrued the basic constituents of reality, since it neglected how the world is made up of nonhuman entities that actually act. These acting entities are composed of an objective as well as a subjective pole, and they are labeled *quasi-objects* accordingly. These *quasi-objects* or hybrids resist localization in nature, society, subjectivity, and language.[65] Being no less active, spontaneous, and constitutive of meaning than humans themselves,[66] they effectively dissolve and undercut any modern paradigm of dichotomous or binary thinking: "Now hybrids, monsters [...] are just about everything; they compose not only our own collectives but also the others, illegitimately called premodern."[67] Hence, we humans have never observed the world of objects from a safe and sovereign position. We falsely entertained the idea, but the truth of the matter is that we have never been modern. Like everything else, we are equally codependent upon and an inseparable part of the actor-networks of quasi-objects.[68] Consequently, the disenchantment of the world never happened.[69]

More recently, Latour has also accentuated the surging need for an enchanted world-picture. In *Facing Gaia* (2017), modeled on his Gifford lectures from 2013, Latour attempts to establish the all-encompassing presence of the antique Earth goddess Gaia in the world of quasi-objects.[70] Dismissing modernity and reimporting mythology, Latour argues that the overwhelming presence of Gaia demonstrates how reality certainly exists independently of human perception, notions, language, and thoughts. Substituting Thomas Hobbes's sovereign (the Leviathan) with Gaia's presence, Latour's world manifests itself tangibly in this new mythology: "It would be more comfortable, as I am quite prepared to recognize, to leave aside the religious question! [...] But it is too late."[71] In other words, taking stock of this would allow humankind to reenter its proper place, finding meaning in the universe as an inhabitant intertwined with and subjected to the sovereignty of an entity transcending any human measure or goal: "Facing the Leviathan, you know who you are and before what authority you have to bow [...] Is it possible that Hobbes's solution is being called into question today by another monster, the hybrid of geology and anthropology [...], a new amalgam of artifice and nature?"[72]

To summarize, it seems clear that Tokarczuk's outspoken longing for *that other world, the world of the teapot*, designates a general trend in recent decades toward a "material turn." Despite substantial internal divergences cutting across disciplinary differences, the passionate call for a reconnection and reconciliation with immediate reality rings out in unison; and theories such as speculative realism, new materialism, object-oriented ontology, and actor-network theory have gained a strong foothold and left a deep impact in the humanities, the social sciences, the artworld, and in cultural and literary studies.

Moreover, the critique of modernity—for having left us with a fatal misconception of human exceptionality that has, in consequence, led us into our current predicaments (and this, above all, means the climate crisis)—has been favorably received and enjoyed widespread attention. With the vow to reembrace immediate reality and to teach us ontological humility, the "material turn" embodies a hopeful promise to revolutionize our understanding of the universe and our place in it. Turning our backs on modernity and embracing a pre-critical and premodern standpoint would allow us to join forces with new politico-ethical communities stretching across the human and nonhuman realms.

In other words, the promise of a deeper connection with the cosmos, boding for a more sustainable and harmonious future and coexistence in a "parliament of things" (including human as well as nonhuman participants),[73] requires a showdown with modernity. The modern conditions constituted by human *finitude*, *secularization*, and *autonomy* need to be disarmed and left behind to pave the way for a more responsible and ethical world cognizant of how "all bodies are kin in the sense of inextricably enmeshed in a dense network of relations,"[74] thus enabling us to "cultivate a more careful attentiveness to the out-side."[75]

Undoing Modernity? The Question of Secularization

In his monumental book *A Secular Age* (2007), Charles Taylor focuses on what it means "to say that we live in a secular world."[76] In continuance of the diminution of faith in or adherence to God or some notion of ultimate metaphysical reality, secularization entails the critical idea of living in a disenchanted universe once enchanted. This will sound familiar to readers of German sociologist and political economist Max Weber, who perceived the process of modern disenchantment (*die Entzauberung der Welt*) as the result of a technical rationalization or intellectualization and objectification of the world (*Zweckrationalität*).[77] But Taylor points to a deeper dimension of secularization, which consists in a strict demarcation of the psychological as now restricted to the minds of humans only. The world of the modern neutral universe is a world "in which the only locus of thoughts, feelings, spiritual élan is what we call minds; the only minds in the cosmos are those of humans [...] and minds are bounded, so that these thoughts, feelings, etc., are situated 'within' them."[78]

In the modern world, meaning, personal agency, and significance are consequently internal features of the human mind that do not inhere in things or the exterior world. Thus, secularization and disenchantment are contingent upon boundaries that sharply distinguish between the interior and the exterior. However, these boundaries are "fuzzy" or "porous," as Taylor has it, in the enchanted, premodern world where "meanings are not only in minds, but can reside in things, or in various kinds of extra-human, but intra-cosmic subjects."[79] What this means, according to Taylor, is that in the enchanted world "power also resided in things": "In fact, in the enchanted world, the line between personal agency and impersonal force was not at all clearly drawn."[80] The boundary between forces and agents was fuzzy, and objects and things were not void of human features or meaning. On the contrary, in the premodern world, things, objects, and natural phenomena could impose a moral meaning upon us and communicate it to us "by bringing us as it were into its field of force."[81] Indeed, in the enchanted world, objects seemingly inanimate could have "what we usually call 'magic' powers."[82] Unlike the modern, disenchanted world of clear-cut boundaries and distinctions, the premodern and enchanted world was a world in which "a clear line between the physical and the moral wasn't drawn."[83]

Charles Taylor's characterization of the modern age of secularism vis-à-vis the premodern age of enchantment aptly elucidates the need for the advocates of the new materialisms necessarily to refute the secularism of modernity. What Latour's *quasi-objects*, Manuel DeLanda's *flat ontology*, Bennett's *thing-power*, and Harman's *polypsychism* (to take some of the towering representatives of the new materialisms) have in common is their preference for the enchanted and premodern worldview in which the clear dividing line between the physical and the moral, the interior and the exterior was not drawn, i.e., where borders between the human and the nonhuman were still *fuzzy* and *porous*. Thus, to take an example among others, Bennett's ontology of re-enchantment, which she characterizes as *quasi-pagan* and *neo-pagan* (see above), advocates for a return to premodern modes of thinking: "Vital materialism as a doctrine has affinities with several non-modern (and often discredited) modes of thought, including animism, the Romantic quest for Nature, and vitalism."[84] Bennett's quest for an undoing of secularism to re-enchant the disenchanted world, where, in the famous words of T. S. Eliot, "[t]he nymphs have departed,"[85] therefore demands the evocation of discredited, premodern, and pre-critical philosophies of nature and a willingness to risk "the taint of superstition, animism, vitalism, anthropomorphism, and other premodern attitudes."[86] Inasmuch as the new materialisms view things as endowed with a kind of self with ethical and political agency, and seeing that the mechanic causality of modern physics does not ascribe such features to the object world, it more or less follows that the new materialists, in Bennett's words, "share a common foe in mechanistic or deterministic materialism."[87]

In sum, Taylor's definition of the premodern enchanted world-picture as one in which thoughts, feelings, agency, and moral features were also present and operational in things suggests that the theories of the new materialists may be less new than they claim to be. Even though the new materialisms mostly ignore the kinds of materiality and materialism found in the Middle Ages, the similarity with the medieval mindset is striking. As a matter of fact, medieval experts like Andrew Cole, Kellie Robertson, Shannon Gayk, and Robyn Malo as well as Anne E. Lester and Katherine C. Little have shown how many of the notions of ontology, agency, and action of the new materialisms are, to a large degree, predicated on their medieval counterparts.[88]

One of the few in this field who does not shy away from explicating the medieval connection is Graham Harman. He explains, for example, how his theory of causality (so-called *vicarious causation*) "owes much to a medieval Islamic [...] current of thought" including "such important figures as Abu al-Hasan al-Ash'ari (874–936) and al-Ghazali (1058–1111)."[89] Although Harman mentions early modern thinkers such as Nicolas Malebranche, he stresses the premodern origins of occasionalism with its assertion that God serves as the direct mediator of causality between things. While "it feels all too easy to laugh at philosophies that imagine the intervention of God in every least event in the world," Harman identifies "a surprisingly similar claim" in contemporary philosophy.[90] Amongst contemporary theorists, Harman highlights Latour "as the founder of a *secular occasionalism*,"[91] and he adds that his own theory of causality should be understood as a variant of Latour's. Where traditional religious occasionalism reserved mediation for a monotheistic and omnipotent God, Harman and Latour's contemporary version expands and extends this feature to apply to all objects, which are endowed with local agency everywhere.

The attribution of agency and psychic features to things and objects is brought about through a quasi-religious and premodern discourse that—as Slavoj Žižek remarks when speaking of new materialism—leaves us with "a kind of spiritualism without gods."[92] In an article preoccupied with identifying what it is exactly that aligns new materialism (e.g., Jane Bennett), object-oriented ontology (e.g., Graham Harman), and actor-network theory (Bruno Latour), Andrew Cole similarly draws attention to their shared employment of "the ancient Logos principle by which things call out to us and speak their being."[93]

In an introduction to a special issue of *English Language Notes* (published in 2015), asking what the growing interest in materiality means for medieval studies, Anne E. Lester and Katherine C. Little ponder what exactly the new materialisms add to the medieval view that objects contained a thing-power that troubled the divide between material objects and human subjects. Duly noting how the similarities are striking indeed, which they exemplify by quoting Bennett's definition of *thing-power* as "the curious ability of inanimate things to animate, to act, to produce effects dramatic and subtle,"[94] Lester and Little point to a critical discrepancy between materialist conceptions then and now when they comment: "Why is the ability of things to live or to have effects 'curious?' It certainly was not in the Middle Ages."[95] In other words, when you dwell inside the *mythos* and inhabit an enchanted world, you are little inclined to find the enchantment of the cosmos unusual. It is only as seen from the outside, posterior to the event of disenchanted secularization, that the magic of the mythological world will appear *curious*. For the premodern, it would only be natural. Pace Latour, Lester and Little's perceptive observation is a beautiful testimony of Taylor's overall argument that "the clearest sign of this transformation [i.e., of modern secularization] in our world is that today many people look back to the world of the porous self [i.e., of the enchanted pre-modern world] with nostalgia."[96]

Undoing Modernity? The Question of Finitude

Strongly opposing secularization and modern disenchantment, the new materialisms are also vehemently pitted against the tradition initiated by Kant, whose critical philosophy imposed the modern condition of finitude upon the human subject. Critique is seen as irrelevant and even misleading, and Karen Barad's assessment is in this regard not exceptional: "I am not interested in critique. In my opinion, critique is over-rated, over-emphasized, and over-utilized."[97] A presence-theoretician like Gumbrecht displays a similar attitude to critique from which he distances himself with tangible sarcasm.[98] In a less scornful tone, Jane Bennett cautions against hermeneutic demystification,[99] warning against searching for a universal reality beyond or behind the sheer existence of things themselves. The discomfort with critique is not limited to Jane Bennett and Karen Barad, but characteristic of the movements as such. Hence, Diana Coole and Samantha Frost assert how "a further trait of new materialism is its antipathy towards oppositional ways of thinking," and accentuate how it favors instead "the creative affirmation of a new ontology."[100]

Hence, the new materialists tend to side with Bruno Latour in his questioning of critique for creating false differences and dichotomies and for presupposing an anthropocentrism given by the idea of a sovereign, worldless subject.[101] Contesting modern finitude, in which humans oppose an exterior world bereft of human traces or echoes, the new materialists seek to reestablish an affirmative unity with the world through re-enchantment, remythologization, or through the reintroduction of religious dogma or sentiments. In their confrontation with what is perceived as the anthropocentrism of modern critique, the new materialists basically extend the qualities (perception, thoughts, and feelings bounded within individual minds as such) that the finitude of modernity had otherwise delimited to humans only to include all things. The anthropocentrism of humans who believe that only they are humanlike is dismantled through ascribing human modes of being to the cosmos—or in the words of Bruno Latour: "Hermeneutics is not a privilege of humans, but, so to speak, a property of the world itself."[102]

Discerning how "any critical interlocutor and, indeed, critique itself—broadly conceived—is portrayed as hubristic, conceited, or resentful, blinded by its anthropocentrism," as Paul Rekret puts it,[103] the new materialisms thus seem to be part and parcel of the movement known as *postcritique*, which seeks to reach beyond the methods of critique, critical theory, and ideological criticism. The most towering proponent of this theoretical movement is most likely Rita Felski. In her *Limits of Critique* (2015), she declares how she found Jane Bennett's *The Enchantment of Modern Life* and *Vibrant Matter* "especially helpful in the course of this project," and adds, "I have also learned much from the work of Graham Harman and of course am deeply influenced by the work of Bruno Latour."[104] Felski, in fact, makes Latour's actor-network theory the new postcritical point of departure in literary and cultural studies. Actor-network would help interpreters appreciate how "many different kinds of entities are engaged in communicating, mediating, signaling, translating; the world is not a dead zone of reification but is as rife with ambiguity as any modernist poem."[105] According to Felski, it is about time that concepts like "attachment" and "enchantment" (rather than diversion, skepticism, suspicion, and distance) come to the fore.

However, not all postcritical theoreticians are sympathetic to the new materialisms. In her postcritical *Revolution of the Ordinary* (2017), which argues for a coherent continuity between language and world in close dialogue with Ludwig Wittgenstein's everyday language philosophy, Toril Moi observed that "the vision of a fully signifying world, a world in which matter speaks [...] has turned out to be attractive to many."[106] For Moi, the contemporary vision, which she exemplifies by quoting posthumanist Karen Barad and new materialists like Rick Dolphijn and Iris van der Tuin, constitutes a "dream of a world in which the gap [between language and the world] has been overcome by the expulsion of the last traces of human subjectivity, human judgement."[107] According to Moi, such theories amount to a denial of the human *tout court* and are thus in keeping with a classic fantasy of "a world in which language, meaning, and knowledge would no longer depend on fallible human subjectivity."[108]

In a sort of ironic, dialectical twist, the importance given to fallible human subjectivity and of human limitations by a postcritical advocate leads directly into the heart of modern finitude and its correlative *need* for critique. Paul Ricœur's characterization of Nietzsche, Marx, and Freud as "the masters of suspicion" is justly famous, as it points to the way that the modern finitude of humans necessitates a certain skeptical and distrustful gaze at our knowledge and our self-consciousness—whether limited in our sovereignty and self-transparency by the will to power (immanent in any will to truth or knowledge), by historical materialism (stressing how the economical material base or substructure predominantly determines the superstructure of the articulations of the human spirit), or by unconscious drives (puppeteering and shaping the conscious ego). In contrast to the rationalism of Descartes, who "does not doubt that consciousness is such as it appears to itself [...] [and] that consciousness, meaning and consciousness of meaning coincide," we have, since Marx, Nietzsche, and Freud, "started to doubt consciousness."[109] In the modern experience, it is the narcissistically humbling recognition of our basic finitude, dictating that being and consciousness can never fully coincide, that entails the inescapable requirement for critique.

In other words, fallibilism and critique go hand in hand, thus bringing us back to Kant's Copernican revolution, which accentuates the finitude of humans and the ensuing need for the self-limitation of human reason. Hence, Kant's first *Critique of Pure Reason*, in which reason comes to terms with itself as reason by delimitating the jurisdiction of theoretical reason, implies a twofold movement. On the one hand, Kant executes his critique of pure reason as a critique of reason (*genitivus obiectivus*), i.e., that of the metaphysical tradition (pure reason) with its claim to an absolute knowledge about the rational nature of the external world. On the other hand, this critique is accomplished by means of an enquiry conducted by reason itself (*genitivus subiectivus*). As the double genitive in the title (*Kritik der reinen Vernuft*) suggests, what is criticized and that which criticizes are one and the same. For Kant, then, critique is always a self-critique involving reason's self-limitation and self-imposed restrictions with respect to its jurisdiction in matters external to itself. As finite, reason takes upon itself to withdraw from any final theoretical judgments about the cosmos as a whole. In contrast to a divine reason (*intellectus archetypes*), human theoretical reason (*intellectus echtypus*)— or, in the Kantian terminology, the understanding (*Verstand*)—is restricted to the use of its categories on finite objects given in intuition. Theoretically, human cognition is thus limited by the liminal concept of the thing in itself (*das Ding an sich*), prohibiting that reason exceeds the area where its categories may justly be applied. Thus distanced from its surroundings, reason can no longer do justice to any claims of absolute knowledge about the world in which it is situated, be it through mediation of its own concepts or by virtue of an immediate access to the things that it dictates. Hence, Kant's criticism ultimately redirects the attention of reason away from the traditional objects of theoretical metaphysics and toward itself, relegating reason to a perpetual self-regulatory praxis.

In *Kant and the Problem of Metaphysics* (1929), which is an interpretation of Kant's *Critique of Pure Reason*, Heidegger argues that the critique of reason demonstrates how sense is a projection of possibilities onto worldly entities based on the temporally finite structure of *Dasein* as essentially mortal, i.e., missing an underlying substance. Intelligibility and meaningfulness of objects and entities— their sense—are rendered possible by the structure of projection upon possibilities of *Dasein*, and sense is ultimately not a property of entities, but rather an existential structure of human existence originating in the constitutive structure of being-in-the-world (*In-der-Welt-Sein*), which in effect forecloses the idea of immediate access to things in themselves. In continuance of Kant, Heidegger argues that human finitude prevents us from understanding things immediately and ontically as God would do, but only indirectly and ontologically through our being. This defines the essence of our finitude and imperfection behind all categories and generality, where every "something" is understood *as* "something." For Heidegger, this is equal to saying that "existence is in itself finitude, and as such it is only possible on the basis of the understanding of Being"; he adds that the "'universality'" of the human understanding of Being (*Seinsverständnis*) "is the originality of the innermost ground of the finitude of Dasein."[110] When Heidegger claims that "transcendence, however, is finitude itself,"[111] that is, that the finite universal essence of our attributing meaning to entities is our way of relating to them, this means that "[w]ith the existence of human beings there occurs an irruption into the totality of beings."

This irruption (*Einbruch*) does not imply that man is a master of beings or of the being which he himself is. On the contrary, human finitude dictates that the human being "can never become master." Seeing that we are not gods endowed with divine reason (*intellectus archetypes*), we come to understand that our existence "harbors in itself the need to require the understanding of Being."[112] Human finitude signifies this need or want (*Not*) according to which human openness is incomplete, never fully self-present, perfect, or self-coinciding. Quoting a Novalis fragment saying that "[p]hilosophy is really homesickness, an urge to be at home everywhere," Heidegger in his 1929–30 lecture course, *The Fundamental Concepts of Metaphysics*, comments and insists that true philosophy is set in motion by taking stock of the fact that we "are *not* at home everywhere."[113] Philosophizing is rooted in finitude, for we would not desire to be at home everywhere if indeed we were. Metaphysical homelessness and finitude mean that we can never achieve full self-presence or immediacy with entities or the world and that we ourselves are "this underway, this transition, this 'neither the one nor the other.'"[114] Our lack of full being and immediacy, amounting to our homelessness and explaining our homesickness, is what makes us human.

If the new materialists are right in their critique of modernity and do offer a way "*to get out of ourselves*, to grasp the in-itself, to know what is whether we are or not,"[115] and if this "extraordinary form of radical realism" is feasible,[116] we would indeed be able to ignore the limitations imposed on reason by Kant's critique, reverse modernity, and reach a state *after finitude*. Moreover, once we have extended the domain of consciousness into objects and entities— *vide*, for example, Harman's pan- and polypsychism, Bennett's strategic anthropomorphization, and Latour's actants—the world would again come our way in our own recognizable human shape. The prodigal sons of modernity could finally return home again.

Reinstalling language, spontaneity, meaning, and knowledge as immanent features of the world, as in premodern and pre-critical thinking, implies that we would no longer be so humiliatingly vulnerable and exposed to our fallible human subjectivity. Inasmuch as the new materialists' declared ambition to redirect the theoretical focus onto the object without the interference of correlating human subjectivity proves, on closer inspection, to be not a move away from but rather a renewed move toward the Subject (with a capital S), unhampered by the restrictions imposed by the critical tradition initiated by Kant, they ironically fall prey to Heidegger's fierce critique directed against a powerful strand of modernity (a critique in which they, on the face of it, seem to partake). What Heidegger targets as the fatal oblivion of Being (*Seinsvergessenheit* or *Seinsverlassenheit*) in the current epoch of the history of Being (*Seinsgeschichte*) is the tradition of modernity's techno-rationalistic humanism, which claims that human finitude and homelessness are no longer an issue and can now be discarded. Human existence originates in a need (*Not* or *Dürftigkeit*), and the essential homelessness of *Dasein* means that the human being is situated in a world entirely other than itself and is, indeed, itself of a being which it itself is not. Finitude thus expresses the humbling recognition by the human being that "for all his culture and technology, he can never become master."[117] In other words, the problem with "contemporary city man, the ape of civilization," as Heidegger acerbically puts it, is that he or she believes to have "long since eradicated" the basic homelessness and homesickness resulting from the finitude of Dasein.[118]

For Heidegger, abandoning the finitude and homelessness so central to the dominant techno-rationalistic humanism has dire consequences, for it implies that "we today do not understand this essential need of our Dasein."[119] Heidegger now argues that "the utmost distress (*Die höchste Not*)" facing us today consists in "the *distress of lack of distress* (*die Not der Notlosigkeit*)."[120] Having cast finitude and homelessness aside and enjoying the mental self-assurance that follows, we unwittingly come to suffer the *distress of lack of distress*.

The mental self-certainty, mastery, and sovereignty at the root of this *distress of lack of distress* are not limited to the techno-rationalistic humanism of modernity. Heidegger shows, furthermore, how premodern thinking partook in the Occidental *Seinsvergessenheit*, as it anthropomorphized the world as *ens creatum*, i.e., as a created thing produced by a (divine) artificer: "[O]n the basis of a religious faith, namely, the biblical faith, the totality of all beings is represented in advance as something created, which here means made."[121] The existential homelessness is discarded both in the techno-rationalistic humanism of modernity and the enchanted world picture before modernity. Both epochs bring about a *Seinsvergessenheit* and domestication of the world through "the power of an enchantment that is enacted by the disenchanting itself," which is the principle that informs the link between "*ens creatum*—modern nature and history—technicity."[122]

In *Totem and Taboo* (1913), Freud is on to something similar when analyzing the "immense domain" of "the theory of the living character of what appear to us to be inanimate objects."[123] For the principle governing magic and the techniques and practices generated by the animistic mode of thinking characteristic of what were then called "primitive" people (or "savages") may be summarized by what he refers to as "the principle of the 'omnipotence of thoughts'"—the principles, techniques, and practices that are also at work in the neurotics, artists, and children of so-called "primitive civilization."[124]

Freud claims that *die Allmacht der Gedanken* behind animistic and enchanted belief systems and specific "civilized" practices ceases with modern secularization—"[t]he scientific view of the universe no longer affords any room for human omnipotence; men have acknowledged their smallness and submitted resignedly to death and to the other necessities of nature."[125] Heidegger, however, demonstrates how this cognitive mode persists in another guise. The diametrical opposition between techno-rationalistic humanism and the new materialisms is only apparent since both partake in *die Allmacht der Gedanken* and the subsequent *Not der Notlosigkeit*.

Undoing Modernity? The Question of Autonomy

The absence of essential finitude, of a lack or need in our understanding of the human being and its world, not only means the abrogation of its existential responsibility. The dissolution of essential finitude and need at the root of human existence, brought to the fore in the contemporary *Not der Notlosigkeit*, concomitantly involves the dissolution of "the *innermost necessity* [Notwendigkeit] *of the freedom of Dasein*."[126]

In the modern, disenchanted world without God—where the meaning of things must be projected onto them from human minds, and where physical objects obey causal laws that in no way turn on the moral meaning things have for humans—finitude encourages human beings to appreciate themselves as both frail and courageous. Heidegger's insistence on the pivotal importance of human finitude and homelessness runs parallel to an appeal to encourage ourselves to be capable of facing a meaningless, hostile universe without faintness of heart, and of rising to the challenge of shaping our own rules of life. This line of thinking is typical of the modern epoch, and thus a young Hegel, one of the first philosophers to systematically ground the modern project, instructs us that the upheaval of modernity implies that "it has been reserved in the main for our epoch to vindicate, at least in theory, the human ownership of treasures formerly squandered on heaven."[127]

Taking a broader look at the epoch of (political) modernity set in motion by the Enlightenment, one notes how the emergence of modern secularity and finitude (in effect, leaving humans unassisted in their moral and eudemonic goals) have been coterminous with the rise of a society in which, for the first time in history, an *exclusive humanism* came to be a widely available option. In a meaningless universe without a transcendent source, bereft of God and an enchanted cosmos, we seem to be the only authorizing agency left. Hence, as modern societies increasingly effected political, public activity without appeals to religion (thus leaving religion or its absence as largely a private matter), they concurrently gave an increasingly important place to individual autonomy.

In other words, autonomy of action and personal responsibility for individual action become emblematic of modernity. The question of freedom comes to the fore in modernity, and the assertion of human freedom is, indeed, perceived to be the key principle of the modern epoch: "The greatness of our time rests in the fact that freedom, the peculiar possession of mind whereby it is at home with itself in itself, is recognized," as Hegel has it in his *Lectures on the History of Philosophy*.[128] No longer does the freedom of the individual mind seek an abode outside of itself, since it itself, independently of larger hierarchical orders, constitutes the true and proper home for itself. Freedom was understood as a quintessential quality of what it means to be a human being and was, as Jean-Jacques Rousseau famously claimed in *The Social Contract* (1762), a birthright for all. Or in the words of another of *les philosophes* from the eighteenth century, Denis Diderot, under the entry "Political Authority" in the *Encyclopedia*, asserted that "[n]o man has received from nature the right to command others. Liberty is a gift from heaven, and each individual of the same species has the right to enjoy it as soon as he enjoys the use of reason."[129] With modernity, political freedom was axiomatically seen as a (natural) right, and modernity's strong emphasis on rights, and the primacy of freedom among these, reflects the principle that society should exist to insure the dignity and freedom of all its members as well as its members' sense of self-authorization through reason or will. The capacity for autonomy basically consists in humans perceiving themselves as the source of their self-representations, institutions, and acts. Inasmuch as being human equals being endowed with reason and will, morality and ethics are defined, posited, and executed on the intrinsic basis of the autonomy enjoyed by humans.

The concept of freedom as autonomy points to a freedom that expresses itself as a law unto itself—a law one renders to oneself, and which one authors. In

Rousseau's famous description, freedom as autonomy exists as "obedience to the law one has prescribed to oneself" and is thus to be distinguished from "natural freedom," which is arbitrary.[130] Autonomy is therefore twofold, as pointing to freedom as obeying a specific law, a law that is, moreover, self-prescribed, not imposed externally.

The Kantian variant of autonomy stipulates that freedom is synonymous with our nature as rational beings, which means that it is because of our rational capacity that we have the power to be self-legislative. Our will, in which our power of lawgiving derives, is free inasmuch as it freely subjects itself to a law that it itself has freely expressed and willed in accordance with reason. Autonomy consists in being bound by one's own law (in Kant's terms, to be *eigengesetzlich*), and Kant therefore asserts that "[a]utonomy of the will is the property of the will through which it is a law to itself."[131] The rational will itself naturally adapts to the form of the law, and the law for which the human being is a legislator as well as a subject is *the categorical imperative* (i.e., you act personally only upon principles that you hold universally valid). As the rational will subjects itself to this law, it is therefore able to deem itself its author and origin. And, as a *rational* agency, the freedom of the will is not lawless, but bound by a lawful prescription issued from and in accordance with its own universal nature. Thus, rational agency can be reduced neither to mechanical causality or instinct (to which inanimate matter and the vegetable and animal kingdoms are subjected) nor to the arbitrary and unrestricted will of sovereignty (Juvenal's "hoc volo, sic iubeo, sit pro ratione voluntas" [it's my wish and my command. Let my will be reason enough][132]): "[F]reedom, even though it is not a quality of the will in accordance with natural laws, is not for this reason lawless, but rather it has to be a causality in accordance with unchangeable laws, but of a particular kind."[133] Autonomy therefore entails subjecting oneself to one's *own* laws that spring from one's *own* nature as rational and free: "The will is thus not solely subject to the law, but is subject in such a way that it must be regarded also as legislating to itself, and precisely for this reason as subject to the law (of which it can consider itself as the author)."[134]

In the end, autonomy precludes external or alien determination, and, according to Kant, the moral realm is in principle *autonomous* and not *heteronomous* (i.e., not caused by something exterior to it). The modern notion of freedom therefore presupposes something absolute that allows beings to act consciously and in accordance with this irreducible faculty. Human existence thus differs from the pure heteronomy of inanimate matter (that blindly obeys the laws of Newtonian physics) and the animal and vegetable kingdoms (that nonetheless do have natural instincts and spontaneity in common with humans, though not autonomy).

In disagreement with the modern concept of freedom, the new materialisms vehemently dispute that inanimate or non-biotic material lacks agency, that human subjectivity calls for a distinct kind of ethical and political consideration, and that entities (whether human or not) can be delimited independently from other materials. For, as Coole and Frost assert, new materialism is a movement that "dislocates agency as the property of a discrete, self-knowing subject inasmuch as the corpus is now recognized as exhibiting capacities that have significant effects on social and political situations."¹³⁵ As agency, according to the new materialists, is no longer a distinct domain of humans, but an inherent dimension not only of other lifeforms than the human, but of materials (or objects) themselves; the consequences are no less radical than the premises: "What is at stake here is nothing less than a challenge to some of the most basic assumptions that have underpinned the modern world, including its normative sense of the human and its beliefs about human agency."¹³⁶ Moral and political self-legislation is an illusion, since agency is indeed distributed within the assemblages of humans and nonhumans alike that, together, make up a flux or mesh of material forces that is hard to pin down as a complex of hierarchically organized individual players. Rather than possessing a discrete individualism or capacity for autonomy, we must understand ourselves as entangled and co-distributed in material networks, which means that action cannot be attributed or isolated to an individual but is always a human–nonhuman congregation, as Bennett explains:

> I think that *human* agency is best conceived as itself the outcome or effect of a certain configuration of human and nonhuman forces. When humans act, they do not exercise exclusively human powers, but express and engage a variety of other actants, including food, micro-organisms, minerals, artefacts, sounds, bio- and other technologies, and so on. There is a difference between a human individual and a stone, but neither *considered alone* has real agency. The locus of agency is always a human–nonhuman collective.¹³⁷

When so-called human agency not only depends upon exterior material conditions to be actualized or executed but originates in a configuration of joined forces involving the active agency of the material realm (rather than something distinctly human), it follows that morality, ethics, and politics can no longer meaningfully be perceived to originate in human reality as distinctly human concerns. The idea of moral laws or goals to be attained, and of shaping the political practices and institutions securing and governing actions to achieve certain ends, must necessarily be extended to involve and address the nonhuman material universe from which we cannot claim distinct moral autonomy. In sum, in accordance with premodern ways of thinking, the new materialists conceive of ontology as practical philosophy.

In Karen Barad's posthumanist theory of "agential realism," for example, which aims to steer clear of social constructivism and scientific realism, "the materialization of all bodies—'human' or 'non-human'" is brought about through what Barad defines as "intra-actions."¹³⁸ Intra-action means that action and agency never emerge as the result of the initiative on the part of an individual since agency is widely disseminated and issued forth from matter itself: "In an agential realist account, agency is cut loose from its traditional humanist orbit. Agency is not aligned with human intentionality or subjectivity. Nor does it merely entail resignification or other specific kinds of moves within a social geometry of anti-humanism. [...] Significantly, matter is an agentive factor in its iterative materialization."¹³⁹ When agency is a matter of shared distribution and entanglement with many exterior factors, that is, when "the space of agency is much larger than that postulated in many other critical social theories," as Barad argues,[140] ethical concerns and responsibility no longer rest solely on human shoulders, but are shared with the surrounding material universe:

> Just as the human subject is not the locus of knowing, neither is it the locus of ethicality [...] What is on the other side of the agential cut is not separate from us—agential separability is not individuation. Ethics is therefore not about right response to a radically exterior/ized other, but about responsibility and accountability for the lively relationalities of becoming of which we are a part.[141]

As human intervention and agency are decentered and found everywhere in the dispersed, distributed, emergent agencies of the pluriverse, and as the new materialisms discard the boundaries between humans and nonhumans, the abolition of the long tradition of liberal humanism and Enlightenment replaces the idea of freedom as autonomy with that of a heteronomy, ordaining that human freedom is merely an effect (not a cause) of a quasi-subjective material world already saturated with self-initiated intentions and spontaneity. When the coherence of agential sovereignty expires in the entangled distribution of agency, the modern idea of distinctly human responsibility tied to autonomy must go, too. With the dissemination of subjective freedom out unto vibrant material assemblages, responsibility is disseminated, too, and can no longer be maintained in the normal political, moral, or ethical sense. The logical consequence, as Barad ascertains, is therefore that "responsibility is not a commitment that a subject chooses but rather an incarnate relation that precedes the intentionality of consciousness."[142] Responsibility cannot be conceived of as individual accountability, but must rather be understood as a broader acknowledgment of our shared participation in a vibrant diversity in which we are always entangled in worldly relations of becoming with other active, material forces and agents. Therefore, responsibility is transformed into the idea of how we (more passively) *respond* to the "ethical call," that is, the "invitation that is written into the very matter of all being and becoming."[143] Bennett makes a quite similar case, when she establishes how "the ensemble nature of action and the interconnections between persons and things" leave individuals "incapable of bearing *full* responsibility for their effects."[144]

Even though the idea of Kant's hypothetical Kingdom of Ends (*Reich der Zwecke*)—composed of autonomous beings, whose free rationality legislates how *autonomous* beings must never treat each other only as means to an end but always also as ends in themselves—is dispersed in *heteronomous* assemblages, it is paradoxically reinstated and expanded to comprise the entire material world after it has been subtracted from the human realm. In a sense, matter, not humans, is worthy of respect. Bennett therefore explains how "[t]hese material powers [...] call for our attentiveness, or even 'respect' (provided that the term be stretched beyond its Kantian sense)."[145]

Having abandoned the ideas and principles comprising the concept of autonomy in the human realm, Barad (like Bennett) reintroduces the Kantian argument about autonomy: she admonishes humans that

> it is crucial that we are mindful of the fact that the point here is not merely to use (non)humans as tools to think with, but in thinking with them to face our ethical obligations to them, for they are not merely tools for our use but real living beings (and I include in this category inanimate as well as animate beings).[146]

Autonomy seems to be a feature of every part of the material universe for the new materialists, if it is stipulated that humans are exempted hereof.

Another good example of this double movement, where *human* freedom is downscaled or even renounced proportionally to a corresponding upscaling of an inherent freedom in *nonhuman* entities, is provided by Morton (who also advances a quasi-animistic worldview not unlike that of Harman's polypsychism, Bennett's vibrant matter, or Barad's agential realism).[147] Morton argues against the traditional Marxist prioritizing of human labor over natural processes—encapsulated in Marx's dictum that "what distinguishes the worst architect from the best of bees is that the architect builds the cell in his mind before he constructs it in wax,"[148] i.e., because architects (humans), contrary to bees (nonhumans), are endowed with imaginative, intentional, and autonomous behavior. Morton even questions the very existence of a human imagination (and the freedom behind it):

> I'm not saying there is no imagination. Far from it. What I require the Marxist to do is to prove that the *architect* has imagination. Prove that I have imagination, as a human being. Prove that I'm not executing an algorithm. More to the point, prove that my idea that I'm not executing an algorithm isn't just the variety of algorithm that I've been programmed to execute.[149]

While the freedom or intentionality shaping a programming and a fashioning of algorithms is questioned or even denied for *human* beings, it is in the same breath said to apply to all other *nonhuman* beings.

By the same line of reasoning, distributed agency means that we need to reassess and dramatically reinterpret the political concept of democracy. Hence, Latour—who since the early 1990s has sought to dissolve the traditional boundaries between culture and nature, subject and object, human and nonhuman—calls for a revolution of politics that would reflect a "political process by which the cosmos is collected in one livable whole."[150] He calls for a political counterrevolution that would include nonhuman actors in the democratic community, and, indeed, embrace "*the voices of nonhumans*."[151] This may sound eccentric to those steeped in Enlightenment thought and its secular humanism, or to those not sharing posthumanist Rosi Braidotti's distrust of "secular scientific rationality."[152] But again, what must be kept in mind is that nonhumans are somehow to be understood in human terms with a human voice of their own: "Nonhumans are endowed with speech, however primitive, with intelligence, foresight, self-control, and discipline, in fashion both large-scale and intimate."[153] Not without a certain pathos, Latour completes the argument, claiming that to "limit the discussion to humans, their interest, their subjectivities, and their rights, will appear as strange a few years from now as having denied the right to vote of slaves, poor people, or women."[154] In the faction of object-oriented ontology, a figure like Levi Bryant has drawn similar political conclusions: "[I]n an age where we are faced with the looming threat of monumental climate change, it is irresponsible to draw our distinctions in such a way as to exclude nonhuman actors."[155]

As the theorization of an autonomous "life" or "agency" of things or objects argues for a more equal footing of humans and nonhumans, it only seems logical at this point that we invoke a premodern, benign animism or vitalism, in which the demos comprises the encompassing dynamics of the cosmos—in the argument of Bennett:

> [I]f human culture is inextricably enmeshed with vibrant, nonhuman agencies, and if human intentionality can be agentic only if accompanied by a vast entourage of nonhumans, then it seems that the appropriate unit of analysis for democratic theory is neither the individual human nor an exclusively human collective but the (ontologically heterogeneous) "public" coalescing around a problem.[156]

As to the question whether rejecting the idea of human distinctness by minimizing the difference between subjects and objects might lead to harmful ethical and political consequences, since humans might now legitimately be treated on a par with mere things or objects, Bennett responds that, well, "the Kantian imperative to treat humanity always as an end-in-itself and never merely as a means does not have a stellar record of success in preventing human suffering or promoting human well-being." The new materialisms' post-secular, anti-Enlightenment ethos is not only critical of what it believes to be a subjectivity of hegemonic sovereignty inherent in the exclusive humanist tradition of the West: as they seek to dismantle human exceptionalism, they also take issue with the idea of autonomy, freedom, and human dignity as an exclusive property of humans. Indeed, the idea of universal autonomy and individual freedom, expressed in the idea of humans as goals-in-themselves and not only means, is as false as it is harmful. At this point in history, what is needed is not more human freedom or an increased recognition or appreciation of every individual human being as endowed with freedom, reason, and self-determination.

On the contrary, it is far from ethically desirable to conceive of humans as end-in-themselves, for the concept of autonomy leaves us with a misleading and harmful sense of ourselves as discrete individuals with distinct human properties qualitatively distinguishing us from other things or objects. Seeing that humans cannot meaningfully be separated ontologically, morally, or politically from the material or objective universe, we should pursue a strategy of an *enhanced* instrumentalization of humans and stop treating them as free and rational individuals that are autonomous ends-in-themselves: "[T]he materialist speaks of promoting healthy and enabling instrumentalizations, rather than of treating people as ends-in-themselves, because to face up to the compound nature of the human self is to find it difficult even to make sense of the notion of a single end-in-itself."[157]

In addition, Bennett argues that getting rid of the modern concept of freedom would be redemptive for downtrodden people all over the world: "Vital materialism would thus set up a kind of safety net for those humans who are now, in a world where Kantian morality is the standard, routinely made to suffer because they do not conform to a particular (Euro-American, bourgeois, theocentric, or other) model of personhood."[158] Humans simply have had too much Kantian autonomy in the sociopolitical treatment of humans in modern times. The exaggerated respect shown them as free ends-in-themselves has worked to the detriment of the truer heteronomous, moral sources. As autonomy has dominated globally, there has been little space for *promoting healthy and enabling instrumentalizations*. Indeed, the concept of autonomy—dictating that each individual human is universally furnished with the capacity of autonomy as a free and rational being regardless of their specific gender, ethnicity, sexuality, culture, race, history, etc.—has been and continues to be a real source of global oppression and suffering. Seeing that the sociopolitical practice in modern times has been engrossed in respecting humans' autonomy as free ends-in-themselves, there has been a tendency not to take stock of more authentic heteronomous sources. Thus, the global hegemony of universal freedom and modern autonomy has suppressed more locally situated voices that hope to establish more natural hierarchical, spiritual, religious, tribalistic, or ethnocentric narratives.

Putting autonomy aside by decentering the human into the encompassing dynamics of the world would help us recognize our primordial unity with an enchanted and engaged material and moral cosmos, thus helping the abovementioned oppressed voices to better heard and uttered.

New Materialisms between Archaism and Hypercapitalism

Taking a hard look at 2008's contemporary world in a debate book with Bernard-Henri Lévy, Michel Houellebecq offers a rather harsh but not entirely unjust portrait of a general spiritual tendency in Western societies (a tendency in which the new materialisms arguably must be said to partake). What we are witnessing today, he says, is:

> a rapidly expanding spiritual movement (the only expanding spiritual movement in Europe these days) based on ecological fundamentalism mixed in some cases with left-wing alter-globalization [the global justice movement] and in others with half-witted New Age cults. This movement does attempt to connect Man to

the Universe, to give him a place in the "balance of nature" (and in particular to keep him in that place); but it also has very little to say about anything that might connect men to each other. Deep down, it's a sort of neopantheism.[159]

Indeed, a spiritualistic impetus seems to have seized a great many people today—even in the academies and universities.

Even if one may find that the theories of the new materialisms and object-oriented ontology are methodologically problematic or inconsistent, one might, nonetheless, be sympathetic toward their ethical vision and utopian sway. One might find that applying the ethical ontology of the new materialisms, highlighting the common materiality and interconnectedness of everything that exists, and taking stock of a wider distribution of agency and responsibility, would help us tame our aggressive human narcissism and protect ourselves and our environment. In addition, one may find that appreciating how the basic material essence of everything in the universe (of which we, too, form part) really is moral and sentient will inspire us to behave more responsibly and humbly, since we would understand that we—if it were not for our exclusive humanism that self-conceitedly sets us apart from our fellow material community—are intimately involved with everything else, part of a whole.

Indeed, would we not be better off forgetting about modernity and simply toss it aside?

Dissolving the distinctiveness of the human while simultaneously formulating firm demands that humans take on political responsibility and assume normative pleas to change the world in a more progressive direction may seem like a blatant performative contradiction. Obfuscating the localization of agency similarly occludes the question of responsibility. In an article criticizing the political and ethical consequences of the new materialisms, Sharon Krause offers a concise description of the problems with effacing human distinctiveness:

> Yet we should not lose sight of [our human agency's] distinctiveness, because it is our distinctive agency that enables us to hold ourselves accountable for the damage we have done and for the good we ought to do. We need to protect the natural world and repair the harm we have inflicted on it because electrons and rocks and bears cannot do this work without us. Likewise, we need to attend to other human beings, to what is broken or stunted or neglected in them, partly because the natural world is indifferent to human suffering, and partly because in many cases—many more than we are used to recognizing—we are in some measure responsible for what has gone wrong.[160]

If objects and things are capable of being moved by moral norms, reflexively regulating and adapting their behavior in response to them, it is obviously no longer solely our responsibility to take ethical or political action—for, as Bennett argues, the thing "will also have to do its part."[161] A case could be made that quietistically relying on heteronomous sources to assist in ethico-political situations only supports the status quo and stalls the implementation of action, leaving the initiative to conservative or reactionary forces.

One may wonder with Krause whether looking for ethical and political assistance from nature, the universe, God, history, the race, or from our fellow positrons or electrons is beneficial for progressive action. Moreover, as the new materialisms dissolve autonomy and self-determination within vibrant assemblages, animated objects, and material networks, they arguably fall victim to the argument that Rousseau, to take one, raises against Christianity, which he deems unfit to govern society. As a religion of resigned suffering, Christianity would only subvert political life by inspiring quietism rather than engagement and commitment. "Render [...] unto Caesar the things which are Caesar's; and unto God the things which are God's," says the Evangelist,[162] and Rousseau paraphrases, "after all what does it matter in this vale of tears whether one is free or a serf? The essential thing is to get to paradise, and resignation is but one more means to that end."[163] Distrusting the public scene of human rational action and sensing a greater affinity with the network of agential forces of which one is only a part, one might, in the face of climate change, for example, feel inclined to withdraw from the public political scene. Hence, Maurizia Boscagli cautions against the "fatalist tendency to the apolitical, or the anesthetic, in the new materialism."[164] In other words, one may find that the new materialisms flirt with romantic escapism and self-indulging reveries that in practice entail a passive stance that shies away from responsibility.

Blurring the boundaries between sheer causality and motivation (dependent on intentionality and a self-reflexive as well as individuated relationship to oneself as responsive to norms), the new materialisms cannot sustain a consistent belief in the personal responsibility and self-determination required by democracy and self-rule. Sharon Krause explains: "In denying the link between agency and a subjectivity that is reflexive and individuated, albeit not sovereign, the new materialism threatens to eviscerate the ground for holding persons responsible. Consequently, it cannot sustain a model of agency that is viable to democratic politics."[165] Even if one acknowledges that nonhuman bodies are external conditions for the execution of human action, that human agency is neither entirely autonomous nor sovereign but indebted to or confined by nonhuman bodies, and that humans are part of the material world, it takes an extraordinary leap of faith to attribute agency to things and to lift the distinction between intentionality and causality, as the new materialisms seem to do. Self-rule necessarily implies a kind of reflexive self, acting within a framework or dimension of order of its own, with its own binding forces and internal rules to acquire the capabilities needed for making truly democratic choices. And so, the demand to bend the knee to heteronomous material forces suspends the prospect of democratic self-determination. A critic like Christian Emden may therefore have a valid point when he argues that the value and legitimacy of democracy "cannot be answered by an appeal to the molecular structure of our cells," even though such normative questions do "depend on what we are as natural beings."[166]

In other words, cleansed of exclusively human traits, a flat ontology would undermine the bedrock of deliberative democracy inasmuch as the latter presupposes the unanimously acknowledged capability of its citizens to engage autonomously and rationally in public life in the firm conviction that fellow citizens act accordingly and respond likewise. To the extent that the democratic community would now include nonhuman entities, which to all intents and purposes do not seem to resonate with human reality, the mutual recognition needed among peers, as defined above, would be rendered null and void. Its takes quite a stretch to square the juxtaposition between humans and nonhuman objects in a way that would meaningfully meet the requirements of John Rawls's criterion of reciprocity, stipulating that, when "terms are proposed as the most reasonable terms of fair cooperation, those proposing them must also think it at least reasonable for others to accept them, as free and equal citizens, and not as dominated or manipulated, or under the pressure of an inferior political or social position."[167] Although the extent and the application of the principle of reciprocity have been debated, its centrality to democratic theorization remains widely uncontested.[168] For many political theorists, the principle means that a modern, liberal democracy should attempt to compensate for or reduce asymmetries due to disabilities or incapacities of one sort or the other through, for example, medical aids or education.

Moreover, the quasi-religious animism of the new materialisms, especially when presupposing a primordial enchanted unity with a benevolent Other, reactualizes the problem of evil. For, as Peter Wolfendale asks, if we extend relations of sympathy, morality, and respect from human agents to nonhuman things and objects, should we then "sympathize with the plight of smallpox, and if not, why not?"[169] When new materialism anthropomorphizes the universe and, in Žižek's words, subscribes to "the New Age topic of a deeper spiritual interconnectedness and unity of the universe," the otherness of matter and the universe "is covered up or facilitated by imaginary identifications which make the Other someone 'like us,' someone we can emphatically 'understand.'"[170] Unwittingly, the new materialists end up illustrating Fernando Pessoa's point, articulated by his anti-idealist and anti-romantic heteronym Alberto Cairo, that "flowers would, if they felt, not be flowers. They would be people."[171] And thus, if we assume that things are endowed with a sense of self and in possession of reflexivity and are thus capable of targeted action, this presupposition seems morally at odds with the catastrophic, painful, chaotic, and seemingly meaningless character of much that happens in the natural and material world.

In his usual provocative and darkly humorous manner, Žižek eminently captures the potential moral unpleasantness following from the premises of the new materialisms when he offers the following example of what a material assemblage could be: "We can think of Auschwitz as an assemblage—in which the agents were not just the Nazi executioners but also the Jews, the complex network of trains, the gas ovens, the logistics of feeding the prisoners, separating and distributing clothes, extracting the gold teeth, collecting the hair and ashes and so on."[172] The erasure of the distinction between intentionality and causality evidently has quite brutal consequences as concerns moral and political responsibility. For, if everybody and everything are accountable, then individual culpability seems to disperse into thin air.

In principle, the premodern gesture that insists upon casting autonomy and secularity aside would allow the emergence of new and quite sinister practical consequences. And so, Christian Abrahamsson seems to have a good case when, in reviewing Bennett's *Vibrant Matter*, he takes issue with the presumption that subjectivizing the world would give rise to better ways of being by noting the malignant influence of vitalist thought on Nazi geopolitics: "To be sure, there are risks with a disenchanted world, but there are also risks with a re-enchanted romantic *Weltanschauung* [...] I am not convinced that Bennett has sufficiently worked through the potential risks that come with disavowing the *I* and avowing the *it*."[173]

When the new materialists team up with the post-secular movement in the humanities and, for example, embrace "quasi-pagan" and "neo-pagan" superstition and animism "because the mood of enchantment may be valuable for ethical life," and when they argue that modern secularization has led us to "a place of dearth and alienation,"[174] one may wonder if the apparent contemporary need for (re)enchantment really springs from a global disenchantment contingent upon an all-encompassing secular, humanist rationality, and if the said secularization really is or would be a regrettable thing. Indeed, in the assessment of the new materialisms, "[t]he problem comes down to whether one agrees that disenchantment, or the related and recently maligned term, 'secularity,' is the source of today's ills," as Sarah Ellenzweig and John Zammito put it.[175]

Taking a hard look at the global situation now raises the question whether secular rationality and liberal self-determination are the sources of the current challenges with, for example, climate crisis, feelings of political impotence, and deep social unrest, or whether it is the other way around, so that the crises are rather consequent upon the failed or insufficient execution of these principles.[176] Are secularization, finitude, and autonomy really hegemonically setting the global agenda today? Or is it not more accurate to say that the severe distrust and unease with the modern project that resound from key voices within the new materialisms themselves resonate deeply with current global political reality? In other words, the passionate call issued from towering figures within the new materialisms to turn toward a re-enchantment and re-mythologization of the world fits nicely with a widespread global sociopolitical hostility to the modern project. Skeptical of liberal and universal rights and principles of modernity (i.e., freedom of speech, religious, political, and sexual tolerance etc.), a highly significant trend in the today's political scene is to enforce more religiously inspired ideologies critical of modern principles of autonomy and secularization, and to endeavor to reintroduce earlier religious, ethnic, and tribalistic political narratives. Secularism, autonomy, and liberal political rights seem to be discredited as tales of re-enchantment or re-mythologization hold more and more sway over more and more people in communities and nations almost everywhere. In the light of the current political reality and challenges, perhaps we should side with Robbins when he argues that the post-secular position may become potentially dangerous "when a break with secularism or rationality is [...] taken as the defining criterion of political resistance."[177]

Inasmuch as the new materialisms propose that we should spend our energy and resources engaging with things and objects that are supposedly alive and morally attuned, several critics have deemed that by doing so they do neoliberalism and capitalism a great favor by claiming that our problems have less to do with social and political conditions than with an insufficient appreciation of or empathy with the inner life of things and objects. Ascribing the responsibility for our present plight to humanity itself and to our disenchanted and insensitive relationship with the material world, these theories may unwittingly serve as decoys and smokescreens that hide the real causes behind the problems and thus obstruct any prospect for change.

Drawing on Karl Marx's theory of commodity fetishism from the *Capital*, Andrew Cole therefore characterizes the philosophy of the new materialisms as "the metaphysics of capitalism."[178] Specifically focusing upon the hubris inherent in human language and concepts, which arguably should be replaced by a personal inner experience of self-abandon that would cultivate our belonging to networks of material agents, the new materialisms tend to ignore those social, economic, or historical forces that shape our reality. This argument is pivotal to Paul Rekret's critique of the political and moral consequences of the new materialisms: "Recent calls on the left for adopting new materialist speculations as means of articulating an ontological 'resistance' to capitalism in nature would thus seem to be misguided insofar as they ask us to disavow the historicity of our own speculations and categories."[179] Seeing that the new materialisms indirectly diminish our distinctly human responsibility in that our problems are no longer issues strictly for us but shared by our nonhuman surroundings, critics like Bonnie Washick and Elizabeth Wingrove have been concerned "that the new terms of agency [...] make it difficult to name and so hold in view the continuities, durabilities and often monotonous predictabilities that characterize systems of power asymmetry (such as capitalism, patriarchy, racism)."[180] Alyson Cole has, furthermore, argued "that destabilizing the object/subject binary and endowing inanimate objects with vitality and agency is actually a constitutive feature of capitalism itself,"[181] while Galloway contends that Latour and speculative realism uncritically mirror the logic and infrastructure of contemporary cyber-capitalism.[182]

When the new materialists interpret human agency as an eventual gathering of a variety of forces interacting in an assemblage, that is, "not [as] a world [...] of subjects and of objects, but of various materialities constantly engaged in a network of relations,"[183] their ontology seems to stage and reaffirm the inner dynamic of capitalism, demanding a continuous creation and erasure of the social materiality and material sociality that comprise human reality. Bruce Robbins has likewise pointed out that the eternal becoming and perpetual unpredictability of matter are hardly an inherent utopian force that would disrupt what the new materialists perceive as the oppressive hegemonic order of the techno-ratio-capitalistic humanism of modernity, but rather a concise expression of global neoliberal capitalism *in actu* today:

> The paradigmatic institution of rationalization is bureaucracy. In the midst of a financial and economic crisis that is extraordinarily severe but historically far from unique, hearing news every day about the sufferings it has caused, we are reminded very forcibly of two things that we ought to have known before: that capitalism has more to do with the shape of our world than bureaucracy does, and although capitalism also uses numbers, it is not a force for rationalization, but a force for chaos. [...] In short, disenchantment is the wrong diagnosis. And reenchantment is the wrong remedy.[184]

In other words, Bennett seems to have a strong case when asserting that, as they avoid critical investment in analyzing structures of historical, economical, or social material conditions, the vital materialisms "will not solve the problem of human exploitation or oppression."[185]

Offering little if anything to reduce suffering or enhance freedom in the *human* realm, the new materialisms, in their efforts to de-center the sovereign human self in worldly processes, reversely make a utopian promise of emancipation in the *nonhuman*, objective realm. And so, the new materialists curiously echo Marx's description of the condition under Capitalist society as one of a "personification of things and a reification of persons"[186]—a characterization well-suited to describe our current situation. For, since the emergence of neoliberalism from the 1970s, extreme inequality and social alienation along with widespread disillusionment with mainstream politics have only increased, especially among the lower and most hard-hit classes.[187] Social and economic insecurity feeds resentment, political dissolution, and defeatism to pave the way for the success of reactionary, antimodern, and illiberal politics that we are witnessing today. Strongman leaders are exemplars of this trend, offering policies like tax cuts for billionaires, obstructing measures to tackle climate emergency, racism, xenophobia, and sexism. The politics enforced by most of these leaders are neoliberal, with tax cuts for the richest, deregulation, privatization, selling of state property and dismantling of social security, thus paradoxically reinforcing the very causes behind the sociopolitical frustration and despair of a large part of their supporters.[188]

According to Marx, the demand for illusions and the appearance of escapist chimeras are expressive of underlying *irrational* socioeconomical structures. He therefore explains that the "religious reflections of the real world can, in any case, vanish only when the practical relations of everyday life between man and man, and man and nature, generally present themselves to him in a transparent and rational manner."[189] Today, we are clearly far from having a transparent and rational relation between man and man as well as between man and nature. As long as this continues to be the case, one should not be too surprised to witness how a pervasive emancipatory craving today demands a return to "that other world, the world of the teapot."[190] What Knausgård described as "the forceful craving for reality that has begun to emerge around us,"[191] which appears more spiritualistic in nature than materialistic, is perhaps best understood as a desperate attempt to make sense of an age in deep crisis, an age that has lost hope that any human initiative can make a meaningful difference. As the human world of modernity is perceived as godforsaken and tainted by humanity, the project of achieving autonomy and freedom in the human realm is effectively disowned, displaced, and relocated into the nonhuman realm. Humans cannot make a positive change by their own effort; only things can save us now.

In that sense, the new materialisms are not as new and daring as sometimes believed. Around the turn of the twentieth century, when modernity entailed capitalistic industrialization, urbanization, massification, and bureaucratization, at a time when "the grand sociological accounts of modernity—by Émile Durkheim, Max Weber, and Georg Simmel—concur[red] in considering the increase in abstraction to be an overarching characteristic of the modernizing world," a modernistic counterresponse, very similar to the current new materialists', emerged, which consisted in the articulation of "aesthetic events meant to release things—or thingness—from the fetters of modernity."[192] This release of things and humans from modernity was frequently evoked by means of a sort of animism, in which the inhumanity of the human world was, as it were, counterbalanced by the humaneness of the nonhuman world.[193] The basic dynamics of this modernistic response against modernity is beautifully and touchingly condensed in a letter by Rilke, written in 1903:

> As a child, when everyone was always unkind to me, when I felt so infinitely forsaken, so utterly astray in an alien world, there may have been a time when I longed to be gone. But then, when people remained alien to me, I was drawn to things, and from them a joy breathed upon me, a joy in being that has always remained equally quiet and strong and in which there was never a hesitation or a doubt.[194]

When a human community is experienced as alien, atomized, and apprehensive, maternal comfort may be sought in the most unexpected places, and the wild, fugitive flight into the realm of things and objects (then and now) may be soothing inasmuch as the finitude of human reality gives way to feelings of infinite immediacy and the omnipotence of thought. But the relief granted by tossing finitude aside and extending the human beyond itself fails to produce more than a spiritualistic freedom of unchecked dogmatism and reveries that, in the material realm, will only be subjected to the whims of what is experienced as the inescapable necessity of the Washington Consensus. The new materialisms can therefore be considered a fascinating symptom of the contemporary crisis in the modern project and a melancholy reminder of Marx's historical materialist principle that "[m]en make their own history, but they do not make it just as they please."[195]

Even though humans are restricted by finitude and material conditions, and even though the project of modernity is perpetually haunted by crisis, one should not forget that it is also in finitude that freedom originates. And even though finitude entails humbling human limitations, it is only by facing this finitude that we can achieve a real possibility and prospect of manifesting freedom.

Today is a time of crisis that undeniably calls for critical self-reflection. A critique of the new materialisms seems like a good place to start.

Notes

1   Olga Tokarczuk, "Nobel Lecture by Olga Tokarczuk: The Tender Narrator," 14, Nobel Foundation, accessed July 30, 2020, available at https://www.nobelprize.org/uploads/2019/12/tokarczuk-lecture-english-2.pdf.
2   Tokarczuk, "The Tender Narrator," 25; Tokarczuk's emphasis.
3   Tokarczuk, "The Tender Narrator," 15.
4   Tokarczuk, "The Tender Narrator," 16.
5   Tokarczuk, "The Tender Narrator," 15.
6   Tokarczuk, "The Tender Narrator," 16.
7   Tokarczuk, "The Tender Narrator," 16–17.
8   Tokarczuk, "The Tender Narrator," 17.
9   See also Bill Brown, who points to a contemporary yearning for "some place of origin unmediated by the sign" ("Thing Theory," *Critical Inquiry* 28, no. 1 [2001]: 1). To that effect, Brown refers to a wonderful scene in A. S. Byatt's *The Biographer's Tale* (2000), where a doctoral student, fed up with poststructuralist and constructionist theories, "looks up at a filthy window and epiphanically thinks, 'I must have things.' He relinquishes theory to relish the world at hand: 'A real, very dirty window, shutting out the sun. A *thing*'" ("Thing Theory," 1–2). Slavoj Žižek has similarly pointed to a dark tendency in the late twentieth century impelled by a "passion for the Real," that is, by a desire to perceive and experience reality unmediated "as opposed to everyday social reality—the Real in its extreme violence as the price to be paid for peeling off the deceptive layers of reality": "The Authentic twentieth-century passion for penetrating the Real Thing (ultimately, the destructive Void) through the cobweb of semblances which constitutes our reality thus culminates in the thrill of the Real as the ultimate 'effect,' sought after from digitalized special effects, through reality TV and amateur pornography, up to snuff movies" (*Welcome to the Desert of the Real!: Five Essays on September 11 and Related Dates* [New York: Verso, 2002], 5–6, 12).
10 Karl Ove Knausgård, *My Struggle, Book 6: The End*, trans. Don Bartlett and Martin Aitken (London: Harvill Secker, 2018), 178. The translators' rendering of Knausgård's original Norwegian "nærvær" (*Min kamp* 6 [Oslo: Forlaget Oktober, 2012], 177) as "closeness" is not incorrect as such, but "presence" is a more concise translation, and the translation has been modified accordingly.
11 Knausgård, *My Struggle* 6, 747–8.
12 See David Shields, *Reality Hunger: A Manifesto* (New York: Knopf, 2010). For an art exhibit and collection of essays calling for a deeper connection with the oblique reality and life of things in modern art and culture, see Anselm Franke and Sabine Folie, ed., *Animismus: Moderne hinter den Spiegeln* (Cologne: Walther König, 2011) as well as Lorraine Daston, ed., *Things That Talk: Object Lessons from Art and Science* (New York: Zone, 2004).
13 Hans Ulrich Gumbrecht, *Production of Presence: What Meaning Cannot Convey* (Stanford, CA: Stanford University Press, 2004), xiv.

14 Gumbrecht, *Production of Presence*, 144.
15 Gumbrecht, *Production of Presence*, 137.
16 Gumbrecht, *Production of Presence*, 136.
17 Graham Harman, "On the Undermining of Objects," in *The Speculative Turn: Continental Materialism and Realism*, ed. Levi Bryant, Nick Srnicek, and Graham Harman (Melbourne: re.press, 2011), 22.
18 Cf. Graham Harman, *The Quadruple Object* (Winchester/Washington: Zero Books, 2011), 12.
19 Harman, *The Quadruple Object*, 63.
20 Harman, *The Quadruple Object*, 63.
21 Graham Harman, "In the Late Afternoon of Modernism: An Interview with Graham Harman," Bad at Sports, Caroline Picard, accessed August 5, 2020, available at http://badatsports.com/2016/in-the-late-afternoon-of-modernism-an-interview-with-graham-harman/.
22 Cf. Graham Harman, *Immaterialism* (Cambridge/Malden, MA: Polity Press, 2016), 27f.
23 Harman, *Immaterialism*, 33.
24 Harman, *The Quadruple Object*, 122; emphasis in original.
25 Cf. Harman, *The Quadruple Object*, 69.
26 Cf. Harman, *The Quadruple Object*, 68.
27 Harman, "On the Undermining of Objects," 24. See also Graham Harman, *Weird Realism: Lovecraft and Philosophy* (Winchester: Zero Books, 2012).
28 Graham Harman, "On the Horror of Phenomenology: Lovecraft and Husserl," *Collapse* 4 (2008): 334.
29 Jane Bennett, *Vibrant Matter: A Political Ecology of Things* (Durham, NC: Duke University Press, 2010), 7.
30 Manuel DeLanda and Rosi Braidotti coined the term "new materialism" in the second half of the 1990s. However, the movement known by the name emerged more recently. Bennet's book *Vibrant Matter* (2010) was one of the first to formulate the basic principles of the movement along with Diana Coole and Samantha Frost's (ed.), *New Materialisms: Ontology, Agency, and Politics* (Durham, NC: Duke University Press, 2010). See especially the editors' introduction to the anthology ("Introducing the New Materialisms"). Exceeding the scope of the singular use of the term "new materialism," we will in the following use the plural term "new materialisms" in a broader sense for convenience and to denote a tendency within recent constellations of materialist and realist thought to put into doubt the theoretical validity and significance of the linguistic turn and cultural materialism. Whatever their internal differences, the materialisms and realisms of theories such as dark ecology, actor-network theory, agential realism, new materialism (in singular), speculative realism, and object-oriented ontology nonetheless share a radical realist commitment critical of all kinds of so-called "correlationism," as they accentuate the need to put human subjectivity under erasure.
31 Bennett, *Vibrant Matter*, 3.
32 Diana Coole and Samantha Frost, "Introducing the New Materialisms," in *New Materialisms: Ontology, Agency, and Politics*, ed. Diana Coole and Samantha Frost (Durham, NC: Duke University Press, 2010), 1–43.
33 Bennett, *Vibrant Matter*, 4.
34 Bennett, *Vibrant Matter*, 30.
35 Bennett, *Vibrant Matter*, 117.

36 Bennett, *Vibrant Matter*, ix.
37 Diana Coole, "Agentic Capacities and Capacious Historical Materialism: Thinking with New Materialism in the Political Sciences," *Millennium: Journal of International Studies* 41, no. 3 (2013): 453.
38 Karen Barad, "Interview with Karen Barad," in *New Materialism: Interviews and Cartographies*, ed. Rick Dolphijn and Iris van der Tuin (Ann Arbor: Open Humanities Press, Michigan Publishing, University of Michigan Library, 2012), 69.
39 See Karen Barad, "On Touching: The Inhuman That Therefore I Am," *Differences* 23, no. 3 (2012): 206–23, see especially 215–19.
40 Barad, "Interview," 59.
41 Bennett, *Vibrant Matter*, 3; Bennett's emphasis.
42 Bennett, *Vibrant Matter*, 2.
43 Bennett, *Vibrant Matter*, xvi.
44 Slavoj Žižek, *Absolute Recoil: Towards a New Foundation of Dialectic Materialism* (London: Verso, 2015), 9.
45 Bennett, *Vibrant Matter*, 122.
46 Alan R. van Wyk, "What Matters Now?" *Cosmos and History: The Journal of Natural and Social Philosophy* 8, no. 2 (2012): 131.
47 Jane Bennett, *The Enchantment of Modern Life: Attachments, Crossings, and Ethics* (Princeton: Princeton University Press, 2001), 12 and 118.
48 Wyk, "What Matters Now?" 131.
49 Timothy Morton, *Ecology without Nature: Rethinking Environmental Aesthetics* (Cambridge, MA/London: Harvard University Press, 2007), 1.
50 Timothy Morton, *Dark Ecology: For a Logic of Future Coexistence* (New York: Columbia University Press, 2016), 10.
51 Morton, *Dark Ecology*, 5.
52 Timothy Morton, *Hyperobjects: Philosophy and Ecology after the End of the World* (Minneapolis/London: University of Minnesota Press, 2013), 1; emphasis in original.
53 Morton, *Hyperobjects*, 28.
54 See, for example, Morton, *Dark Ecology*, 110.
55 Morton, *Dark Ecology*, 11 and 6.
56 Morton, *Dark Ecology*, 6 and 11; emphasis in original.
57 Morton, *Dark Ecology*, 116.
58 Cf. Morton, *Dark Ecology*, 117.
59 Cf. Morton, *Dark Ecology*, 17.
60 Morton, *Dark Ecology*, 16.
61 Timothy Morton, *Being Ecological* (Cambridge, MA: MIT Press, 2018), 80. See also Morton, *Dark Ecology*, 137.
62 Latour's critique of modernity is taken up by Bennett and Harman, whose works directly engage with Latour's theories (Bennett's concept of "thing-power" from *Vibrant Matter* is inspired by Latour's idea of an "actant" as a source of action that can be human as well as nonhuman, and Graham Harman has devoted an entire book to him; see *Prince of Network: Bruno Latour and Metaphysics* [Melbourne, Australia: re.press, 2009]). Meillassoux praises Latour's break with correlationism (cf. Ray Brassier et al., "Speculative Realism," *Collapse* 3 [2007], 423), while Morton, though he departs from Latour's claim that we have never been modern, acknowledges "shared philosophical concerns" (Morton, *Hyperobjects*, 19) between the two.
63 Bruno Latour, *We Have Never Been Modern*, trans. Cathy Porter (Cambridge, MA: Harvard University Press, 1993), 10–11.

64 Latour, *We Have Never Been Modern*, 47.
65 Cf. Latour, *We Have Never Been Modern*, 65.
66 Cf. Latour, *We Have Never Been Modern*, 128.
67 Latour, *We Have Never Been Modern*, 47.
68 See, for example, Bruno Latour, *An Inquiry into Modes of Existence* (Cambridge, MA: Harvard University Press, 2013).
69 Latour, *We Have Never Been Modern*, 128.
70 See Bruno Latour, *Facing Gaia: Eight Lectures on the New Climate Regime*, trans. Cathy Porter (Cambridge/Medford, MA: Polity Press, 2017).
71 Latour, *Facing Gaia*, 150.
72 Latour, *Facing Gaia*, 149.
73 Latour, *We Have Never Been Modern*, 144.
74 Bennett, *Vibrant Matter*, 13.
75 Bennett, *Vibrant Matter*, 17.
76 Charles Taylor, *A Secular Age* (Cambridge, MA: The Belknap Press of Harvard University Press, 2007), 1.
77 See Max Weber's famous *Science as a Vocation* (the text of a lecture given in 1918 at Munich University), in *The Vocation Lectures*, ed. David Owen and Tracy Strong, trans. Rodney Livingstone (Indianapolis, IL: Hackett Books, 2004), 1–31.
78 Taylor, *A Secular Age*, 29–30.
79 Taylor, *A Secular Age*, 33.
80 Taylor, *A Secular Age*, 32.
81 Taylor, *A Secular Age*, 33.
82 Taylor, *A Secular Age*, 35.
83 Taylor, *A Secular Age*, 40.
84 Bennett, *Vibrant Matter*, xviii.
85 T. S. Elliot, *The Wasteland*, ed. Michael North (New York: W. W. Norton & Company, 2001), 11.
86 Bennett, *Vibrant Matter*, 18.
87 Jane Bennett, "A Vitalist Stopover on the Way to a New Materialism," in *New Materialisms: Ontology, Agency, and Politics*, ed. Diana Coole and Samantha Frost (Durham, NC: Duke University Press, 2010), 48.
88 See Andrew Cole, "The Call of Things: A Critique of Object-Oriented Ontologies," *The Minnesota Review* 80 (2013): 106–18; Kellie Robertson, "Medieval Materialism: A Manifesto," *Exemplaria* 22, no. 2 (2010): 99–118; Shannon Gayk and Robyn Malo, "The Sacred Object," *Journal of Medieval and Early Modern Studies* 44 (2014): 457–67; and Anne E. Lester and Katherine C. Little, "Introduction: Medieval Materiality," *English Language Notes* 53, no. 2 (2015): 1–8.
89 Graham Harman, *Object-Oriented Ontology: A New Theory of Everything* (London: Pelican Books, 2017), 150 and 164.
90 Harman, *Object-Oriented Ontology*, 154.
91 Harman, *Object-Oriented Ontology*, 166; emphasis in original.
92 Žižek, *Absolute Recoil*, 9.
93 Cole, "The Call of Things," 107.
94 Bennett, *Vibrant Matter*, 6.
95 Lester and Little, "Introduction," 7n7.
96 Taylor, *A Secular Age*, 38.
97 Barad, "Interview with Karen Barad," 49.
98 See Gumbrecht, *Production of Presence*, 142–5.

99 See Bennett, *Vibrant Matter*, xiii–xiv.
100 Coole and Frost, "Introducing the New Materialisms," 9.
101 For the *locus classicus* of Bruno Latour's critique of critique, see his article "Why Critique Has Run Out of Steam," *Critical Inquiry* 30 (2004): 225–48.
102 Bruno Latour, *Reassembling the Social: An Introduction to Actor-Network-Theory* (Oxford: Oxford University Press, 2005), 245.
103 Paul Rekret, "A Critique of New Materialism: Ethics and Ontology," *Subjectivity* 9, no. 3 (2016): 227.
104 Rita Felski, *The Limits of Critique* (Chicago: University of Chicago Press, 2015), 195–96n4.
105 Felski, *The Limits of Critique*, 175.
106 Toril Moi, *Revolution of the Ordinary: Literary Studies after Wittgenstein, Austin, and Cavell* (Chicago: University of Chicago Press, 2017), 124.
107 Moi, *Revolution of the Ordinary*, 128.
108 Moi, *Revolution of the Ordinary*, 127.
109 Paul Ricœur, *Freud and Philosophy: An Essay on Interpretation*, trans. Denis Savage (Yale: Yale University Press, 1977), 33.
110 Martin Heidegger, *Kant and the Problem of Metaphysics* (fifth edition, enlarged), trans. Richard Taft (Bloomington/Indianapolis: Indiana University Press, 1997), 160.
111 Heidegger, *Kant and the Problem of Metaphysics*, 64.
112 Heidegger, *Kant and the Problem of Metaphysics*, 160.
113 Martin Heidegger, *The Fundamental Concepts of Metaphysics: World, Finitude, Solitude*, trans. William McNeill and Nicholas Walker (Bloomington/Indianapolis: Indiana University Press, 1995), 5; emphasis in original.
114 Heidegger, *The Fundamental Concepts of Metaphysics*, 6.
115 Quentin Meillassoux, *After Finitude: An Essay on the Necessity of Contingency*, trans. Ray Brassier (New York: Continuum, 2008), 27; emphasis in original.
116 Bruno Latour, *Pandora's Hope: Essays in the Reality of Science Studies* (Cambridge, MA: Harvard University Press, 1999), 4.
117 Heidegger, *Kant and the Problem of Metaphysics*, 160.
118 Heidegger, *The Fundamental Concepts of Metaphysics*, 5.
119 Heidegger, *The Fundamental Concepts of Metaphysics*, 165.
120 Martin Heidegger, *Contributions to Philosophy (From Enowning)*, trans. Parvis Emad and Kenneth Maly (Bloomington/Indianapolis: Indiana University Press, 1999), 75; emphasis in original; German original quoted from Martin Heidegger, *Beiträge zur Philosophie (Vom Ereignis)* (Frankfurt am Main: Vittorio Klostermann, 1989), 107.
121 Martin Heidegger, *Poetry, Language, Thought*, trans. Albert Hofstadter (New York: HarperCollins, 2001), 29.
122 Heidegger, *Contributions to Philosophy*, 75.
123 Sigmund Freud, *Totem and Taboo: Some Points of Agreement between the Mental Lives of Savages and Neurotics*, trans. James Strachey (London/New York: Routledge Classics, 2001), 87 and 88.
124 Freud, *Totem and Taboo*, 99.
125 Freud, *Totem and Taboo*, 103.
126 Heidegger, *The Fundamental Concepts of Metaphysics*, 166; emphasis in original.
127 G. W. F. Hegel, "The Positivity of the Christian Religion," in *On Christianity: Early Theological Writings by Hegel*, trans. T. M. Knox (Chicago: University of Chicago Press, 1948), 159.

128　G. W. F. Hegel, *Hegel's Lectures on the History of Philosophy*. Vol. 3, trans. E. S. Haldane (New York: Routledge and Kegan Paul, 1968), 423.
129　Denis Diderot (attributed), "Political authority [abridged]," in *Denis Diderot's The Encyclopedia: Selections*, ed. and trans. Stephen J. Gendzier (New York: Harper Torchbooks, 1967).
130　Jean-Jacques Rousseau, *The Social Contract*, in *"The Social Contract" and Other Later Political Writings*, ed. and trans. Victor Gourevitch (Cambridge: Cambridge University Press, 1997), 54.
131　Immanuel Kant, *Groundwork of the Metaphysics of Morals*, ed. and trans. Allen W. Wood (New Haven/London: Yale University Press, 2002), 58.
132　Persius Juvenal, *Juvenal and Persius*, Loeb Classical Library, ed. and trans. Susanna Morton Braund (Cambridge, MA: Harvard University Press, 2004), VI.223.
133　Kant, *Groundwork*, 63.
134　Kant, *Groundwork*, 49.
135　Coole and Frost, "Introducing the New Materialisms," 20.
136　Coole and Frost, "Introducing the New Materialisms," 4.
137　Gulshan Khan, "Agency, Nature and Emergent Properties: An Interview with Jane Bennett," *Contemporary Political Theory* 8 (2009): 101; emphasis in original.
138　Karen Barad, *Meeting the Universe Halfway: Quantum Physics and the Entanglement of Matter and Meaning* (Durham, NC: Duke University Press, 2007), 66.
139　Barad, *Meeting the Universe Halfway*, 177–8.
140　Barad, *Meeting the Universe Halfway*, 177.
141　Barad, *Meeting the Universe Halfway*, 393.
142　Barad, *Meeting the Universe Halfway*, 392.
143　Barad, *Meeting the Universe Halfway*, 396.
144　Bennett, *Vibrant Matter*, 37; emphasis in original.
145　Bennett, *Vibrant Matter*, ix.
146　Karen Barad. "Nature's Queer Performativity." *Qui Parle* 19, no. 2 (2011): 127.
147　Cf. Morton, *Dark Ecology*, 16 and 137.
148　Karl Marx, *Capital: Volume 1: A Critique of Political Economy*, trans. Ben Fowkes (London: Penguin, 1990), 284.
149　Morton, *Dark Ecology*, 30–1. For this line of critique, see also Morton, *Dark Ecology*, 26–31.
150　Latour, *Pandora's Hope*, 304.
151　Bruno Latour, *Politics of Nature: How to Bring Sciences into Democracy*, trans. Cathy Porter (Cambridge, MA: Harvard University Press, 1999), 69; emphasis in original.
152　Rosi Braidotti, *The Posthuman* (Malden, MA: Polity Press, 2013), 37.
153　Latour, *Pandora's Hope*, 203–4.
154　Latour, *Politics of Nature*, 69.
155　Levi R. Bryant, *The Democracy of Objects* (Ann Arbor, MI: Open Humanities Press, 2011), 12.
156　Bennett, *Vibrant Matter*, 108.
157　Bennett, *Vibrant Matter*, 12.
158　Bennett, *Vibrant Matter*, 13.
159　Michel Houellebecq and Bernard-Henri Lévy, *Public Enemies: Dueling Writers Take on Each Other and the World*, trans. Miriam Rachel Frendo and Frank Wynne (New York: Random House, 2011), 164–5; Houellebecq's emphasis.
160　Sharon Krause, "Bodies in Action: Corporeal Agency and Democratic Politics." *Political Theory* 39, no. 3 (2011): 312.

161 Bennett, *Vibrant Matter*, 30.
162 *Matthew* 22: 21 (King James version).
163 Rousseau, *The Social Contract*, 148.
164 Maurizia Boscagli, *Stuff Theory: Everyday Objects, Radical Materialism* (London: Bloomsbury, 2014), 27.
165 Krause, "Bodies in Action," 317.
166 Christian Emden, "Normativity Matters: Philosophical Naturalism and Political Theory," in *The New Politics of Materialism: History, Philosophy, Science*, ed. Sarah Ellenzweig and John H. Zammito (New York City: Routledge, 2017), 289.
167 John Rawls, "The Idea of Public Reason Revisited," *The University of Chicago Law Review* 64, no. 3 (1997): 770.
168 See, for example, Jürgen Habermas, "Religion in the Public Sphere," *European Journal of Philosophy* 14, no. 1 (2006): 1–24.
169 Peter Wolfendale, *Object Oriented Philosophy: The Noumenon's New Clothes* (Falmouth, England: Urbanomic, 2014), 383.
170 Žižek, *Absolute Recoil*, 12.
171 Fernando Pessôa, *O Guardador de Rebanho*, in *Poemas de Alberto Cairo*, ed. João Gaspar Simões and Luiz de Montalvor (Lisbon: Ática, 1946), XXVIII.9–10; our translation.
172 Žižek, *Absolute Recoil*, 8n8.
173 Christian Abrahamsson, "Book Review Forum. Vibrant Matter: A Political Ecology of Things," *Dialogues in Human Geography* 1, no. 3 (2011): 401.
174 Bennett, *The Enchantment of Modern Life*, 3, 12, and 118.
175 Sarah Ellenzweig and John H. Zammito, "Introduction: New Materialism: Looking Forward, Looking Back," in *The New Politics of Materialism: History, Philosophy, Science*, ed. Sarah Ellenzweig and John H. Zammito (New York City: Routledge, 2017), 6.
176 One may, for example, ask oneself whether it is a reflection of an obsession with secular rationality and the democratic rights of popular self-determination when (according to an analysis from the Center for American Progress Action Fund) 150 members of the 116th American Congress—all Republicans (nearly 60 percent of Republican members)—do not believe in the scientific consensus that human activity is making the Earth's climate change (notably, since the previous Congress, the number of climate deniers has decreased by thirty members, in part, because forty-seven former deniers retired, resigned, or were defeated in their 2018 re-election contests)? A number that, by the way, according to a Monmouth University poll, does not line up with public opinion, where close to 80 percent believe that climate change is real and leading to severe weather impacts.
177 Bruce Robbins, "Why I Am Not a Post-Secularist," *Boundary 2* 40 no. 1 (2013): 60.
178 Andrew Cole, "Those Obscure Objects of Desire," *Artforum Summer* (2015): 323.
179 Rekret, "A Critique of New Materialism," 240.
180 Bonnie Washick and Elizabeth Wingrove, "Politics That Matter: Thinking about Power and Justice with the New Materialists," *Contemporary Political Theory* 14, no. 1 (2015): 66.
181 Alyson Cole, "The Subject of Objects: Marx, New Materialism, and Queer Forms of Life," *Journal for Cultural Research* 22, no. 2 (2018): 167.
182 Alexander R. Galloway, "The Poverty of Philosophy: Realism and Post-Fordism," *Critical Inquiry* 39, no. 2 (2013): 347–66.

183 Jane Bennett, "The Force of Things: Steps toward an Ecology of Matter," *Political Theory* 32, no. 3 (2004): 354.
184 Bruce Robbins, "Enchantment? No, Thank You!," in *The Joy of Secularism: 11 Essays for How We Live Now*, ed. George Levine (Princeton, NJ: Princeton University Press, 2011), 92.
185 Bennett, *Vibrant Matter*, 13.
186 Marx, *Capital*, 209.
187 For the history and definition of neoliberalism, see David Harvey, *A Brief History of Neoliberalism* (Oxford: Oxford University Press, 2007). For the story and economical logics behind the capitalistic rise of inequality, see Thomas Piketty, *Capital in the Twenty-First Century* (Cambridge: Belknap Press, 2014).
188 In its annual report on global inequality, presented at the first day (January 21, 2020) of the Annual Meeting of the global elites, World Economic Forum, in the Swiss city, Davos, the development organization Oxfam concluded: "Economic inequality is out of control. In 2019, the world's billionaires, only 2,153 people, had more wealth than 4.6 billion people. The richest 22 men in the world own more wealth than all the women in Africa. These extremes of wealth exist alongside great poverty. […] This broken economic model has accumulated vast wealth and power into the hands of a rich few, in part by exploiting the labour of women and girls, and systematically violating their rights. At the top of the global economy a small elite are unimaginably rich. Their wealth grows exponentially over time, with little effort, and regardless of whether they add value to society" (Oxfam International, *Time to Care: Unpaid and Underpaid Care Work and the Global Inequality Crisis* 9, accessed February 5, 2021, available at https://oxfamilibrary.openrepository.com/bitstream/handle/10546/620928/bp-time-to-care-inequality-200120-en.pdf). For the complex causality between the rise of right-wing populism and the increased crises of democratic legitimation and representation along with rising politico-social alienation, see Kirk Hawkins, Madeleine Read, and Teun Pauwels, "Populism and Its Causes," in *The Oxford Handbook of Populism*, ed. Cristóbal Rovira Kaltwasser, Paul Taggart, Paulina Ochoa Espejo, and Pierre Ostiguy (Oxford: Oxford University Press, 2017), 267–86, Cas Mudde, *Populist Radical Right Parties in Europe* (Cambridge: Cambridge University Press, 2007), and "The Populist Zeitgeist," *Government and Opposition* 39, no. 4 (2004): 541–6.
189 Marx, *Capital*, 173.
190 Tokarczuk, "The Tender Narrator," 17.
191 Knausgård, *My Struggle* 6, 748.
192 Bill Brown, "Materialities of Modernism: Objects, Matter, Things," in *A Handbook of Modernism Studies*, ed. Jean-Michel Rabaté (Chichester, West Sussex: Wiley-Blackwell, 2013), 281.
193 The story of this interest of the modernists in the inner and secret life of things as a safe haven from a relentless modernity cannot be told here; but see, for example, Bill Brown's article quoted above as well as Brook Henkel, *Animistic Fictions: German Modernism, Film, and the Animation of Things* (PhD diss., Columbia University, 2013).
194 Rainer Maria Rilke, *The Letters of Rainer Maria Rilke, 1892-1910*, trans. Jane Bannard Greene and M. D. Herter (New York: W. W. Norton, 1969), 102.
195 Karl Marx, *The Eighteenth Brumaire of Louis Bonaparte* (Moscow: Progress Publishers, 1972), 10.

Cited Works

Abrahamsson, Christian. "Book Review Forum: Vibrant Matter: A Political Ecology of Things." *Dialogues in Human Geography* 1, no. 3 (2011): 399–402.
Barad, Karen. *Meeting the Universe Halfway: Quantum Physics and the Entanglement of Matter and Meaning*. Durham, NC: Duke University Press, 2007.
Barad, Karen. "Nature's Queer Performativity." *Qui Parle* 19, no. 2 (2011): 121–58.
Barad, Karen. "Interview with Karen Barad." In *New Materialism: Interviews and Cartographies*, edited by Rick Dolphijn and Iris van der Tuin, 48–70. Ann Arbor, MI: Open Humanities Press, 2012.
Barad, Karen. "On Touching: The Inhuman That Therefore I Am." *Differences* 23, no. 3 (2012): 206–23.
Bennett, Jane. *The Enchantment of Modern Life: Attachments, Crossings, and Ethics*. Princeton: Princeton University Press, 2001.
Bennett, Jane. "The Force of Things: Steps toward an Ecology of Matter." *Political Theory* 32, no. 3 (2004): 347–72.
Bennett, Jane. *Vibrant Matter: A Political Ecology of Things*. Durham, NC: Duke University Press, 2010.
Bennett, Jane. "A Vitalist Stopover on the Way to a New Materialism." In *New Materialisms: Ontology, Agency, and Politics*, edited by Diana Coole and Samantha Frost, 47–69. Durham, NC: Duke University Press, 2010.
Boscagli, Maurizia. *Stuff Theory: Everyday Objects, Radical Materialism*. London: Bloomsbury, 2014.
Braidotti, Rosi. *The Posthuman*. Malden, MA: Polity Press, 2013.
Brassier, Ray, Iain Hamilton Grant, Graham Harman, and Quentin Meillassoux. "Speculative Realism." In *Collapse: Philosophical Research and Development*. Vol. 3, edited by Robin Mackay, 307–449. Falmouth, England: Urbanomic, 2007.
Brown, Bill. "Thing Theory." *Critical Inquiry* 28, no. 1 (2001): 1–22.
Brown, Bill. "Materialities of Modernism: Objects, Matter, Things." In *A Handbook of Modernism Studies*, edited by Jean-Michel Rabaté, 281–95. Chichester, West Sussex: Wiley-Blackwell, 2013.
Cole, Alyson. "The Subject of Objects: Marx, New Materialism, and Queer Forms of Life." *Journal for Cultural Research* 22, no. 2 (2018): 167–79.
Cole, Andrew. "The Call of Things: A Critique of Object-Oriented Ontologies." *The Minnesota Review* 80 (2013): 106–18.
Cole, Andrew. "Those Obscure Objects of Desire." *Artforum Summer* (2015): 317–23.
Coole, Diana. "Agentic Capacities and Capacious Historical Materialism: Thinking with New Materialism in the Political Sciences." *Millennium: Journal of International Studies* 41, no. 3 (2013): 451–69.
Coole, Diana and Samantha Frost. "Introducing the New Materialisms." In *New Materialisms: Ontology, Agency, and Politics*, edited by Diana Coole and Samantha Frost, 1–43. Durham, NC: Duke University Press, 2010.
Diderot, Denis, (attributed). "Political authority [abridged]." In *Denis Diderot's The Encyclopedia: Selections*. Edited and translated by Stephen J. Gendzier, 254–6. New York: Harper Torchbooks, 1967.
Ellenzweig, Sarah, and John H. Zammito. "Introduction: New Materialism: Looking Forward, Looking Back." In *The New Politics of Materialism: History, Philosophy, Science*, edited by Sarah Ellenzweig and John H. Zammito, 1–15. New York: Routledge, 2017.

Elliot, T. S. *The Wasteland*, edited by Michael North. New York: W. W. Norton & Company, 2001.

Emden, Christian. "Normativity Matters: Philosophical Naturalism and Political Theory." In *The New Politics of Materialism: History, Philosophy, Science*, edited by Sarah Ellenzweig and John H. Zammito, 269–99. New York: Routledge, 2017.

Felski, Rita. *The Limits of Critique*. Chicago: University of Chicago Press, 2015.

Freud, Sigmund. *Totem and Taboo: Some Points of Agreement between the Mental Lives of Savages and Neurotics*. Translated by James Strachey. London and New York: Routledge Classics, 2001.

Gayk, Shannon, and Robyn Malo. "The Sacred Object." *Journal of Medieval and Early Modern Studies* 44 (2014): 457–67.

Gumbrecht, Hans Ulrich. *Production of Presence: What Meaning Cannot Convey*. Stanford, CA: Stanford University Press, 2004.

Harman, Graham. "On the Horror of Phenomenology: Lovecraft and Husserl." In *Collapse: Philosophical Research and Development*. Vol. 4, edited by Robin Mackay, 333–64. Falmouth, England: Urbanomic, 2008.

Harman, Graham. *The Quadruple Object*. Winchester/Washington: Zero Books, 2011.

Harman, Graham. "On the Undermining of Objects." In *The Speculative Turn: Continental Materialism and Realism*, edited by Levi Bryant, Nick Srnicek, and Graham Harman, 21–40. Melbourne: re.press, 2011.

Harman, Graham. *Immaterialism*. Cambridge/Malden, MA: Polity Press, 2016.

Harman, Graham. *Object-Oriented Ontology: A New Theory of Everything*. London: Pelican Books, 2017.

Harman, Graham. "In the Late Afternoon of Modernism: An Interview with Graham Harman." By Caroline Picard. *Bad at Sports*, (August 2, 2016). Available at http://badatsports.com/2016/in-the-late-afternoon-of-modernism-an-interview-with-graham-harman/. Accessed August 5, 2020.

Hegel, G. W. F. "The Positivity of the Christian Religion." In *On Christianity: Early Theological Writings by Hegel*, translated by T. M. Knox. Chicago: University of Chicago Press, 1948.

Hegel, G. W. F. *Hegel's Lectures on the History of Philosophy*. Vol. 3. Translated by E. S. Haldane. New York: Routledge and Kegan Paul, 1968.

Heidegger, Martin. *Beiträge zur Philosophie (Vom Ereignis)*. Gesamtausgabe 65. Frankfurt: Vittorio Klostermann, 1989.

Heidegger, Martin. *The Fundamental Concepts of Metaphysics: World, Finitude, Solitude*. Translated by William McNeill and Nicholas Walker. Bloomington/Indianapolis: Indiana University Press, 1995.

Heidegger, Martin. *Kant and the Problem of Metaphysics*. Translated by Richard Taft. Fifth edition, enlarged. Bloomington/Indianapolis: Indiana University Press, 1997.

Heidegger, Martin. *Contributions to Philosophy (From Enowning)*. Translated by Parvis Emad and Kenneth Maly. Bloomington/Indianapolis: Indiana University Press, 1999.

Heidegger, Martin. *Poetry, Language, Thought*. Translated by Albert Hofstadter. New York: HarperCollins, 2001.

Houellebecq, Michel, and Bernard-Henri Lévy. *Public Enemies: Dueling Writers Take on Each Other and the World*. Translated by Miriam Rachel Frendo and Frank Wynne. New York: Random House, 2011.

Jacob, Margaret C. "Reflections on Bruno Latour's Version of the Seventeenth Century." In *A House Build on Sand: Exposing Postmodernist Myths about Science*, edited by Noretta Koertge. Oxford: Oxford University Press, 2006, 240–54.

Juvenal, Persius. *Juvenal and Persius*. Edited and translated by Susanna Morton Braund. Loeb Classical Library. Cambridge, MA: Harvard University Press, 2004.

Kant, Immanuel. *Groundwork of the Metaphysics of Morals*. Edited and translated by Allen W. Wood. New Haven/London: Yale University Press, 2002.

Khan, Gulshan. "Agency, Nature and Emergent Properties: An Interview with Jane Bennett." *Contemporary Political Theory* 8 (2009): 90–105.

Knausgård, Karl Ove. *Min Kamp 6*. Oslo: Forlaget Oktober, 2012.

Knausgård, Karl Ove. *My Struggle, Book 6: The End*. Translated by Don Bartlett and Martin Aitken. London: Harvill Secker, 2018.

Krause, Sharon. "Bodies in Action: Corporeal Agency and Democratic Politics." *Political Theory* 39, no. 3 (2011): 299–324.

Latour, Bruno. *We Have Never Been Modern*. Translated by Cathy Porter. Cambridge, MA: Harvard University Press, 1993.

Latour, Bruno. *Pandora's Hope: Essays in the Reality of Science Studies*. Cambridge, MA: Harvard University Press, 1999.

Latour, Bruno. *Politics of Nature: How to Bring Sciences into Democracy*. Translated by Cathy Porter. Cambridge, MA: Harvard University Press, 1999.

Latour, Bruno. *Reassembling the Social: An Introduction to Actor-Network-Theory*. Oxford: Oxford University Press, 2005.

Latour, Bruno. *Facing Gaia: Eight Lectures on the New Climate Regime*. Translated by Catherine Porter. Cambridge, MA: Polity Press, 2017.

Lester, Anne E., and Katherine C. Little. "Introduction: Medieval Materiality." *English Language Notes* 53, no. 2 (2015): 1–8.

Marx, Karl. *Capital: Volume 1: A Critique of Political Economy*. Translated by Ben Fowkes. London: Penguin, 1990.

Meillassoux, Quentin. *After Finitude: An Essay on the Necessity of Contingency*. Translated by Ray Brassier. London/New York: Continuum, 2008.

Moi, Toril. *Revolution of the Ordinary: Literary Studies after Wittgenstein, Austin, and Cavell*. Chicago: University of Chicago Press, 2017.

Morton, Timothy. *Ecology without Nature: Rethinking Environmental Aesthetics*. Cambridge, MA/London: Harvard University Press, 2007.

Morton, Timothy. *Hyperobjects: Philosophy and Ecology after the End of the World*. Minneapolis/London: University of Minnesota Press, 2013.

Morton, Timothy. *Dark Ecology: For a Logic of Future Coexistence*. New York: Columbia University Press, 2016.

Morton, Timothy. *Being Ecological*. Cambridge, MA: MIT Press, 2018.

Oxfam International. *Time to Care: Unpaid and Underpaid Care Work and the Global Inequality Crisis*. Accessed February 5, 2021. Available at https://oxfamilibrary.openrepository.com/bitstream/handle/10546/620928/bp-time-to-care-inequality-200120-en.pdf.

Pessôa, Fernando. *O Guardador de Rebanho*. In *Poemas de Alberto Cairo*, edited by João Gaspar Simões and Luiz de Montalvor. Lisaon: Ática, 1946.

Rawls, John. "The Idea of Public Reason Revisited." *The University of Chicago Law Review* 64, no. 3 (1997): 765–807.

Rekret, Paul. "A Critique of New Materialism: Ethics and Ontology." *Subjectivity* 9, no. 3 (2016): 225–45.

Ricœur, Paul. *Freud and Philosophy: An Essay on Interpretation*. Translated by Denis Savage. Yale: Yale University Press, 1977.

Robbins, Bruce. "Enchantment? No, Thank You!" In *The Joy of Secularism: 11 Essays for How We Live Now*, edited by George Levine, 74–94. Princeton, NJ: Princeton University Press, 2011.

Robbins, Bruce. "Why I Am Not a Post-Secularist." *Boundary 2* 40 (2013): 55–76.

Robertson, Kellie. "Medieval Materialism: A Manifesto." *Exemplaria* 22, no. 2 (2010): 99–118.

Rousseau, Jean-Jacques. *"The Social Contract" and Other Later Political Writings*. Edited and translated by Victor Gourevitch. Cambridge: Cambridge University Press, 1997.

Taylor, Charles. *A Secular Age*. Cambridge, MA: The Belknap Press of Harvard University Press, 2007.

Tokarczuk, Olga. "Nobel Lecture by Olga Tokarczuk: The Tender Narrator." Nobel Foundation. Available at https://www.nobelprize.org/uploads/2019/12/tokarczuk-lecture-english-2.pdf. Accessed July 30, 2020.

Washick, Bonnie, and Elizabeth Wingrove. "Politics That Matter: Thinking about Power and Justice with the New Materialists." *Contemporary Political Theory* 14, no. 1 (2015): 63–79.

Wolfendale, Peter. *Object Oriented Philosophy: The Noumenon's New Clothes*. Falmouth, England: Urbanomic, 2014.

Wyk, Alan R. van. "What Matters Now?" *Cosmos and History: The Journal of Natural and Social Philosophy* 8, no. 2 (2012): 130–6.

Žižek, Slavoj. *Welcome to the Desert of the Real!: Five Essays on September 11 and Related Dates*. New York: Verso, 2002.

Žižek, Slavoj. *Absolute Recoil: Towards a New Foundation of Dialectic Materialism*. London: Verso, 2015.

Chapter 1

OBJECT-ORIENTED ONTOLOGY AND
THE PASSION FOR THE REAL

Zahi Zalloua

An unmistakable hunger for the "real thing" drives the movement of object-oriented ontology (OOO). It shares with speculative realism (SR) a deep suspicion for anything that smells of correlationism, a widely used term coined by Quentin Meillassoux to designate the enemies of pure ontology. Any conceptual approach that qualifies its access to exteriority, to the "great outdoors,"[1] is effectively guilty of correlationism: "The thesis of the correlationist [...] is that I can't know what reality would be *without me*."[2] A correlationist must, then, always add "for me" (the categories of the mind, consciousness, language, power, and so on) to any claim that he or she makes about the external world. If, for SR and its sympathizers, Immanuel Kant was the first to inaugurate a regressive paradigmatic shift away from metaphysical inquiry to (the limits of) epistemology (his Copernican Revolution was in fact a "Ptolemaic Counter-Revolution"[3]), it is the "linguistic turn," along with what it spawned (postmodernism, Lacanian psychoanalysis, deconstruction), that has plagued and hamstrung contemporary continental philosophy. The remedy for this prison house of '68 theory was simple: initiate a return to ontology. This return, or rather revolt, was fueled by a "passion for the real,"[4] a passion for something beyond mediation, untainted by the exhausted categories of subjectivity and representation. With OOO, this desire for more reality (and less humanity) takes the form of a passion for objects, or what I have described elsewhere as "object fever."[5]

OOO's frontal attack on continental philosophy, seen as currently impaired by its linguistic preoccupations, can also be formulated in terms of *prima philosophia*. If, with Kant, epistemology frames the conditions for philosophy—philosophers must start with a recognition of what is within the realm of knowledge and appropriately curtail their will to speculate about the nature of world (the aim of *Critique of Pure Reason*)—with OOO, aesthetics is the new contender for *prima philosophia*. Graham Harman, one of the founders and leading figures of OOO, draws on Emmanuel Levinas's own corrective intervention, on his assertion of "ethics as first philosophy."[6] For Harman, the gift of Levinas is his disclosure of a different way of relating to the external world. Unlike Martin Heidegger,

Levinas refuses to reduce external objects to virtual equipment, to inscribe them in the system of being. Rather, he foregrounds the body and its enjoyment of the elements; the self's exposure to the environment is not a cognitive matter but an affective manner. Against Heidegger's "fundamental ontology" as first philosophy (which is said to repeat epistemology's insistence on mastery and domination), Levinas champions ethics, considering it the true *prima philosophia*, since it refuses to subordinate the other to the question of Being.

In what follows, I take up Harman's critical engagement with Levinas (his rejection of the latter's anthropocentric biases), focusing on the ways he rewrites Levinas's claim of ethics as first philosophy in order to champion "aesthetics as first philosophy." Next, I address the kind of aesthetics Harman favors, exploring his commitment to what he dubs "weird realism." As an alternative to the realism of OOO, I turn to Jean-Paul Sartre's novel *Nausea* (1938). I argue that the novel stages a passion for the real in his protagonist Antoine Roquentin. And this passion is very much oriented toward the uncanny objects in Roquentin's world. But whereas a OOO reading would too quickly celebrate the novel's displacement of Roquentin as subject (in the name of inanimate objects), I trace the persistence of the subject in *Nausea*. This subject, however, is not the "mega-actant"[7] so derided by OOO and other posthumanists. The subject in question here is better understood psychoanalytically as a subject fundamentally out of joint with itself, marked by its relation to what Jacques Lacan calls "*objet petit a*." Roquentin's passion for the real, his "extraordinary adventures"[8] with objects, illustrates and enacts the limitations of OOO, producing a *realism of the Real*, stranger than Harman's vaunted weird realism.

Aesthetics and the Sensible Ego

For Levinas, the ego comes into being through a "radical separation"[9] between itself and the world (Being as *totality*). In a sense, the ethical journey begins with enjoyment, with my "living-from" the world, that is, the self's appropriation of its surroundings for the purposes of nourishment, comfort, and familiarity: "[T]he transmutation of the other into the same [...] an energy that is other [...] becomes, in enjoyment, my own energy, me."[10] Enjoyment, for its own sake, characterizes the human condition: "To enjoy without utility, ... this is the human."[11] Enjoyment possesses "no ulterior meaning beyond what we encounter."[12] Enjoyment is synonymous with the sheer love of life; it is "an exaltation, a peak that exceeds the pure exercise of being. [...] The love of life does not love Being, but loves the happiness of being."[13]

The enjoyment of the sensible ego is clearly not the result of a cognitive act. Enjoyment reminds us of the primacy of the affective register. It is "entirely nonsignifying."[14] As Levinas avers, enjoyment does not involve "any intentional relationship of cognition and possession,"[15] nor does it belong "to the order of thought but to that of sentiment, that is, the affectivity wherein the egoism of the I pulsates."[16] It is not enough to fault Heidegger for neglecting the corporeality of the body; the joy of food is wholly foreign to a Heideggerian framework: "*Dasein* in Heidegger is never hungry. Food can be interpreted as an implement only in a world of exploitation."[17] Without enjoyment, I would remain entrenched in totality. The separated ego—dislodged from totality—paves the way for ethics, for my exposure to the infinity of the other, which radically takes me out of my comfort, placing me, as it were, "*outside* enjoyment."[18] The move from enjoyment to the other, from egoism to generosity, defines the priority of ethics.

Harman's intervention seeks to slow down Levinas's teleological move from enjoyment to ethics, and dwell longer in enjoyment, taking in what it discloses about the world of objects. He repeats Levinas's insight that we encounter objects via enjoyment, but adds that enjoyment itself never exhausts what an object *is*, never fully instrumentalizes it for egoistical ends. The object resists, its inner reality is immune from the "sleek power struggle of totality."[19] Harman, however, interrupts the next step in the Levinasian journey toward the (human) other's infinity.

He deems Levinas's reform of philosophy wanting insofar as it restricts the excesses of the face to humans. Steven Shaviro is also disappointed with Levinas's human exceptionalism, the anthropocentric belief that "we are alone in our aliveness: trapped in a world of dead, or merely passive, matter."[20] For Harman, ethics, as articulated by Levinas, is irremediably limited to the realm of humans and thus disqualifies it as *prima philosophia*: "[Levinasian] ethics cannot be first philosophy, since ethics unjustly divides the world between full-fledged humans and robotic causal pawns, in a manner little different from Descartes."[21] If the face of the other enables Levinas to exit the orbit of correlationism (it unsettles the self's state of immanence, problematizing its enjoyment and "egoist spontaneity"[22]), Harman democratizes the face; he generalizes the conditions for what might jolt the sensible ego out of its humanist, narcissistic slumber, distributing, in turn, the privilege of the face to all objects. Indeed, OOO regards all beings as agential objects, objects whose ontology exceeds their epistemological account, and thus noncompliant with our hermeneutic desires.

It is at the level of the aesthetic—in the realm of sensibility—that I encounter objects and enjoy their singularity. *Aesthetics as first philosophy* foregrounds and sustains the nonrelationality of objects. My encounters with objects are always incomplete; I can approach them only *obliquely*,[23] meeting them at the surface. Objects are irreducible to my will, to my interpretive system; my being never infringes on the autonomy of objects nor can I penetrate their "volcanic core."[24] The love of objects is not a moment in the ethical journey toward the other's infinity: it is the final destination of OOO.

Weird Realism

Harman's project is to restore the dignity of objects or things, to recognize their dutiful place in world. Their ontological status has been neglected for too long by continental philosophy and even science. His aim is to correct philosophy's idealist penchant, which fetishizes self-reflexivity and mediation, by refocusing our attention on objects of all kinds:

> Nothing could be more urgent for present-day philosophy, which for two centuries has lost touch with all the specific real and fictional entities that populate the cosmos. My claim is that reality is object-oriented, and that a corresponding shift is needed from the analysis of consciousness and written words towards an ontology of dogs, trees, flames, monuments, societies, ghosts, gods, pirates, coins, and rubies.[25]

Science does not fair better: "The thing as portrayed by the natural sciences is the thing made dependent on our knowledge, and not the thing in its untamed, subterranean reality."[26]

Materialism is also a concern for Harman:

> For it either undermines objects from below, reducing them downward to their material underpinnings, or it overmines them from above, reducing them upward to their appearance for human beings. Both strategies have abundant prestige, but both are disasters, since they strip objects of their autonomy and enslave them to a less worthy principle.[27]

And unlike the New Materialism championed by Jane Bennett, Harman's OOO warns against its overinvestment in process-oriented frameworks, which always risk eclipsing the "inner depth"[28] of objects, "deny[ing] the existence of individual objects in favor of a more primordial, vibrant continuum."[29] Harman prefers the flat ontology of Bruno Latour's actor-network theory (ANT) for its attentiveness to different types of objects: "The greatness of ANT [...] consists largely in its return to individual entities as opposed to throbbing or static wholes, and in its willingness to allow all entities an equal claim to participating in its theory: human and nonhuman, natural and cultural, real and imaginary."[30]

Still, the primacy that ANT attributes to relationality over the irreducibility and withdrawnness of objects troubles Harman. Latour ignores that "the being of any object is always deeper than how that object appears to us."[31] Upholding the doxa of relationism, Latour and Bennett ultimately betray objects "by abolishing any hidden depth in things while reducing them to their actions."[32] Only OOO does justice to the autonomous reality of objects. It actively promotes realism, but not in its epistemological version. Harman's realism is not about our capacity to know the world. This is realism under epistemology as *prima philosophia*. What Harman is after instead is a realism of the "great outdoors." To that end, OOO espouses a realism that boldly theorizes or speculates about the independent existence of the world. If philosophy is to take objects seriously, or *sincerely*,[33] it must adopt a realist orientation: "Philosophy must be realist because its mandate is to unlock the structure of the world itself."[34] Harman further qualifies this ontological realism as "weird": "It must be weird because reality is weird"[35]; "reality itself is weird because reality itself is incommensurate with any attempt to represent or measure it."[36]

In literature, no author, for Harman, performs this "weird realism" better than H. P. Lovecraft: "[N]o other writer is so perplexed by the gap between objects and the powers of language to describe them."[37] Harman admires the extent to which Lovecraft's art, his passion for the real, is "violently anti-idealist."[38] With his horror fiction, Lovecraft puts the metaphorical powers of language in the service of disclosing a reality that is itself "incommensurate with any attempt to represent or measure it."[39] Lovecraft's language is marked by its exposure to a reality that is through and through untranslatable. What we get in his stories is not so much the representation of reality as the reminder and remainder of language's failure to translate reality:

> The meaning of being might even be defined as untranslatability. Language (and everything else) is obliged to become an art of allusion or indirect speech, a metaphorical bond with a reality that cannot possibly be made present. Realism does not mean that we are able to state correct propositions about the real world. Instead, it means that reality is too real to be translated without remainder into any sentence, perception, practical action, or anything else.[40]

Lovecraft's description of his famous monster Cthulhu demonstrates what Harman appreciates about the author:

> If I say that my somewhat extravagant imagination yielded simultaneous pictures of an octopus, a dragon, and a human caricature, I shall not be unfaithful to the spirit of the thing. A pulpy, tentacled head surmounted a grotesque and scaly body with rudimentary wings; but it was the *general outline* of the whole which made it most shockingly frightful.[41]

Declining the style of representational realism, Lovecraft stages a more powerful scene for his readers by making their encounter with Cthulhu indirect, inviting them to experience/imagine the horror of the monster as something that exceeds the sum of his parts:

> Lovecraft hints at an octopoidal dragon while also suspending that literal depiction in three separate ways: (1) he downplays it as merely the result of his own "extravagant imagination"; (2) he evasively terms his description "not unfaithful to the spirit of the thing" rather than as dead-on correct; (3) he asks us to ignore the surface properties of dragon and octopus mixed with human and to focus instead on the fearsome "general outline of the whole," suggesting that this outline is something over and above a literal combination of these elements.[42]

The art of Lovecraft is to proceed obliquely, opening an "*indirect* access" to things-in-themselves, earning him the designation of "Kantian writer of 'noumenal' horror."[43] Lovecraft is at his best when he "poise[s] his creatures forever on the very brink of knowability."[44] Lovecraft's aesthetics produces worlds that are disturbingly not mine, unfiltered by my concerns and desires. Readers are constantly disabused of their correlationist bias and made to confront a *world-without-them*.

The Subject and objet petit a

A world-without-us characterizes OOO's passion for the real. Any (indirect) encounter with reality must pass through a radical suspension of the subject. "Getting out of the subject" and "getting the subject out,"[45] as Alenka Zupančič stresses, are *the sine qua non* of OOO. All of philosophy's problems begin and end with the subject. From its death ("the death of man"; "the death of the author") and endless resurrection (or its substitution with language or power), the subject stands for mediation—and all of its discontents. Harman's promotion of weird realism is a kind of "realism without a subject," pointing to an exit out of correlationism. It is a realism predicated on the demotion of the subject, removing its exceptionalism, treating it as an object among other objects. As fellow OOO traveler Timothy Morton observes: "We've become so used to hearing 'object' in relation to 'subject' that it takes some time to acclimatize to a view in which there are only objects, one of which is ourselves."[46] OOO's passion for the real is decidedly subject-free. There are no subjects—only objects. The subject's demotion is now complete and permanent.

This liquidation of the subject and elevation of the object simplify a great deal. Do you really need to choose between the subject or the object? This anti-correlationist blackmail—anything short of a full endorsement of the autonomous reality of things (the *parti pris* of objects) commits you to the unfavorable position of human exceptionalism or narcissistic idealism—is rejected by psychoanalysis on two grounds: first, the subject is not a "mega actant"; second, the object is not always distinct from the subject. Jacques Lacan's notion of *objet petit a* complicates OOO's simultaneous separation and dissolution of the subject/object distinction (it separates the two by positing the subject as a relic of correlationism and it dissolves the distinction by affirming that the subjects are in fact objects in line with the truth of flat ontology). *Objet petit a* compels us to consider the logic of desire when accounting for the object, since it is, strictly speaking, not exclusively in the object. *Objet petit a* is not only in the object—as the object-cause of desire; the unattainable object of desire—but also *in* the subject.[47] The desires of the subject are always mediated by the symbolic order—*desire is always desire of the Other*. My desires are never purely my own; to paraphrase Marx, they "have their origin in society."[48] Simply put, I am taught how to desire. This is the (ideological) function of social scripts and fantasies.

To trace the relation between the subject, object, and desire, psychoanalysis returns to the conditions and formation of the child. Prior to the Symbolic, the child's fusion with the mother—their symbiotic unity—constitutes pure gratification. The mother *occupies* the position of *das Ding*, the site of unity and plenitude.[49] The child's contact with the body of the mother—the unmediated or pure (m)other—is thus the originary scene of wholeness. But after the Symbolic, once the child exits this phantasmatic state of bliss—following the prohibition against incest, the Law of the Father/the Father's No (*le nom/non du Père*)—pure enjoyment is forever out of reach. After this profound loss, what is left then is *objet petit a*, "that which remains of the Thing [*Das Ding*] after it has undergone the process of symbolization."[50] Thus, social subjects, all we are allowed to enjoy, or have access to, are partial objects (*objets petit a*), with only partial gratification.

In the Symbolic, nostalgia sets in. People dream of a prior symbiosis, a lost wholeness—a distant *das Ding*. Žižek, however, warns against "substantializing" *das Ding*. To counter this impulse to ontologize, Žižek draws attention to the play of language in any conceptualization of *das Ding*. Consequently, *das Ding* must be seen as an *effect* or fiction generated by the symbolic order:

> What we experience as "reality" discloses itself against the background of the lack, of the absence of it, of the Thing, of the mythical object whose encounter would bring about the full satisfaction of the drive. This lack of the Thing constitutive of "reality" is therefore, in its fundamental dimension, not epistemological, but rather pertains to the paradoxical logic of desire—the paradox being that this Thing is retroactively produced by the very process of symbolization, i.e. that it emerges from the very gesture of its loss. In other (Hegel's) words, there is nothing—no positive substantial entity—behind the phenomenal curtain, only the gaze whose phantasmagorias assume different shapes of the Thing.[51]

The psychoanalytic account of the subject and *objet petit a* is a bit of a nuisance for OOO since it does not obey the strict separation between subject and object. If Harman is generous in attesting to the richness of the "quadruple" object, foregrounding the object's four facets ("real object," "real qualities," "sensual object," "sensual qualities"[52]), he is rather parsimonious when it comes to the subject. For those who *care* about the subject—Lacan and Žižek are named—they are simply described/dismissed as "enamored with the human subject,"[53] plagued by their attachment to the human, enthralled by its exceptionalism. But the very idea of *objet petit a* troubles OOO's passion for objects, the righteous labor of "getting out of the subject" and of "getting the subject out." OOO is ill-equipped to take up the psychoanalytic insight that the cathexis that magically turns an ordinary thing into a desirable object necessarily implicates the subject.

Roquentin's Passion for the Real

Sartre's existentialist novel *Nausea* tells the story of Roquentin's struggle with objects while undergoing something of an existential crisis. The link between the two appears to be causal: objects are revolting, his identity deteriorating. The origins of Roquentin's existential malaise preoccupy him from the start. No longer at home in the provincial town of Bouville (Mudville), where he has spent the last three years doing research on the biography of the Marquis de Rollebon, an eighteenth-century diplomat and adventurer, Roquentin is unsure as to why he now feels uneasy in the presence of everyday, inoffensive objects, like the pebble he picks up at the beach, provoking his first attack of nausea. As he disquietly notes:

> Objects should not *touch* because they are not alive. You use them, put them back in place, you live among them: they are useful, nothing more. But they touch me, it is unbearable. I am afraid of being in contact with them as though they were living beasts.[54]

A OOO reading seems almost irresistible here. Roquentin's sensible ego is discovering that objects are "actants" too, that the philosophical separation between human and object is fading away.

Hoping to reestablish his human privilege over the domain of object, and thus to reaffirm his superior status as subject, Roquentin sets out to implement an aggressive phenomenological regime to cope with his new situation. His diary—the novel we're reading—meticulously documents his progress and setbacks. Through writing down his observations, a passion for the real starts to take shape: "Let none of the nuances or small happenings escape even though they might seem to mean nothing. And above all, classify them. I must tell how I see this table, the street, the people, my packet of tobacco ... I must not put in strangeness where there is none."[55] Here Roquentin might pass for a OOO enthusiast *avant la lettre* given the movement's strong urge to make lists of objects, as Harman's "diamonds, rope, neutrons ... armies, monsters, square circles, and leagues of real and fictitious armies" attests.[56] To be sure, there is a difference in the intent behind the listing of objects. Roquentin is naming the physical objects around him in order to better control them, whereas Harman is seeking to expand our understanding of what constitutes an object—which for him does not have to be "physical nor even real."[57] Still, Roquentin develops an eye for objects. Their affective force is highlighted from the start in his cognitive project "to see clearly."[58] Epistemology and aesthetics, we might say, are co-originary when it comes to Roquentin's quasi-philosophical orientation.

Roquentin does not seem to belong to his bourgeois environment[59] and human community. He cannot understand how Bouvillians go about living their lives, and decries the Bouvillians' penchant for reducing the unknown to the known, for systematically ignoring anything that does not align with established *doxa*: "They explain the new by the old—and the old they explain by the older still, like those historians who turn Lenin into a Russian Robespierre, and a Robespierre into a French Cromwell: when all is said and done, they have never understood anything at all."[60] Roquentin's passion for the real is a passion for what lies beyond Bouville's homogenizing ideology and assimilative logic. He disidentifies with their sense of exceptionalism, with the ways they consider themselves "indispensable to something or someone."[61] Roquentin for his part is *de trop*, ontologically irrelevant: "[I]t seems as though I belong to another species"; "I hadn't the right to exist. I had appeared by chance, I existed like a stone, a plant or a microbe."[62] We might characterize Roquentin as a "postsubject object"—a subject dispossessed of the privileges of being human(ist).

How Roquentin got to this point remains a mystery. Aside from the pebble that triggered his first bout of nausea, Roquentin was experiencing a crisis at the professional level. As a would-be biographer of the Marquis de Rollebon, he becomes skeptical of the project. After critically assessing his research, Roquentin comes to realize to his chagrin that his arrangements of events lack any genuine coherence, any deep hidden truth. "What is lacking in all this testimony is firmness and consistency. They do not contradict each other, neither do they agree with each other; they do not seem to be about the same person."[63] History possesses no inherent meaning. Consequently, his project of portraying the actual events of Rollebon's past is as fake as the Bouvillians' mystification of their lifeworld. Both engage in fiction and the distortion of the reality of things.

What is noteworthy from a OOO perspective is the status of Rollebon as an *object* of study. Existentialism makes a sharp distinction between a living human and a dead human; the latter is subjected to the former, to the interpretive wills of the living. The claim that "Hell is other people" from Sartre's play *Huis Clos* illustrates that point, as the three dead figures of the play find themselves reduced to their facticity, to the pure status of *en soi*—the "in itself" that it shares with inanimate objects—unable to change who they are, having lost their freedom. But the dead Rollebon behaves as if he were alive, resisting Roquentin's will, disrupting his biographical desire for coherence. The loss of Rollebon's *pour soi* (the "for itself," that which makes transcendence possible) does not diminish the object's capacity to withdraw.

Roquentin is driven by a passion for the real. He is not satisfied with the semblance of the Marquis de Rollebon; he does not want to settle for a proximate image—he wants the real thing. But since it is not available, he decides to abandon the project altogether. The ramifications of this decision are significant. As Andy Leak rightly observes, "Rollebon was far more than simply *any* project for Roquentin, he had been a paternal guarantor of the latter's identity."[64] Rollebon was no mere object of biographical investigations; he guaranteed Roquentin's identity. He was his *objet petit a*. Rollebon, a minor historical figure, was magically transformed into someone who mattered, who mattered to Roquentin. The promise of the biography gave Roquentin hope and purpose, satisfying his hunger for meaningful and pleasurable plenitude. It helped to remedy, as much as possible, the void left by the cut of the signifier. Rollebon as *objet petit a* compensated for Roquentin's socialization and loss of fully enjoyment. With the dissolution of this magical object, existential alienation sat in, or rather returned with a vengeance.

Roquentin's alienation reaches its apogee when his own hand appears as other, as an obtrusive object affectively detached from its proprietor: "I see my hand spread out on the table. […] no matter where I put it it will go on existing; I can't suppress it, nor can I suppress the rest of my body."[65] Amidst his self-estrangement, Roquentin decides to mutilate himself as if to intervene at the material level by (re)claiming his hand: "My saliva is sugary, my body warm: I feel neutral. My knife is on the table. I open it. Why not? It would be a change in any case. I put my left hand on the pad and stab the knife into the palm."[66] Roquentin wants to feel something, something that would allow some reprieve from the absurdity of existence.

If everything around him is losing its symbolic veneer, the rippling effects of contingency (the feeling *de trop*), Roquentin wants to bypass the Social (an engine of ideological mystification) and reaffirm an immediate and authentic relation between himself and his body. Self-violence is an acceptable price for Roquentin's passion for the real. But here this bold act of revolt is rapidly neutralized by contingency: "I wonder. I watch the small, monotonous trickle of blood. Now it is coagulating. It's over. My skin looks rusty around the cut. Under the skin, the only thing left is a small sensation exactly like the others, perhaps even more insipid."[67]

This is in many ways a lesson in existentialist thought. We have a textbook case of ontological nausea brought about by an "*insipid* taste"[68] of contingency. Denis Hollier however asks us to pause before proceeding with this existentialist reading and its inauguration of a new kind of realism, a "subject realism," the realism proper of phenomenology:

> It should be recalled here that Roquentin, who is writing this at the same time he is doing it, knows quite well ... that in order to write one has to make use of both hands, one to hold the pen, the other to prevent the paper from moving. All of which gives him four in this case: two real—or better, plausible—ones, those that are before his eyes and that he evokes on this page (one with the knife, the other with the wound), and then their shadowy twins, which give them utterance, the phantom hands of his double.[69]

The novel's "subjective realism" is a ruse, ironizing, as it were, the reader's imagined passion for the real: he or she wants to read characters who are real, raw—not fake or conventionally narrated as in nineteenth-century realism. Irony—the most "inhuman trope"[70] of all—robs Roquentin and his readers of their humanist aspirations, their hunger for a precious piece of authenticity.[71]

Are OOO readers any different? Their focus would undoubtedly be on Roquentin's weak sovereignty, on his status a mere actant, who is finally waking up to the autonomy of objects. Roquentin, of course, experiences this wake-up call as a trauma. The revolt of objects against symbolic (that is, human) domestication crystallizes the reality of flat ontology. Roquentin and objects are on the same footing. Or worse, to the extent that Roquentin finds himself on the losing end of his semiotic encounters with objects.

The Real(ity) of Objects

Roquentin is a failed Adam, dispossessed of his powers of the logos, unable to dominate nature and the world of objects. Indeed, objects are not obeying him but breaking free from their linguistic domestication: "Things are divorced from their name. They are there, grotesque, headstrong, gigantic and it seems ridiculous to call them seats or say anything at all about them: I am in the midst of things, nameless things."[72] Roquentin, nevertheless, persists in his commitment "to see clearly." At the public park, Roquentin encounters a chestnut tree and is tested once again. This time, though, he claims to have seen: "And suddenly, suddenly, the veil is torn away, I have understood, I have *seen*."[73] The epiphany was presumably pre-linguistic:

> The word absurdity is coming to life under my pen; a little while ago, in the garden, I couldn't find it, but neither was I looking for it, I did not need it: I thought without words, *on* things, *with* things.[74]

Roquentin whets the appetite of philosophical readers, sparks the interest of OOO: Is Roquentin an epistemological realist? Is he going to share his knowledge of the things-in-themselves? Roquentin suggests that he is, but right when we expect him to give us a definitive account of naked existence, he upsets these expectations, proliferating instead a series of uncanny metaphors:

> Absurdity was not an idea in my head, or the sound of a voice, only this long serpent dead at my feet, this wooden serpent. Serpent or claw or root or vulture's talon, what difference does it make.[75]

A OOO reading would signal the shift from epistemological realism to ontological realism, that Sartre like Lovecraft is making his own weird realism, a realism that cultivates an *indirect* contact with the thing-in-itself.

A psychoanalytic reading goes further, appreciates that more is at stake in *Nausea*. Roquentin's metaphors do not simply move obliquely from the appearance of the chestnut tree to its volcanic core but work to undermine the noumena/phenomena distinction itself. The metaphors destroy what he knows about his world and the objects in it; they overwhelm Roquentin's phenomenological *epoché* (his bracketing of presuppositions about the objective world), sabotaging his narrativization of the event, its gentrification of the Real. Roquentin's metaphors gesture to the Real but they do so in a way that is different from Lovecraft's/Harman's "indirect access" to the things-in-themselves. As Slavoj Žižek puts it, the Real is "not an external thing that resists being caught in the symbolic network, but the fissure within the symbolic network itself."[76] The Real is not located outside the Symbolic "but a constant companion to 'reality.'"[77] The ontological lesson of *Nausea* rails against OOO and correlationists alike. Why? Simply because there are no noumena. OOO's passion for the Real involves a specious Kantianization[78] of the Real. *Nausea* invites a different path. The novel frustrates a readerly passion for the real; it avoids Kantianizing or substantializing the Real. Rather, *Nausea* discloses inconsistency and incompleteness as constitutive of reality. The realism of the Real is stranger than Harman's weird realism. The Real does not create the gaps and inconsistencies in the symbolic order; the former is counterintuitively an effect the latter. What is unknowable or unmasterable about the chestnut tree is not external to Roquentin's field of knowledge (in some inaccessible, extra-linguistic realm) but internal to it. The Real is beyond reality—but with the added twist: the "beyond" in question is also immanent to reality itself.

Notes

1 Quentin Meillassoux, *After Finitude: An Essay on the Necessity of Contingency*, trans. Ray Brassier (New York: Continuum, 2008), 7.
2 Quentin Meillassoux, *Time without Becoming*, ed. Anna Longo (Haverton: Mimesis International, 2014), 23, emphasis added.

3 Graham Harman, *Quentin Meillassoux: Philosophy in the Making* (Edinburgh: Edinburgh University Press, 2011), 51.
4 Following Alain Badiou, Žižek muses on the "passion for the Real" of the late twentieth century. He describes it as a desire to experience reality without mediation, absent the "deceptive layers of reality" (*Welcome to the Desert of the Real! Five Essays on September 11 and Related Dates* [New York: Verso, 2002], 5–6). See Alain Badiou, *The Century* trans. Alberto Toscano (Cambridge: Polity Press, 2007).
5 Zahi Zalloua, "On Not Selling Out the Subject," *symplokē* 27, no. 1–2 (2019): 299; Zahi Zalloua, *Being Posthuman: Ontologies of the Future* (New York: Bloomsbury, 2021).
6 Emmanuel Levinas, "Is Ontology Fundamental?" in *Entre Nous: On Thinking-of-the Other*, trans. Michael B. Smith and Barbara Harshav (New York: Columbia University Press, 1998), 1–11.
7 Slavoj Žižek, *Sex and the Failed Absolute* (New York: Bloomsbury, 2020), 367.
8 Sartre had suggested "'The Extraordinary Adventures of Antoine Roquentin" as a title for his novel.
9 Emmanuel Levinas, *Totality and Infinity: An Essay on Exteriority*, trans. Alphonso Lingis (Pittsburgh: Duquesne University Press, 1969), 54.
10 Levinas, *Totality and Infinity*, 111.
11 Levinas, *Totality and Infinity*, 133.
12 Graham Harman, "Aesthetics as First Philosophy: Levinas and the Non-Human," *Naked Punch* (2012), available at http://www.nakedpunch.com/articles/147, accessed April 19, 2020.
13 Levinas, *Totality and Infinity*, 144.
14 Harman, "Aesthetics as First Philosophy."
15 Emmanuel Levinas, *Otherwise than Being: Or beyond Essence*, trans. Alphonso Lingis (The Hague: Martinus Nijhoff, 1981), 73.
16 Levinas, *Totality and Infinity*, 135.
17 Levinas, *Totality and Infinity*, 134.
18 Stella Sandford, *The Metaphysics of Love: Gender and Transcendence in Levinas* (London: Athlone Press, 2000), 116.
19 Harman, "Aesthetics as First Philosophy."
20 Steven Shaviro, *The Universe of Things: On Speculative Realism* (Minneapolis: University of Minnesota Press, 2014), 46.
21 Harman, "Aesthetics as First Philosophy."
22 Levinas, *Totality and Infinity*, 43. "A calling into question of the same—which cannot occur within the egoist spontaneity of the same—is brought about by the other. We name this calling into question of my spontaneity by the presence of the Other ethics. The strangeness of the Other, his irreducibility to the I, to my thoughts and my possessions, is precisely accomplished as a calling into question of my spontaneity, as ethics" (Levinas, *Totality and Infinity*, 43).
23 Graham Harman, *Weird Realism: Lovecraft and Philosophy* (Winchester: Zero Books, 2012), 52.
24 Graham Harman, *Guerrilla Metaphysics: Phenomenology and the Carpentry of Things* (Chicago: Open Court, 2005), 171.
25 Graham Harman, "Realism without Materialism," *SubStance* 40, no. 2 (2011): 52.
26 Harman, *The Quadruple Object* (Ropley: Zero Books, 2011), 80.
27 Harman, "Realism without Materialism," 52.
28 Harman, *Guerrilla Metaphysics*, 110.

29 Graham Harman, *Immaterialism: Objects and Social Theory* (Cambridge: Polity, 2016), 96.
30 Harman, *Immaterialism*, 96.
31 Graham Harman, *Prince of Networks: Bruno Latour and Metaphysics* (Melbourne: re.press, 2009), 180–1.
32 Harman, *Immaterialism*, 2.
33 Following Levinas, Harman describes sincerity as everything that is what it is, that "does not pass elsewhere by means of relations; each point of reality stands in itself, candidly being just what it is" (Harman, "Aesthetics as First Philosophy").
34 Graham Harman, "On the Horror of Phenomenology: Lovecraft and Husserl," *Collapse* IV (2008): 334.
35 Harman, "On the Horror of Phenomenology," 334.
36 Harman, *Weird Realism*, 51. "Any realism that is not weird is simply a capitulation, an agreement to become the handmaid of either common sense or natural science" (Harman, *Speculative Realism*, 91).
37 Harman, *Weird Realism*, 3.
38 Harman, *Weird Realism*, 3.
39 Harman, *Weird Realism*, 51.
40 Harman, *Weird Realism*, 16.
41 Howard Phillips Lovecraft, "The Call of Cthulhu," *Weird Tales* (1928), H. P. Lovecraft Archive, available at http://www.hplovecraft.com/writings/texts/fiction/cc.aspx, accessed April 21, 2020.
42 Harman, *Weird Realism*, 24.
43 Harman, *Weird Realism*, 17, 27.
44 Harman, *Weird Realism*, 148. Harman acknowledges that Lovecraft at times fail to live up to his own ideal, deviating from "the proper path of H.P. Lovecraft" (Harman, *Weird Realism*, 148).
45 Alenka Zupančič, *What Is Sex?* (Cambridge: MIT Press, 2017), 119.
46 Timothy Morton, "Here Comes Everything: The Promise of Object-Oriented Ontology," *Qui Parle* 19, no. 2 (2011): 165.
47 Slavoj Žižek, "Afterword: Objects, Objects Everywhere," in *Slavoj Žižek and Dialectical Materialism*, ed. Agon Hamza and Frank Ruda (New York: Palgrave Macmillan, 2016), 188.
48 Karl Marx, *Wage-Labour and Capital* (New York: International Publishers, 1933), 33.
49 Jacques Lacan, *Seminar VII: The Ethics of Psychoanalysis*, trans. Dennis Porter (New York: Norton, 1992), 67.
50 Slavoj Žižek, *The Plague of Fantasies* (New York: Verso, 1997), 81.
51 Slavoj Žižek, *Tarrying with the Negative: Kant, Hegel, and the Critique of Ideology* (Durham: Duke University Press, 1993), 37.
52 See Harman, *The Quadruple Object*. In his formulation of the "quadruple object," Harman adopts Heidegger's key thing/object distinction, without, however, assigning a positive value to the former and a negative one to the latter (5).
53 Harman, *Immaterialism*, 97.
54 Jean-Paul Sartre, *Nausea*, trans. Lloyd Alexander (New York: New Directions, 1964), 10.
55 Sartre, *Nausea*, 1.
56 Harman, *The Quadruple Object*, 5.
57 Harman, *The Quadruple Object*, 5.
58 Sartre, *Nausea*, 1.

59 Roquentin, though, does at times feel ensconced in his environment, and when that is the case he characterizes his feeling as *bourgeois*: "I am quite at ease this evening, quite solidly *terre-à-terre* [*bien bourgeoisement*] in the world" (Sartre, *Nausea*, 2).
60 Sartre, *Nausea*, 69.
61 Sartre, *Nausea*, 111.
62 Sartre, *Nausea*, 58, 84.
63 Sartre, *Nausea*, 13.
64 Andy Leak, "Nausea and Desire in Sartre's *La Nausée*," *French Studies* 43, no. 1 (1989): 68.
65 Sartre, *Nausea*, 98–9.
66 Sartre, *Nausea*, 100.
67 Sartre, *Nausea*, 100.
68 Jean-Paul Sartre, *Being and Nothingness: An Essay on Phenomenological Ontology*, trans. Hazel E. Barnes (New York: Philosophical Library, 1956), 338.
69 Denis Hollier, *The Politics of Prose: Essay on Sartre*, trans. Jeffrey Mehlman (Minneapolis: University of Minnesota Press, 1986), 117.
70 Lee Edelman characterizes irony in a similar fashioning, describing it as "that queerest of rhetorical devices" (Lee Edelman, *No Future: Queer Theory and the Death Drive* [Durham: Duke University Press, 2004], 23).
71 The note from "the Editors" that precedes the diary and purportedly guarantees the authenticity of the document ("These notebooks were found among the papers of Antoine Roquentin. They are published without alteration" [1]), a literary practice which harks back to eighteenth-century literary convention, further plays with a readerly passion for the real.
72 Sartre, *Nausea*, 125.
73 Sartre, *Nausea*, 126.
74 Sartre, *Nausea*, 129.
75 Sartre, *Nausea*, 129.
76 Slavoj Žižek, *How to Read Lacan* (New York: Norton, 2006), 72.
77 Benjamin Noys, "Žižek's Reading Machine," in *Repeating Žižek*, ed. Agon Hamza (Durham: Duke University Press, 2015), 76.
78 Žižek, "Afterword: Objects, Objects Everywhere," 185.

Cited Works

Badiou, Alain. *The Century*. Translated by Alberto Toscano. Cambridge: Polity Press, 2007.
Edelman, Lee. *No Future: Queer Theory and the Death Drive*. Durham: Duke University Press, 2004.
Harman, Graham. *Guerrilla Metaphysics: Phenomenology and the Carpentry of Things*. Chicago: Open Court, 2005.
Harman, Graham. *Prince of Networks: Bruno Latour and Metaphysics*. Melbourne: re.press, 2009.
Harman, Graham. *The Quadruple Object*. Ropley: Zero Books, 2011.
Harman, Graham. *Quentin Meillassoux: Philosophy in the Making*. Edinburgh: Edinburgh University Press, 2011.
Harman, Graham. "Realism without Materialism." *SubStance* 40, no. 2 (2011): 52–72.

Harman, Graham. *Weird Realism: Lovecraft and Philosophy*. Winchester: Zero Books, 2012.
Harman, Graham. *Immaterialism: Objects and Social Theory*. Cambridge: Polity, 2016.
Hollier, Denis. *The Politics of Prose: Essay on Sartre*. Translated by Jeffrey Mehlman. Minneapolis: University of Minnesota Press, 1986.
Lacan, Jacques. *Seminar VII: The Ethics of Psychoanalysis*. Translated by Dennis Porter. New York: Norton, 1992.
Leak, Andy. "Nausea and Desire in Sartre's *La Nausée*." *French Studies* 43, no. 1 (1989): 61–72.
Levinas, Emmanuel. *Totality and Infinity: An Essay on Exteriority*. Translated by Alphonso Lingis. Pittsburgh: Duquesne University Press, 1969.
Levinas, Emmanuel. *Otherwise than Being: Or Beyond Essence*. Translated by Alphonso Lingis. The Hague: Martinus Nijhoff, 1981.
Levinas, Emmanuel. "Is Ontology Fundamental?" In *Entre Nous: On Thinking-of-the Other*, translated by Michael B. Smith and Barbara Harshav, 1–11. New York: Columbia University Press, 1998.
Lovecraft, Howard Philips. "The Call of Cthulhu." *Weird Tales* (1928). H. P. Lovecraft Archive. Accessed June 12, 2022. Available at http://www.hplovecraft.com/writings/texts/fiction/cc.aspx.
Marx, Karl. *Wage-Labour and Capital*. New York: International Publishers, 1933.
Meillassoux, Quentin. *After Finitude: An Essay on the Necessity of Contingency*. Translated by Ray Brassier. New York: Continuum, 2008.
Meillassoux, Quentin. *Time without Becoming*, edited by Anna Longo. Haverton: Mimesis International, 2014.
Morton, Timothy. "Here Comes Everything: The Promise of Object-Oriented Ontology." *Qui Parle* 19, no. 2 (2011): 163–90.
Noys, Benjamin. "Žižek's Reading Machine." In *Repeating Žižek*, edited by Agon Hamza, 72–83. Durham: Duke University Press, 2015.
Sandford, Stella. *The Metaphysics of Love: Gender and Transcendence in Levinas*. London: Athlone Press, 2000.
Sartre, Jean-Paul. *Being and Nothingness: An Essay on Phenomenological Ontology*. Translated by Hazel E. Barnes. New York: Philosophical Library, 1956.
Sartre, Jean-Paul. *Nausea*. Translated by Lloyd Alexander. New York: New Directions, 1964.
Shaviro, Steven. *The Universe of Things: On Speculative Realism*. Minneapolis: University of Minnesota Press, 2014.
Zalloua, Zahi. "On Not Selling Out the Subject." *symplokē* 27, nos. 1–2 (2019): 291–300.
Zalloua, Zahi. *Being Posthuman: Ontologies of the Future*. New York: Bloomsbury, 2021.
Žižek, Slavoj. "Afterword: Objects, Objects Everywhere." In *Slavoj Žižek and Dialectical Materialism*, edited by Agon Hamza and Frank Ruda, 177–92. New York: Palgrave Macmillan, 2016.
Žižek, Slavoj. *Tarrying with the Negative: Kant, Hegel, and the Critique of Ideology*. Durham: Duke University Press, 1993.
Žižek, Slavoj. *The Plague of Fantasies*. New York: Verso, 1997.
Žižek, Slavoj. *Welcome to the Desert of the Real! Five Essays on September 11 and Related Dates*. New York: Verso, 2002.
Žižek, Slavoj. *How to Read Lacan*. New York: Norton, 2006.
Žižek, Slavoj. *Sex and the Failed Absolute*. New York: Bloomsbury, 2020.
Zupančič, Alenka. *What Is Sex?* Cambridge: MIT Press, 2017.

Chapter 2

CORRELATIONIST STERILITY: A CRITIQUE OF THE ABSOLUTIZATION OF CONTINGENCY IN MEILLASSOUX

Diana Khamis

Meillassoux's *After Finitude* is a masterful attempt to overcome what Meillassoux calls correlationism—the position that thought does not have a direct access to reality but has access only to thought's correlation with it.[1] "Correlationism" follows from the post-Kantian separation between thought and being as manifest in the distinction in-itself/for-us, central to critical philosophy. The separation between thought and being occurs through the painfully simple "correlationist circle" argument,[2] as Meillassoux calls it: we cannot think the in-itself without making it for-thought, i.e., we cannot access it independently of our thought's conditions of access. The correlationist argument has invalidated constructing dubious dogmatic absolutes and making inferences about necessary reality from concepts, but it has also done away with all ground for ascertaining the truth of any particular discourse by shutting off all knowledge about being-itself. Post-Kantians have made reality even further inaccessible by showing that there is nothing necessary even in the categories of thought postulated by Kant, and with this extension of critical philosophy, the skeptical spirit came to taint thought with its "it-can-be-otherwise" stance. To any account of reality, the correlationist believes himself entitled to answer: "[R]eality cannot be accessed, because it is independent from thought, and we cannot think what is independent from thought." Our pleaded ignorance about the nature of reality puts on an ontological par all statements about it and opens the door to all kinds of irrationalisms and fideisms, as Meillassoux points out.[3] All statements about the unknowable reality become permissible and equally acceptable under correlationism. It is against this equal acceptability that Meillassoux aims his arguments in an attempt to rediscover an absolute which would ground our thought, but would not be dogmatic and metaphysical,[4] i.e., an absolute discovered *within* correlationism.

Meillassoux thinks this is necessary in order to explain a central feature of post-Galilean science: its ability to think the world apart from its manifestation in thought. This reasoning of the correlationist gives scientific statements a double meaning: a literal (for the correlationist, a naïve realist) meaning, whereby statements are treated as literal truths about a mind-independent reality, and a "deeper" meaning, whereby same statements are treated as facts "for scientists," but ones which cannot be literally true in the terms in which the scientists themselves understand them, and which are therefore meaningless if interpreted literally as statements about mind-independent reality.[5] Most scientific statements are thus meaningful only with the qualifier "for the scientist," and this goes against the whole scientific enterprise. Science is rendered impossible, since its significance lies in that it provides us with an account of reality independent from thought, and it is precisely the possibility of such an account that the correlationist denies. The case is even more bizarre for scientific statements made about ancestral reality, as Meillassoux calls it, that reality that pre-existed all thought. Since, for the correlationist, the givenness of a particular state of affairs to consciousness is what makes statements about that state of affairs meaningful, the reality which pre-existed human (or even all) consciousness, and therefore givenness, cannot be conceptualized. Statements about ancestral reality are thus rendered nonsensical because their referent is not (and cannot be) correlated with thought.[6]

The only absolutizing move Meillassoux can afford to make in order to break this vicious anti-scientific correlationist circle is the absolutization of contingency, and it is this move I will criticize in this chapter. Meillassoux's absolutization is ingenious; yet, I will argue that it is not enough to break thought free from the snares of Kantian philosophy. I will show that Meillassoux's breaking of the correlationist circle is incomplete, since it is impossible to drag any result of negative reasoning into a positive statement about thought-independent being, even if that being is absolute contingency.

Thought's Divorce from Being

Meillassoux's breakout from the circle remains incomplete because he, try as he may, cannot overcome one of the principles which correlationism is based on, i.e., that purely negative discourse, one which deals with the "whatness" of things, cannot make inferences into the positive, into the real existence of those things. This principle stems from the primary Kantian division between thought and being-itself, insofar as this division invalidates the connection between the concept and the real being of the referent of that concept and disqualifies the possibility of thinking the object's reality-in-the-world as based on the idea of that object.

Of all post-Kantians, it is Schelling who emphasizes this division most, in drawing the distinction between positive and negative philosophies. His discussion of these ideas is relevant here, even though the exact conclusions he made and the direction his philosophy took as a result of these conclusions are not necessarily so. Schelling completely agreed with Kant in that Kant has constructed a complete "science of pure reason," one to which there is hardly anything to add, save for the fact that this "science" constructed by Kant is only one kind of philosophy needed in order to successfully think about the world. Kant's philosophical system is what Schelling calls a "negative philosophy," since it sets limits for our thought; tells us what things are *not* and what we can*not* know.⁷ In Kant's case, of course, we are told that the in-itself is *not*—at least not necessarily—identical to appearance and that we can*not* know the in-itself. This embargo on definitely thinking anything apart from its manifestation for thought is what has established limits for our thinking and rendered Kantian philosophy negative.⁸ It has also led to thought's entrapment within its own boundaries: since we cannot access being, since our concepts, thoughts, and ideas do not have to connect to the world or reflect it in any way, we cannot say anything about things in the world that extends beyond their appearance to us. For Kant, we only know that there is an in-itself, so the real being of things in the world is not something that appears to us, and we cannot make any statements about it. Kant makes this clear with his disqualification of the ontological argument for the existence of God: besides the fact that being is not a predicate, let alone one that grants reality to that of which it is predicated, Kant's refutation tells us that our concept of anything can never be extended beyond thought into the "realm" of being in order to tell us about the real existence of that anything. Because of this incapacitation of reason, the laws of logic are rendered not necessarily applicable to the real world, and the derivation of an entity's being (let alone its necessary being) from the concept of the entity is shown to be impossible. In other words, nothing about the conceptual reality of a certain representation or concept could grant us access to real being, to something that is in reality. Schelling says, on this point: "Kant shows in general how futile it is for reason to attempt through inferences to reach beyond itself to existence (in this effort, however, reason is not dogmatic, since it does not reach its goal, but simply dogmatizing)."⁹

Meillassoux himself invokes this impossibility of access when he argues that Kant has made obsolete the principle of sufficient reason: "As we know, this Kantian refutation of the ontological argument has implications extending well beyond its Cartesian proof, for it is not just a matter of rejecting the proof of God's existence, but of refuting every proof that would presume to demonstrate the absolute necessity of a necessary entity."¹⁰

And yet, it is not just the derivation of the necessary existence of an entity that the Kantian refutation invalidates, it is the derivation of any conclusions about the existence or nonexistence of any entity. It follows from Kantian philosophy that our thinking cannot extend itself beyond what it is purely possible—in the sense of conceivable. We cannot say: "God does not exist" any more than we can say "God does exist" within the framework of Kantian or post-Kantian correlationism.¹¹ Strictly speaking, from within that framework we also cannot make statements like "trees really exist," if what we mean by these statements is along the lines of: "in the in-itself, beyond our representation, in the *real* reality there really exist objects which have the characteristics of trees." We also cannot make the same statements in the negative or make them about any entity or nonentity of our choice. We cannot even make statements about the physical possibility of the existence of an entity or a nonentity, but only about its conceivability, since statements like "There is a real possibility that God really exists" is still meaningless within a Kantian framework, as it might be that the in-itself is such that it necessitates the nonexistence of God.[12] We can only maintain that something is conceivable or inconceivable, the state of affairs inconceivable being a contradiction. And even then, though a contradiction within the in-itself is impossible for Kant, it becomes possible for those post-Kantians who came after him.

The relevance of all this to Meillassoux is that the correlationist philosophy he sets out to attack is, obviously, a negative philosophy. It is enclosed within the "conceivable" and explicitly disavows all capacity to make statements about being. This means that Meillassoux cannot begin breaking the correlationist circle from outside; he has to do it from within, since the circle is claimed to be the limit of our thought. Positing thought at a starting point outside the circle would mean an illegitimate return to dogmatic metaphysics and unwarranted claims about the nature of being. Therefore, Meillassoux has to accept the correlationist invalidation of the principle of sufficient reason and agree with the correlationists in that any attempt to put thought and being into a direct relation with each other would be a dogmatizing attempt. The fact that Meillassoux is attacking the correlationist on the correlationist's terms also means that he has to accept the principle that being (whether necessary or contingent) cannot be derived from pure thought, and therefore that the absolute regardless of its nature cannot be derived by reason alone. Yet, Meillassoux claims he has found an exception to this principle and proceeds to derive his absolute precisely in the manner forbidden by it: from correlationist discourse about thought he concludes the existence of an absolute—of contingency. As Meillassoux puts it, "*we are going to put back into the thing itself what we previously took to be an incapacity in thought.*"[13] Such a positive leap from thought to existence needs to be carefully articulated and justified in case Meillassoux is to continue with his project. It has to be assessed how adequate Meillassoux's arguments and his absolute are in order to connect the negative with the positive, thought with being.

The Correlationist's Facticity

Meillassoux begins his derivation with distinguishing between two kinds of correlationism, the weak and the strong.[14] Within this division, the weak correlationism is the correlationism of Immanuel Kant, that which still allows the philosopher to think the in-itself, though limitedly, only through the knowledge that the in-itself exists and is not contradictory. The strong correlationist view, on the other hand, claims that the in-itself is completely inaccessible even for thought. There is no way we could decisively prove that the in-itself is not contradictory or unthinkable, and so we have no reason to say that we can think it. This is the kind of correlationism under which our inability to access being and therefore ground our discourse in any independent reality can lead to fideism and skeptical irrationalisms a-la "it can be otherwise," which Meillassoux is most opposed to, since with this type of correlationism intellectually dominant, no criteria for philosophical rigor can be provided. The strong correlationist view is, then, the most rigorous challenge to any absolutization maneuvers, and so

2. Correlationist Sterility

Meillassoux decides to break the correlationist circle from within precisely strong correlationism—if he defeats the view which prohibits any thought of the absolute, no other view can provide counterarguments strong enough.

So, Meillassoux plans to spot an implicit absolutization within the strong correlationist's chain of reasoning. To that end, he analyzes the argument of the correlationist against both the dogmatic realist and the subjective idealist and comes to the conclusion that it is precisely the move that the correlationist has to make in order to refute the latter that hides the absolutization of contingency. Moreover, Meillassoux deliberately spells out his argument[15] in order to prove that this absolutization is indeed a positive one, and that the resulting absolute is uncorrelated and independent of thought. How he does it will be examined in what follows.

Meillassoux starts by giving the refutation of dogmatizing thought by the correlationist. The dogmatist would like to argue for the existence of a certain accessible absolute entity, and invalidating this position was achieved with weak Kantian correlationism; the correlationist circle prohibits metaphysical statements about the nature of the absolute by severing thought from being. Then, to invalidate dogmatic statements about being, it is enough to say that we cannot think being as it is in-itself without making it for-us. Thus, we cannot access any absolute, and mind-independent reality could be completely other than the one described by the dogmatist. Meillassoux gives an example: that of our post-mortem. A religious dogmatist could claim that we spend an eternity contemplating God (or whatever else it is he wants to maintain), and an atheist dogmatist would like to claim that our existence stops after death; yet, both those dogmatists do not have access to our post-mortem in-itself, and thus no account given by one of them is more conceivable than the other.

This line of response—the "meshes of the correlation,"[16] as Meillassoux puts it—is effective against the dogmatic philosopher, but it cannot be used to refute the subjective idealist, who absolutizes this correlation. For the idealist, not only is the in-itself unknowable, but there is no good reason to deem it thinkable. For Kant, the in-itself was thinkable only because it was noncontradictory, but if being is separated from thought—and from logic, insofar as logic is the body of principles which governs thought—then there is nothing about the in-itself which makes it necessarily noncontradictory. But then, since the in-itself is unthinkable, the whole concept of the in-itself as distinct from our thought can be dealt away with, so that only the correlation remains. This way, the correlation, i.e., our thought, is equated with being.

The subjective idealist's position is unacceptable for the correlationist, since the correlationist wants to insist that the distinction between the in-itself and the for-us must stand and that thought cannot access being. Idealism is refutable from within the correlationist position only if the correlationist accepts the unthinkability of the in-itself suggested by the idealist, i.e., becomes a strong correlationist. Once that is done, however, the correlationist can argue against the idealist much in the same way that he argued against the dogmatist: just as the in-itself could be otherwise than any dogmatic depiction of it, it can be other than equivalent to the for-us. The crux of the correlationist argument is that the thesis of the subjective idealist is not any more conceivable than the thesis of any of the dogmatists. The subjective idealist would like to claim that his thesis is more conceivable, since the dogmatist in-itself that is not equivalent to the for-us is independent of us and admits the real possibility[17] of our own nonexistence. This possibility is inconceivable for the idealist, and so is the dogmatist thesis, since our own nonexistence cannot be a correlate of thought. Yet, the correlationist would argue that even though the thesis of the realist dogmatist is unthinkable, its possibility is thinkable, as Meillassoux puts it, "by dint of the unreason of the real."[18] To clarify this with Meillassoux's post-mortem example: the idealist would claim that, since our nonbeing is inconceivable, nothing will change after our death, we would persist in our being. The correlationist, however, would have to reply that all those positions—those of the dogmatist and that of the idealist—are all equally possible; that it is possible we contemplate God, are annihilated, or remain completely the same after our death. Even unthinkable or inconceivable possibilities are possible: though our annihilation might be unthinkable, the possibility of the unthinkable is thinkable. The correlationist, then, can argue that both the idealist and the dogmatists claim to have identified a necessary state of affairs—whether a dogmatically metaphysical or an idealist reality—and this is precisely what cannot be done, since being could always be other than what we think it is.

Dragging Facticity into the Great Outdoors

Being can be other—this is the conclusion a strong correlationist reaches, and this is where Meillassoux claims the implicit absolutization lies. Yet, this absolutization must be made explicit by Meillassoux in order to show how contingency can pass through the gap between thought and being and prove that it is a property of the in-itself. Meillassoux has to show that the correlationist claim about contingency is a claim about the real possibility of being and not about our inability to know being: "being can become wholly other," rather than "being can be wholly other than we think it is."

The first step Meillassoux makes is attempting to prove that contingency can be attributed to the in-itself, and his argument is given in the following passage:

> How then are we able to claim that this capacity-to-be-other is an absolute—an index of knowledge rather than of ignorance? The answer is that it is the agnostic herself who has convinced us of it. For how does the latter go about refuting the idealist? She does so by maintaining that we can think ourselves as no longer being; in other words, by maintaining that our mortality, our annihilation, and our becoming-wholly-other in God, are all effectively thinkable. But how are these states conceivable as possibilities? On account of the fact that we are able to think—by dint of the absence of any reason for our being—a capacity-to-be-other capable of abolishing us, or of radically transforming us. *But if so, this*

2. Correlationist Sterility

capacity-to-be-other cannot be conceived as a correlate of our thinking precisely because it harbours the possibility of our own non-being. In order to think myself as mortal, as the atheist does—and hence as capable of not being—I must think my capacity not-to-be as an absolute possibility, for if I think this possibility as a correlate of my thinking, if I maintain that the possibility of my non-being only exists as a correlate of my act of thinking the possibility of my not-being, *then I can no longer conceive the possibility of my not-being*, which is precisely the thesis defended by the idealist. [...]Thus, the correlationist's refutation of idealism proceeds by way of an absolutization (which is to say, a de-correlation) of the capacity-to-be-other presupposed in the thought of facticity—this latter it the absolute whose reality is thinkable as that of the in-itself as such in its indifference to thought; an indifference which confers upon it the power to destroy me.[19]

This means the following: this facticity the correlationist speaks about, this equivalence of all possibilities of being subsumes at least one possibility which is a possibility of our nonbeing, and our nonbeing cannot be correlated with our thought—if we are not, then we, obviously, do not think. Therefore, our nonbeing is decorrelated from thought, but the decorrelation of absolute contingency is not so obvious. This is one of the most important points in Meillassoux's argument, so it needs examining. Bear in mind that Meillassoux has not yet established that contingency is the real in-itself, and so he has not yet established that the possibilities contingency contains are real possibilities—for now we can work under the assumption that they can be possibilities of ignorance, and so, just like the strong correlationist, we can assume we have no evidence for any of the alternatives contingency holds. In the argument, Meillassoux gives the move a strong correlationist has to make in order to refute the idealist. But, the strong correlationist does not wish to prove that the position embraced by the idealist (or by anyone for that matter) is wrong, he merely wishes to show that it impossible to prove that any of them is right. It is only in this sense that the correlationist is "refuting" the idealist. All the things Meillassoux says in this argument would apply and be perfectly to the point if the correlationist were really refuting the idealist, i.e., showing that the idealist if wrong. In that case, the correlationist would have to maintain that "we can think ourselves as no longer being," that "we are able to think a capacity to be other abolishing us or radically transforming us," and that we consequently must think of our capacity-not-to-be as a possibility uncorrelated with our thought. The correlationist, however, does not want to show that the idealist position is wrong, and neither does he want to show that the atheist's possibility of our nonbeing is a real possibility. He merely wants to demonstrate that all possibilities that could be given for the nature of the in-itself are possibilities of ignorance, and this is what he does. It is not that we can think ourselves as not-being that the correlationist wants to assert, it is that we can think the possibility of our own nonbeing because we do not know what kind of an in-itself there is—one that will cause our nonbeing, or one that will forbid it. For the correlationist, we are not able to think *being's* capacity to be otherwise, we are simply able to think the *possibility* of it being-otherwise, and even that possibility is a possibility of ignorance: we do not know whether it can be otherwise, we do not know whether it can stay completely the same. This—the inability of our thought to access any quality of the in-itself—cannot be absolutized in the way that Meillassoux suggests in the above passage. The capacity-to-be-other of being which Meillassoux claims the correlationist absolutizes is simply not postulated by the correlationist, whether as absolute or not.

However, let's suppose that one alternative account of reality is the existence of absolute contingency (since it clearly is, no correlationist would deny it) and look at the second argument Meillassoux makes in order to show that a consistent correlationist has to accept contingency as his absolute. If absolute contingency is taken to be a possible absolute, and Meillassoux wants to defend this absolute, he has to show that a correlationist cannot use his "being can be other" card and say that this newly suggested absolute, this "capacity-to-be-other" can be other. Meillassoux argues that the correlationist cannot do this, because by his very suggestion that being can be other, he absolutizes this facticity, this contingency and capacity-to-be-other which is present within all being. To restate: when faced with an absolute, it suffices for a strong correlationist to utter the magical "it can be completely other" in order to disqualify the attempt at absolutization. Yet, if what is absolutized is being's capacity-to-be-other—being's facticity—the correlationist cannot make his standard move, since he uses this facticity within the move, implicitly presupposing the absolution within his refutation. For the strong correlationist, being's capacity to be other cannot be other—it is absolute. This is Meillassoux's absolute—it is necessary, but not a necessary entity, and is therefore non-metaphysical.

However, I would argue that Meillassoux fails again, and that nothing, not even contingency, can have its existence derived from the pure thought of the correlationist circle. Meillassoux argues that in order to make contingency a possibility of our ignorance, the correlationist has to think it as a real possibility, and this is precisely what he does while refuting the idealist. Yet, I've shown that there is reason to doubt that this is what the correlationist does, and when Meillassoux tells the correlationist that "the core of your [strong correlationist's] argument is that we can access everything's capacity-not-to-be, or capacity-to-be-other,"[20] he is actually being too charitable to the correlationist. The core of his thesis is not that we can access everything's capacity-not-to-be, but that we can access our thought's capacity to think everything as not-being or being other. The correlationist does not make any implicit absolutizing moves and does not make any statements about reality. In fact, it is Meillassoux who makes the absolutizing move he wants to see the correlationist making: Meillassoux is the one who equates everything's logical possibility not-to-be with an ontologically significant possibility, and "frames" the correlationist with doing it. Instead of breaking the correlationist circle from within and turning the difference between thought and being into their equivalence, Meillassoux simply assumes this equivalence down the road. When thinking about contingency, the correlationist does not really hypostatize it as an independent entity; he rather admits that he cannot *think* without thinking *it*. It is an absolute of thought, and not of being. The correlationist circle is thus not really broken, it is rather finalized—at most Meillassoux has proven that in order to think anything, we have to think contingency. We cannot think but contingency, but this in no way relates to what Being is. Rather, it seems that while searching for an absolute, Meillassoux found a *real* category of thought, without which there can be no correlationist thinking. Therefore, Meillassoux has given us a limit to correlationist thought but he failed to establish its link to being. Meillassoux does decisively disprove a possible strong correlationist counterargument to his thesis: the correlationist indeed cannot say that the capacity-to-be-other can be other, since being's *logical* capacity-to-be-other lies as an indispensable condition of correlationist thought. Meillassoux's thesis is indeed more conceivable than any other dogmatic realist or idealist alternative, at least from the point of view of the correlationist. Yet it doesn't really matter what is more conceivable if we are trying to access what is real, and therefore I am not reiterating the strong correlationist's "being could be otherwise, no matter what you say it is," argument, but am rather claiming that the views of anyone thinking from within strong correlationism cannot relate to what being really is.

In order to verify that the above reading of Meillassoux's argument gives him due, we will now examine Graham Harman's reading, which comes from his book *Quentin Meillassoux: Philosophy in the Making*. Harman has an exposition of the argument for absolutizing contingency in the first chapter of the book.[21] He provides a useful summary of Meillassoux's argument:

> The entire drama can be summarized briefly as follows. The Atheist and the Believer are both derailed by the Kantian point that we cannot have access to reality outside our conditions of access to it. The Idealist is defeated by Meillassoux's point that the meaninglessness of thinking a world outside thought does not mean a world outside thought is impossible. And finally, the Correlationist is defeated by being transformed into a Speculative Materialist. For the Correlationist avoids being an Idealist only by insisting that there *might* be an in-itself different from the for-us, and this "might" has to refer to a real in-itself, not just an "in-itself-for-us". The Correlationist claims to abstain from any form of the absolute, but can only be Correlationist by holding that there are *absolutely* a number of different possibilities. Meillassoux concludes: "We have now identified the faultline that lies at the heart of correlationism; the one through which we can breach its defences" (AF 59)—namely, there is no way to avoid making *either* facticity *or* the correlate absolute. If we say that everything is the correlate of an act of thought, then we have absolutised the correlate and become Subjective Idealists. Or, we can escape this position by de-absolutising the correlate and saying that, after all, there might be something outside it. But this means *absolutising facticity*, by saying that it is absolutely true that there might be something outside the correlate of thought and world. The Correlationist cannot have it both ways by saying: "there absolutely might be something outside thought, yet maybe this is absolutely impossible." In other

words, once we escape the prison of Dogmatism, we can only be Idealists or Speculative Materialists. The standard agnostic version of Correlationism turns out not to be entirely agnostic, in spite of itself.[22]

If we now look at this summary and examine it to try and locate the fault that we have located in the original *After Finitude* argument, we find it here: Meillassoux starts from a "standard agnostic version" of correlationism. And yet, as Harman points out, Meillassoux claims that the correlationist has to absolutize either the correlate or facticity, and thus has to either become a subjective idealist of a speculative materialist. However, this is a false dilemma. Meillassoux gives no reasons for the correlationist to fail in his agnosticism. He gives us no reasons to treat the various possibilities for the absolute a correlationist has in his mind as anything but possibilities of ignorance, and so the statement "there absolutely might be something outside thought, but maybe this is absolutely impossible" is a perfectly legitimate statement which simply means "we do not know whether there is something outside thought or whether this is absolutely impossible."

Meillassoux attempts, yet again, to make a positive claim about absolute contingency later in his book. He has to ask himself the Leibnizian question: "Why is there something rather than nothing?" Why it is that absolute facticity exists at all? Instead of answering this question with the principle of sufficient reason, as the philosophers of Enlightenment did, Meillassoux introduces the principle of "unreason." This principle follows from the absolutization of contingency: it states that there is no reason for being to be this or that way, and that being consequently can always be other than it is. In order to show that this principle grants access to being, Meillassoux proposes two interpretations of this principle: a "weak" and a "strong" interpretation.[23] The weak interpretation takes the principle to mean "if something exists, it is contingent." The strong interpretation, however, treats the principle as an affirmation "something exists, and that something is contingent." Limiting oneself to the weak interpretation would mean that facticity is a mere fact of the world and is therefore possibly contingent just like all the other facts of the world. Meillassoux thus wants to prove that the strong interpretation is the only possible, again securing the positive absolute existence of contingency. He proceeds as follows: we can suppose that the weak interpretation is valid. Then, we would have to say that the existence of contingent things is factual, asserting a second-order "facticity of facticity." This logic Meillassoux calls "self-refuting," since he believes it has refuted itself in his previous argument against the correlationist. In order to doubt facticity, we have to think it as an absolute. I have shown the mistake within this logic: in order to doubt facticity, we cannot help but think it, and yet we could never simply prove its absoluteness. Meillassoux then fails to connect thought to being through the strong interpretation of the principle of unreason, just as he has failed to connect them through his arguments against the correlationist. Needless to say, he also does not prove that there has to be something rather than nothing, and thus cannot decisively claim that the in-itself exists.

Once a shadow is thrown upon Meillassoux's main argument, we see that a challenge is raised to his absolutization of noncontradiction. The absolutization of the principle of noncontradiction is also based on Meillassoux's "principle of unreason." Meillassoux argues that a contradictory entity is impossible, since it has to be a necessary entity: everything can be predicated of it, it is simultaneously X and *not-X* and therefore it cannot become—it has no "other" to change into, it subsumes everything within itself and thus cannot be except as it is. A contradictory being is not capable of being other, and since Meillassoux thinks he has absolutized contingency already, this inability-to-be-other cannot exist for Meillassoux, and neither can a contradictory being.[24] When it comes to assessing this absolutization, it must be noted that there seems to be a problem already, as I have argued, with Meillassoux's account of absolutizing contingency, and the process of absolutizing noncontradiction has to include absolute contingency within its premises. Without contingency as an absolute, noncontradiction falls prey to the same argument from separation between thinking and being to which absolutization of contingency fell. Noncontradiction is a logical principle; it tells us about our thought, and not about its correlates. It, just as contingency logically presupposed within the thought of correlationist, cannot access being or be dragged into it through argumentation. It could be replied to me that there is a link between noncontradiction and being insofar as contradictory being implies necessary being. Yes, but the way the two are linked does not mean that if we think contradiction, we think a necessary being that necessarily is—all contradiction could give us is the statement "if a contradictory being exists, then it is necessary," which follows perfectly from Meillassoux's reasoning concerning the impossibility of contradictory being to become otherwise. Again, no link between thought and being is made through Meillassoux's reasoning.

Conclusion

Meillassoux's agenda was modeled on Descartes's: he intended to prove the existence of an absolute and use that absolute in order to derive the absoluteness of mathematics from it, in turn, to establish a firm foothold for science's access to being. Had he succeeded in showing that contingency was a real absolute, it would have been questionable even then whether mathematics is derivable from an absolute capacity to be otherwise. But Meillassoux fails to establish the absoluteness of contingency, or link thought to being through his arguments against correlationism. Correlationism, based on thought's sterile inability to access being, remains sterile even in Meillassoux's hands. It is therefore evident that the arguments of *After Finitude* cannot be used to absolutize mathematics or ground science. In fact, Meillassoux's attempts to vindicate science seem to give ironic results, not unlike Kant's attempts. Kant tried to protect the growing field of scientific enquiry against skepticism, and, to vindicate a Galilean revolution in science, he drew the distinction between thought and being. This led to, as Meillassoux puts it, the correlationist's "Ptolemaic counter-revolution" which pulled the rug from underneath science, apparently voiding scientific statements from any content about the world and rendering them equal to any unscientific statements. Meillassoux's attempt to vindicate science gives an ironic result as well: attempting to rediscover thought's positive ability to access the "great outdoors," he instead discovers what seems to be the utmost negative point of philosophy: the limit of correlationist thought. Absolute contingency is, as a result of Meillassoux's arguments, shown to be the final limit of correlationism, that outside which the correlationist cannot think. For the correlationist, Meillassoux's contingency serves as a "category of thought" of sorts, the only form without which, for the correlationist, there could be no thought.

Meillassoux's failure is telling. It reaffirms the claim that positive statements about being cannot be possibly derived from negative thought. It is another consequence of the impossibility to reach the positive from within a negative course of thought, the impossibility to access what being is through setting limits to our thought, and through telling us what being is not. The power of the distinction between the negative and the positive, the power of the principle of separation between thought and being which correlationism is based on is once again demonstrated. Yet, Meillassoux's criticisms of the correlationist are also telling because they show that correlationism is not a desirable path for philosophy to take. Correlationism "enables" thought to engage in fideisms and irrationalisms, without allowing thinkers to evaluate their claims about being, even in terms of rational criteria or plausibility, but only in terms of conceivability. Moreover, the critique Meillassoux bases on his principle of ancestrality remains a rather effective argument against correlationism[25]: the correlationist cannot give or accept an account of the events that have happened so early in the history of our world that they have happened anterior to all givenness or exposure to a mind which would prevent them from being nonsensical. The conclusion one must derive from Meillassoux's book is not that the correlationist thesis must be upheld and defended just because Meillassoux fails to refute it. Instead, Meillassoux's project does not lose its urgency: philosophy has the pressing need to overcome correlationism (or any negative thought, for that matter) as its solely valid counterpart,[26] and to overcome it all the more efficiently because of the realization that the overcoming is impossible to accomplish from within. What Meillassoux has showed us is, in effect, the need to formulate an account of the world that allows us to articulate both thought and being, the conceptual and the nonconceptual. It seems it is also most fruitful to articulate this distinction through a dialectic of two currents in philosophy: the negative, giving us the limits of our thought, and the positive, dealing with a direct access toward being, an access which does not treat being as that which is not-thought. Of course, the main problem of philosophy is again: what is this "positive," and how can we access being directly? Several possible answers can be given as to how to forge a positive philosophy. A possible hint is given by Meillassoux himself, whereby he suggests that we must "discover, in our grasp of facticity, the veritable *intellectual intuition* of the absolute."[27] It remains to be seen what Meillassoux will make out of this intellectual intuition in subsequent works, and possibly, alternatives to a renewed search for human faculties should be envisioned in order to bring thought and being together. And that has to be done, even if it cannot happen through the filters of thought about thought.

Notes

1. Quentin Meillassoux, *After Finitude: An Essay on the Necessity of Contingency*, trans. Ray Brassier (New York: Continuum, 2008), 5.
2. Meillassoux, *After Finitude*, 5.
3. Meillassoux, *After Finitude*, 44–9.
4. Meillassoux accepts the Kantian critique; he is truly a post-Kantian philosopher. For Meillassoux, we must accept Kant, but overcome him.
5. Meillassoux, *After Finitude*, 13–14.
6. Meillassoux, *After Finitude*, 17–26.
7. Negative philosophy thus takes thought as its starting point and proceeds by separation of thought from being. Positive philosophy, on the other hand, takes the human mind's access to being as its starting point, and not our thought's limitation.
8. Kant, of course, does think that the in-itself is accessible to thought, but in a very limited way: Thus, we can definitely think it as existent and noncontradictory, but no more.
9. Friedrich Wilhelm Joseph Schelling, *The Grounding of Positive Philosophy: The Berlin Lectures*, trans. Bruce Matthews (New York: SUNY Press, 2007), 147.
10. Meillassoux, *After Finitude*, 32.
11. The distinction between Kantian and post-Kantian correlationism is the distinction between weak and strong correlationism. Kantian correlationism is that which allows us to think the in-itself without, however, allowing us to know anything about it. Instead of having access to being, we have access only to the correlation between thought and being. Post-Kantian strong correlationism, on the other hand, absolutizes the correlation whereby we are unable to even think the in-itself. See Meillassoux, *After Finitude*, 35–8.
12. In any case, modality is not a property of the in-itself for Kantians, and neither it is so for all kinds of correlationists.
13. Meillassoux, *After Finitude*, 53.
14. Meillassoux, *After Finitude*, 35–8.
15. Meillassoux, *After Finitude*, 54–9.
16. Meillassoux, *After Finitude*, 51.
17. "Real possibility" is distinguished from the possibility of ignorance, a distinction that Meillassoux makes and that will serve an important purpose in his argument later. A real possibility is a possibility that exists in the world, in the it-itself, and a possibility of ignorance is a possibility due to our inability to know which is the real state of affairs that pertains to being. For this point, however, an in-itself that is distinct from the for-us presupposes that it is independent for us, relying on the real possibility that the subject will cease to exist.
18. Meillassoux, *After Finitude*, 56.
19. Meillassoux, *After Finitude*, 57.
20. Meillassoux, *After Finitude*, 58.
21. Namely, here: Graham Harman, *Quentin Meillassoux: Philosophy in the Making* (Edinburgh: Edinburgh University Press, 2011), 25–30.
22. Meillassoux, *After Finitude*, 29.
23. Meillassoux, *After Finitude*, 74–5.
24. Meillassoux, *After Finitude*, 69–70.
25. Of course, this applies if the correlationism Meillassoux describes is a position people indeed hold, which is a separate question, not investigated here.

26 For a different take on this matter, a take which however leads to a similar conclusion, i.e., the untenability of a solely negative philosophy, see Graham Priest, *Beyond the Limits of Thought* (Oxford: Oxford University Press, 2002).

27 Meillassoux, *After Finitude*, 82. Meillassoux probably uses intellectual intuition here in a Kantian sense: intuition, for Kant, is that operation of our faculties which puts them in direct contact with their objects. Kant argues that human faculties are restricted to having one kind of intuition: the sensory intuition, whereby it is the faculty of sensibility that is being put in direct touch with the objects. An intellectual intuition, for Kant, is a direct link between our faculty of intellection, i.e., the understanding, and the objects of knowledge. See Immanuel Kant, *Critique of Pure Reason*, trans. Paul Guyer and W. Wood, Allen (Cambridge: Cambridge University Press, 1998), 191–2.

Cited Works

Harman, Graham. *Quentin Meillassoux: Philosophy in the Making*. Edinburgh: Edinburgh University Press, 2011.

Kant, Immanuel. *Critique of Pure Reason*. Translated by Paul Guyer and Allen W. Wood. Cambridge: Cambridge University Press, 1998.

Meillassoux, Quentin. *After Finitude: An Essay on the Necessity of Contingency*. Translated by Ray Brassier. New York: Continuum, 2010.

Priest, Graham. *Beyond the Limits of Thought*. Oxford: Oxford University Press, 2002.

Schelling, Friedrich Wilhelm Joseph. *The Grounding of Positive Philosophy: The Berlin Lectures*. Translated by Bruce Matthews. New York: SUNY Press, 2007.

Chapter 3

FACTS, NOT FOSSILS: NEW VS SPECULATIVE REALISM

Markus Gabriel

On account of its long and varied history, "realism," like well-nigh every philosophical expression, is used in many ways.[1] Nevertheless, we might distinguish between two general intellectual currents that can find expression in a commitment to realism. On the one hand, realism consists in a series of *epistemological* positions united in their belief that we enjoy unproblematic access to reality or some aspect thereof. Realism in this sense maintains that we can know whichever aspect of reality is under scrutiny. On the other hand, realism is also considered a *metaphysical* thesis, whose advocates work on the premise that something real (or even reality or the "world") is largely or entirely independent of the conditions under which we can grasp or represent it. To be sure, there are prominent attempts to show a common semantic denominator underlying both enterprises; these, for their part, can appeal to the tradition that understood realism (in contrast to nominalism) as a theory of the meaning of those general expressions that play a fundamental role in our cognition of the structures of the real.

In what follows, I will contrast two much-discussed contemporary variants of realism, both of which advance proposals for pursuing the various epistemological, metaphysical/ontological, and sematic realism debates in light of central problems of recent philosophy. In particular, I will examine these different options—namely speculative and New Realism respectively—in light of the question of what their potential contributions might be to understanding the position of thought with respect to nature.

I understand this as a question about which premises a realistic philosophy of nature has to deploy in tackling a further question: to what extent should nature be regarded as knowable? The issue, therefore, is to clarify what the relation between epistemological and metaphysical/ontological realism looks like in light of issues in the philosophy of nature.

Against this background, I urge against neglecting the semantic dimension of the realism debate. Whether and in what sense some form of realism recommends itself always depends, at least in part, on which beliefs concerning the decomposition of our truth-apt thoughts about some particular domain one deems defensible.

With this in mind, I consider the opening move of speculative realism to be problematic for both semantic and generally epistemological reasons. This form of realism typically builds upon Quentin Meillassoux's critique of correlationism. On closer inspection, however, "correlationism" is not in fact a notion that is sufficiently delineated to be an object of focused debate, but rather an epistemologically somewhat indeterminate field of philosophical conflict.

In the first part of my contribution, I shall argue against the theoretical setup of speculative realism. In particular, I regard "correlationism" as an indeterminate phantom. In the second part, I will take a position on the question of which foundational consequences for the philosophy of nature follow from the kind of realistic ontology of facts advocated by my own contribution to the debate surrounding New Realism: fields of sense ontology (*Sinnfeldontologie*).

Fossils

The systematic starting point of the various divergent programs grouped under the banner of "speculative realism" is Meillassoux's much-discussed attempt to break through what he calls "correlationism."[2] Yet it is ultimately unclear what precisely the object of his critique, i.e., correlationism, is really meant to be. In his critical discussion of Meillassoux's anti-phenomenological orientation, Dan Zahavi, by closely following Meillassoux's account, summarizes the content of correlationism as follows:

> Correlationism is the view that subjectivity and objectivity cannot be understood or analyzed apart from one another because both are always already intertwined or internally related. It is the view that we only ever have access to the correlation between thinking (theory) and being (reality) and never to either in isolation from or independently of the other. On this view, thought cannot get outside itself in order to compare the world as it is "in itself" with the world as it is "for us". Indeed, we can neither think nor grasp the "in itself" in isolation from its relation to the subject, nor can we ever grasp a subject that would not always-already be related to an object.[3]

Zahavi believes that Husserl, Heidegger, and Merleau-Ponty advocate positions of this form, and he ascribes it to phenomenology quite generally (the tradition of which he counts himself an adherent). But what exactly is correlationism meant to be? If we take what Meillassoux and Zahavi tell us about it at face value, the idea is that we have access only ever to a correlation between being and thought, but never to either one in isolation from the other. But what coherent meaning could be attached to this surprising claim? If the correlation for its part is something belonging to being, a vicious infinite regress results, because one *ipso facto* has to have access to infinitely many correlations in order to have access to anything at all. If, however, the correlation belongs to thought, the very same problem emerges. Accordingly, one could have no access to the correlation, and this hardly speaks in favor of correlation, as it undermines the conditions of its own assertability. Thus, the very formulation of the "position" of correlationism is immediately threatened by incoherence.

In order to avoid this flat incoherence, the defender of the very intelligibility of correlationism might tell us that a correlation is a specific form of relation. The idea might be that the relation of cognition or intentionality that is supposed to obtain between subject and object is a specific form of relation, which we are meant to understand as correlation. Yet what distinguishes a correlation from other relations? If one formulates what correlationism asserts, one necessarily mentions two relata (being and thinking, or subject and object), which stand in a determinate relation. But one thus requires an access to the relata that is independent of this relation. Otherwise, we fall back into the threat of a vicious infinite regress which bars us from formulating the very idea of a correlation.

Accordingly, if correlationism is meant to represent an intelligible position at all, specific assumptions about the nature of the correlation have to be made. One could, for example, interpret Kant as maintaining that appearances are correlates that would literally not exist if there was nobody around who found or could find themselves in an epistemically relevant relation to them. There would then be a sense in which the correlates are not relata to which one could have access independently of this specific relation. Yet, once again, it does not simply follow without supplementary assumptions that this is a problematic position, one that undermines any desirable realism. Firstly, the position is explicitly meant to be understood as empirical realism, which means that one can have truth-apt beliefs about appearances, such that our appearance-beliefs have objective reality. And secondly, things in themselves are not correlates of the appearance correlation, meaning that there's no room left here for metaphysical realism as well. Thus, if Kant is a correlationist in that sense, correlationism is fully compatible with realism and no problematic, suspiciously anti-realist maneuver has been performed in virtue of thinking of appearances as essentially related to thinkers.

In any event, as long as a correlation is a specific form of relation between the two relata, thinking and being (or subject and object), immediate access to the relata has to be granted, and as a result, the undesirable results Meillassoux claims to derive from correlationism simply do not follow at all.

Accordingly, if one believes that there is something wrong with correlations between subject and object, thinking and being, mind and world or what have you, it is necessary to tackle the (supposed) problem of correlationism differently and find an alternative to Meillassoux's and Zahavi's formulations.

Presumably, what Meillassoux has in mind is the epistemic/semantic problem that the truth conditions for the articulated beliefs we state whenever we make a knowledge claim always depend in some sense on which "picture" we form of the fact we have in our sights, the fact whose obtaining we assert. In the wake of Kant, this problem tends to be negotiated via a theory of imagination, which is introduced in order to be able to raise knowledge claims "from the human standpoint."[4] It is part of the human standpoint that we can reflect on something only if we can have "mental access" to something of the relevant sort in the first place.⁵ Yet the existence of mental access conditions merely entails that objects are always given to us in some determinate manner. Objects that cannot in any manner be given to *us* cannot, *trivialiter*, be objects epistemically individuated in the usual way, i.e., as objects of truth-apt beliefs, insofar as these are involved in the practices of justifiable knowledge claims.

From the standpoint of epistemology, it would seem at first blush that the very opposite of Meillassoux's analysis of the situation follows from the analysis of our knowledge claims: whoever knows that p by having mental access to p does not thereby *ispso facto* stand in a relation to this relation, but rather maintains a relation to being (p) itself, which is not further mediated. The facts themselves thus serve as a regress blocker, and they are not undermined by standing in a relation whose structure might rightly be classified as some form of correlation or some other form of tight relation between thinking and being.

Nevertheless, Meillassoux has found a new way of reminding us of an old problem, one that also in fact emerges within the Kantian framework. This problem stems from the fact that epistemology right down to the nineteenth century tended to work on the premise not only that the human being is the epistemological center of its cognitive universe—which need not be a problematic assumption—but also that reality as a whole is either itself tailored to the event of its becoming known by human beings or could remain utterly unknowable. In this connection, Kant assumes without hesitation in his *Universal Natural History and Theory of the Heavens* that every planet in the known universe hosts intelligent life designed to observe nature and exercise moral capacities.⁶

With the extremely widespread discussion of fossil discoveries, especially in the Romantic period, the concept of the embeddedness of the knowing human being in natural history undergoes a radical change. These discoveries raised the question of the origin of human mindedness in a particularly pointed fashion.⁷ Meillassoux objects to correlationism that it has fundamental difficulties with the existence of "arche-fossils," which he discusses in terms of the concept of ancestrality.⁸ He thereby means to refer to the domain of that which existed or was the case prior (in time) to the emergence of intelligent life on our planet. How, goes the somewhat more modally refined question, can one think of a reality that would also have existed if creatures like us had not existed—a reality, therefore, that cannot have those structures we ascribe to it when we experience it as cognisable *post festum* inscribed within it *qua* thing-in-itself?

One could, of course, say that the imagination can also reel the past into the "field of possible experience"⁹ retroactively. As soon as creatures like us are on the scene, we can also survey the pre-existing domain of the ancestral. Yet this immediately invites the speculative realist response that we do not thereby grasp the ancestral to the extent that it would have had the character of a thing-in-itself if creatures like us had not existed. Otherwise put, Meillassoux's critical response is to ask how it can be that some of what could have remained a thing-in-itself, retrospectively, with our access, reveals itself to be knowable and thus as appearance, whilst other things continue to remain things-in-themselves and thus elude our cognition. At this point, one could of course respond that Kant does not think that any thing-in-itself can ever be cognized. Rather, what transpires with the emergence of human epistemic subjects is that the appearances that we count as belonging to the past are admitted into the temporal series because we now assign them this position. This response, however, then raises the question of what exactly it means to say that something is past only if there is a present consisting of appearances, some of which can be cognized by human epistemic subjects. In this respect, Meillassoux's critique of the attitude underlying expressions of something like correlationism rightly points out that views like transcendental idealism about time owe us an explanation of how they manage to accommodate the fact that there was a time when no one equipped with pure forms of intuition was around.

How does it come about that our modes of registration process information in such a way that certain domains of reality become knowable through the constitutive bracketing out of other domains? It cannot be because reality, in some ultimately mysterious way, is always already tailored to its being known, i.e., before it was even certain that cognition could in fact occur.[10] It is against just this kind of mysterious, teleological assumption that Meillassoux levels his objections.

Nevertheless, his conclusion that (transcendental) idealism, which he targets as an instance of correlationism, embroils itself in problems concerning an "ancestral" nature is misguided.[11] The problem cannot be how that which already existed before creatures like us did becomes partly knowable as soon as we know it. For this problem can be quickly dispatched with recourse to Kant's famous thesis that the conditions of knowability that we spell out in transcendental philosophy are not real predicates. It is not only being that is not a real predicate: the entire conceptual framework articulated by transcendental philosophy is precisely not supposed to present us with an ontology in the sense of universal knowledge of things as such.[12]

According to the Kantian framework, what makes the real knowable is precisely not any metaphysical property that inheres in the real independently of its being known. Yet, contrary to what Meillassoux assumes, this is not to assert that the real is not independent of its being known, but only that known reality, *trivialiter*, is subject to those conditions that have to be fulfilled if we are to know it. The statement that the real arises within the horizon of cognition, so to speak, says something about this horizon in its relation to first-order reality, but nothing about how that first-order reality would have been had nobody known it.

Yet this does not exclude our knowing how the reality we have come to know would have been had we not come to know it. Against this background, we can make a first attempt to determine the concept of a *natural ancestral fact* more precisely. The concept of such a fact is, firstly, the concept of something that would also have been the case if there had been nobody around to notice its being the case. Secondly, it is the concept of something belonging to the object domain of our best-established—that is to say: epistemically successful—natural sciences. My *terminus technicus* for this domain is "the universe," as the expression "nature" is by now fraught with too many outmoded connotations. The question then becomes how we can conceive of the universe's constitutive independence of its relation to mental episodes of finite thought occurring within it.

At this point, Meillassoux might possibly challenge the idea that there are even conditions of our capacity to know something. Yet that would surely be to go too far; after all, he himself relies on a very classical conception of the scope of logic in drawing far-reaching metaphysical-speculative consequences from the principle of non-contradiction.[13] Moreover, Meillassoux does not want to contest the idea that there are appearances that exist only because creatures like us do; to thematize these, he draws on the early modern concept of secondary qualities.[14]

The problem with correlationism is thus not that there are conditions of our being able to know anything whatsoever; this much is compatible with any desirable form of realism. Yet a variant of the difficulties to which Meillassoux has done so much to draw our attention arises all the same: for, if the real in part stands under conditions of knowability and is in part potentially cut off from these, we face the question of why some of reality eludes cognition. This problem domain, to be sure, is not opened up by diachronic ancestrality, since its synchronic manifestation is no less significant. Nature coexists with us and cannot have suddenly disappeared when we started to come to know it.

Facts—Nature and Neutral Realism

Contrary to Meillassoux's assessment of the epistemological landscape of modern and contemporary philosophy, there is in fact a widespread temptation to overestimate the ancestral. The overestimation of the ancestral, to which Meillassoux himself ultimately falls victim as well, consists in entertaining the following (world-)picture of how knowledge is metaphysically embedded in nature: in the beginning, the universe was an environment hostile to life. Aeons had to pass before the physical, and then the specifically biochemical, conditions were in place for the emergence of species. Then, once again after many aeons, the biological process of the differentiation of the animal kingdom led to the occurrence of thinkers capable of retrospectively reconstructing this very process of emergence. Such a world-picture receives a paradigmatic representation at the start of Terence Malick's *Tree of Life*.

This story contains various cutoff points, which mark structural transformations that give rise to problems in the philosophy of nature and the philosophy of science: what accounts for the emergence of bio-chemical, organic, and then sociohistorical structures? Or, if we choose to eschew deploying the magic word "emergence": how can we develop a suitable reductionist metaphysics that allows us to think of nature as the all-encompassing, unified domain (as all of spacetime, say, or the universe as a whole), in which the event of this whole becoming known through one of its parts (human beings) can be rendered intelligible?

Against this worldview, which I shall simply label "the naturalistic worldview," the line of argument I pursue in my own contribution to New Realism recommends a quite different point of departure, namely a "neutral realism."[15] Neutral realism considers it *prima facie* unproblematic that many of the sentences with which we express truth-apt beliefs are concerned with the real and are true independently of their somehow or other being referentially anchored in "nature," "the universe," or the "cosmos." It is true that 2+2=4; true that Angela Merkel is the Chancellor of Germany; that Picasso was a better artist than George Braque; that it is evil to torture creatures capable of suffering on a whim, etc.[16] The objects just mentioned are real and they really are as these true thoughts present them to be. At this level of analysis, the realism problem is not in any way connected with the question of how we can think of an ancestral reality. We can quite evidently think of ancestral realities without thereby being somehow stuck in a correlation that places the ancestral reality at a distance.

This is just what Hegel intends when he emphasizes that thinking consists in having thoughts.[17] What he calls "intelligence" is just the supposition that we are able not only to experience nature as something impenetrably other, but also to know it as something within which intelligence is embedded. Thus, says Hegel, "[i]t knows that what is *thought*, *is*; and that what *is*, only *is* in so far as it is a thought."[18] He also calls this "simple identity of the subjective and objective."[19] By this point, however, speculative realists will have instinctively wanted to level the accusation of correlationism or—perhaps worse still—of idealism. Yet caution is required. What Hegel asserts here (Frege *avant la lettre*!) is precisely that a thought is something grasped by thinking and not something that is itself any kind of psychological state or process. The decisive point of his reflections is that true thoughts are not trapped on this side of a "limit which completely separates"[20] them from reality.

The supposition that reality could elude our thought cannot be a legitimate constraint on realism in general. It seems to be only if we have already endorsed a problematic picture of thinking as a correlationistic distortion of reality. This picture underlies not only Meillassoux's version of speculative realism, but also those of Ray Brassier and Gilbert Harman, all of which work on the supposition that nature loves to hide itself.[21] In their way of thinking, the real or the natural is opposed to appearances, which ultimately, in all three cases, exhibit precisely the logical form they ascribe to correlationism. They therefore also believe that one can escape from the correlationsist circle only with recourse to nonphilosophical forms of knowledge. In the case of Badiou/Meillassoux, this is mathematics/physics; for Harman/Heidegger it is primarily art, whilst for Brassier/Sellars, it is future science, which will, step-by-step, have dismantled the manifest image of human beings.

Against the option I am sketching here, Maurizio Ferraris has objected that it involves an idealist sleight of hand.[22] However, his worry is based on his understanding of thoughts as something that only comes to be through a human achievement. However, neutral realism draws on the concept of objective thoughts, which are precisely not mental states of individuals.[23] Against this, Ferraris wants to claim Schelling for his own "negative realism" and believes that to exist means to resist any conceptual penetration (esistere = resistere, as he puts it in Italian). Such an approach thus returns us to an understanding that wants to tie the necessity of realism to the idea that the natural somehow withdraws from being known.[24]

But why should something be real only if it presents difficulties for cognition? It is this very supposition which reveals an ontological overestimation of cognition.

Firstly, one thereby makes it constitutive of being that it stands in a negative relation to cognition. Secondly, one thus lays claim to knowledge of reality as a whole, which can only be justified by citing some reason why the real should dwell in the epistemic distance. To insist that the real holds surprises in store for us is simply not pertinent to the question at issue; for, no party in this debate wants to contest the fact that reality is frequently different from how we believe it to be.[25]

Neutral realism approaches the question of realism by building on the concept of fact. A *fact* is something which is true of something. What something is true of is an *object*.[26] Much would still have been true in that sense had nobody existed to verify these truths. Truth is thus not purely a property of propositions or statements, but rather a formal structure whose obtaining is not bound to—though nor does it exclude—somebody's encountering it and communicating it, say, in the form of an assertion.

Many facts are natural. Specifically, a fact might be called *natural* if it is maximally modally robust, i.e., if it would also have obtained had nobody noticed, and it belongs to the universe. We might have been permanently mistaken about what it means to have true thoughts without this having changed the fact *that* we have true thoughts. One can model the truth conditions of obviously true statements and combine these models with theoretical constructions in a variety of ways. Accordingly, thoughts themselves belong to reality, which is thus not something to be found "out there" in the epistemic distance, even if there is indeed much that we do not (and cannot) know.

A misconceived theoretical construction of the truth conditions of statements concerning the ancestral assumes that we have to make a choice between correlationism or speculative realism. On the first option, a statement about the ancestral like

(A) "the presence of fossils proves that dinosaurs existed before there were any human beings"

somehow expresses a proposition of the following form:

(P_C^A) The presence of fossils proves that it looks to us as though dinosaurs existed before there were human beings.

But why should one accept such an analysis? There are, to be sure, reasons for formulating some suspicion of a similar form; yet Meillassoux does not, so far as I can tell, give us any convincing account of such reasons.[27]

Speculative realism, by contrast, formulates (A) as follows:

(P_{SK}^A) The presence of fossils, which, since not really graspable from the human standpoint, is in principle unverifiable, proves that something existed before there were any human beings, whereby what existed was presumably quite different from how it presents itself to us.

Neither Meillassoux, nor Harman or Brassier is in a position to assume that fossils themselves are proofs for the ancestral presence of dinosaurs. Fossils, after all, are essentially colored and thus have secondary qualities (meaning that, for Meillassoux and Brassier, they cannot be real or ancestral in the full sense). Fossils qua objects accessible to the senses, which can be cited as evidence for the real existence of something ancestral, differ from what would be a real proof—hence Meillassoux's shift to arche-fossils. Neither Meillassoux nor Brassier allows sensibly accessible proofs for their speculative realism, because they regard the sensible as a world of manifest illusion that arises only via our epistemic mechanisms. Both, therefore, accept a projectivist reading of early modern empiricism, according to which secondary qualities do not feature in the "great outdoors [*grand dehors*],"[28] but only in the correlationist internal space of the subject.

We thus have a worrying dilemma on our hands. Either the correlationist is right and fossils do not prove what they are supposed to prove, or the speculative realist is right and there are no fossils that can prove anything at all, for every candidate proof we could consider distorts what would really be a proof.

In both cases we have a false picture of what it means to make a knowledge claim. Yet one cannot avoid explaining how exactly, on the basis of manifest perceptual knowledge, we are supposed to acquire reasons for switching to the speculative mode. And unless one delivers a corresponding theory of science, mere reference to the natural sciences or mathematics does not get us any further.

World and Universe

This epistemological sketch cannot by itself, of course, avoid the question of what it means to account for nature or the universe. To begin with, some conceptual clarification is in order here. The concepts "world," "cosmos," "universe," "actuality," "reality," and "nature" frequently function as synonyms, all of which indicate, somewhat imprecisely, an absolute whole the existence of which is supposed to be, in some equally imprecise sense, independent of language, consciousness, thought, and theory-construction. On a pre-theoretical understanding of the term, a (metaphysical) realist is therefore someone who commits to there being such a reality, which has the modal status of being real primarily because only those things that we can *grasp*, but not *produce*, in thought belong to it. This accords with the traditional usage of our concepts concerning the natural, insofar as nature is meant to be that whose secrets we uncover via extensive experiment and modeling based on an elaborate division of scientific labor—not something that exists or is as scientific research shows it to be *because* scientific research shows it to be that way. This is a realistic platitude bound up with the concept of nature. Since its coinage in Greek philosophy, the concept has indicated that some things grow and flourish of their own accord, in contrast to the arts of rhetoric and poetry on the one hand and the technical production of artifacts on the other, both of which inhabit the cultural space of the polis.

Yet the concept of nature has of course undergone numerous transformations over the centuries—so many, indeed, that its philosophical rehabilitation seems to be a fairly hopeless prospect. Today, it stands in too great a proximity to the naturalistic worldview, which is based on the idea that nature is the domain in which all legitimate, i.e., nonsupernatural, things occur. At the same time, it continues to draw strength from the Spinozistic intuition of membership in an all-encompassing whole.

In order to remove the residual connotations of the concept of nature from the term *natural* science and render it more analytically precise, I suggest referring to the object domain of the natural sciences as "the universe." The universe is the object domain investigated by natural scientific research in all its unsurveyable variety. We can thus take up an insight that was given a clear elaboration by Milton Munitz: we have no scientific evidence that *the universe* as a whole even exists, where everything "natural"—i.e., everything belonging to the universe—can be shown to be a part of this whole.[29] We thus have no sufficiently well-grounded reason to assume that there is a reality—"the universe"—composed of ultimate particles, as though out of Lego bricks, configured as objects of different orders of magnitude at different scales.[30]

Nevertheless, it still makes sense to distinguish the object domain of the natural sciences from other domains, which is why I use the expression "the universe." From our standpoint as creatures of a particular magnitude located in a tiny corner of the Milky Way, the cosmological scope of the universe certainly seems impressive; yet, it is really one "ontological province"[31] amongst others. It is simply false that all objects that (really) exist have to fall within the universe in the specified sense. Put more cautiously, there are at least no scientifically credible reasons to assume as much, since the natural sciences, even taken as an ensemble, do not investigate all objects that exist. So much is trivially true; after all, they do not investigate the history of the Federal Republic of Germany, intergenerational justice, the refugee crisis, or the Epic of Gilgamesh.

Housing all objects that (really) exist in a single domain and identifying this domain with the universe is neither a scientifically nor an ontologically legitimate move, but a coup de main achieved through brute philosophical stipulation. We therefore need to think differently about the objectivity conditions of natural scientific enquiry.

Neither the vast ensemble of disciplines and sub-disciplines comprising the contemporary natural sciences, nor the idealized unifying science (physics) of antiquated logical positivism should be identified with metaphysics *qua* the science that investigates the absolute whole of reality. Nevertheless, it cannot be disputed that the natural sciences are, to a large extent, subject to realistic conditions of objectivity. It is doubtless true of many natural scientific statements that the objects that have to exist if they are true have a maximally modally robust status. That is, they would still have existed even if there had been nobody around to formulate corresponding statements about them.

It is usually by this point at the latest that my argument encounters resistance from certain quarters. Such resistance takes something like the following form: it certainly seems to be the case that we physically anchored creatures find ourselves at a location belonging to spacetime. Spacetime *qua* large-scale system (perhaps also *qua* maximal system) has developed. The initial state of spacetime, as we understand this today, was such that at that time (if such a temporal formulation is even permissible) there could not yet be sufficient conditions for intelligent life on any planet—if only because planetary structures emerged only later on. The universe developed in such a way that life, then various lifeforms arose within it, leading eventually, by means of processes of which we as yet have little understanding, to the evolution of species to which we ascribe both consciousness and, ultimately, the capacity to grasp their place in the universe. Against this background, it seems sensible to locate everything that exists somewhere along the time axis of the permanent structural construction site of spacetime—although this already presents us with the problem that, from a physical perspective, spacetime does not in fact feature a time axis on which we might plot an event like the Thirty Years' War or the lifespan of a human being.

By contrast, neutral realism recommends switching to a completely different perspective, namely that of ontology. The question is not how one might choose to depict the unfolding of the universe from the Big Bang, but how it is possible to understand what exists in light of the idea that we can make truth-apt statements about it—statements that are the original impetus for our legitimately assuming that something exists. We do not leap outside of our own thought and discover that there is a universe "out there," which began with a Big Bang and, after several aeons, began to spit out knowing creatures—creatures who until recently found this all so puzzling that they regarded the sheer existence of anything at all as itself a *mysterium tremendum et fascinosum*. This genealogical simplification of intellectual history is a falsification that has unfortunately become common currency, including in philosophy. It entirely ignores that metaphysics originally grew out of the assumption that the whole to which we thinkers belong must be constitutively open to the possibility of our comprehending it. It would otherwise be impossible to explain how it can so much as be an object of wonder.[32] I take the assumption that there is such a whole to be false. Yet it originally gave voice to a consciousness that we belong to the very domains that we know—even if it does not follow that there is precisely one all-embracing domain of objects which we can know.

The point of departure of the ontology of neutral realism can be understood in terms of Frege's insight that objects are accessible only within the framework of facts. Objects are essentially embedded in contexts without which we could not assume that the objects exist in the first place. Facts have a modal status, which can be measured relative to the appearance of cognitively equipped creatures. Against this background, it is quite correct to judge that those objects to which we ascribe an extremely broad cosmological role are—in the successful case—already as we grasp them to be independently of our grasping them.[33]

The modal status of facts, which marks out certain facts as "natural," does not pertain to them on the level at which pre-critical thought locates objects. Pre-critically, we locate objects "out there," outside of the "window frame" of our subjective visual field. What does not appear in the cave of our subjectivity can be real and dangerous, which is an obviously anthropological primitive constant. But we wildly overestimate our sense of sight if we locate the relevant source of realism in the fact that most of what we can literally see is not produced through sight and therefore is a cause for particular caution. This error was already denounced in the *Sophist* by Plato, the first great speleologist amongst the ontologists, when he made fun of the "earth-born" who regard as real only that which they can touch.[34]

Against this, it is vital to guard against confusing facts with fossils. Fossils are documents that support statements that ascribe a particular modal status to their objects. Fossils are not ancestral by their very nature. They do not resist their being known or their incorporation into the "parliament of things" which—as the recent political ecology stemming from Latour rightly insists—consists equally of "natural" (in the pre-critical sense) and "social" objects.[35] We know all this from the standpoint of an ontology whose operative concept of realism, since it does not draw on pre-critical ontological stipulations, is neutral. What this means for the philosophy of nature is that we are entitled to reject an atomistic metaphysics according to which the universe consists merely of objects to which we may ascribe nothing that transcends their presence in the fabric of the world qua "big physical object."[36]

But we cannot know anything about the universe (let alone about the world, which many equate with the universe as an enormous physical thing) if we suggest that it is merely a mosaic of particulars. For, we have to assume that the objects that we somehow or other discover are constitutively apt to be discovered in this or that way. The conditions of knowability of the known are communicable and thus essentially public. The known is not known because it is singular down to the last detail, but rather because it exhibits a form that allows it to be embedded in a fact.

We must therefore finally overcome the Cartesian metaphysics of *res extensa* and the Humean edifice built upon it. The latter presents the universe as a heap of particulars and recommends this conception by claiming, of all things, that it thus ties the universe to its knowability (its being mathematizable).[37] A universe of particulars would be unknowable if it had no more form than that of a mere heap. A mosaic (which, like a heap, is also a kind of aggregate) already exhibits a form. Even if one sees the universe merely as a disjointed assemblage of a given multiplicity of sets, one can do so only because one assigns an extensional semantics to statements about the universe, which itself assumes a structural framework that includes more than just particulars. Facts are unavoidable in any thinkable scenario. They cannot be replaced by fossils.

However, in doing their utmost to use nonphilosophical forms of knowledge to smuggle a pre-critical ontology of bare particulars past epistemological reflection, Meillassoux, Harman, and Brassier all fall prey to a constellation of ideas that regards facts as reducible and supposes an all-encompassing reality composed of contingently existing particulars. Speculative realism's conception of realism is thus, as many of its advocates eagerly and militantly stress, pre-critical.[38] The problem is that it has not convincingly shown us a path that avoids the snares and pitfalls of Kant's Copernican revolution. Instead, it hypostatizes a one-sided conception of truth-apt statements into a world-picture by isolating the subject of such statements from the predicates and relations with which they are essentially associated in true thoughts. This gives rise to the assumption that there is precisely one, mathematizable reality, which consists of lawless particulars whose only law (whose only necessity) is the complete absence of objective order.

In the debate over universals, this position would be classed not so much as realism as nominalism, for it denies that reality actually possesses the variety of structures that, supposedly, first pertain to it when we make judgments. Yet this is just to take the correlationist circle at face value, in the form of the claim that true judgments do not represent what is the case, but rather somehow construct it or conjure it into being.

Conclusion

In short: current incarnations of speculative realism suffer from the absence of an epistemology and semantics that allow for a demarcation between statements that are about reality and statements of a different kind (including speculative realism's methodological statements concerning its own statements, which evidently do not deal with fossils or ancestral facts). This is made all the more difficult by the tendency of the speculative metaphysical positions on offer to conceive of nature as something that loves to hide itself to such an extent that it has nothing further to do with our concepts. Reality thereby collapses into an empty ostensive gesture that assures us that there are natural objects out there, beyond the reach of the supposed correlationist circle. But such an empty assurance requires epistemologically informed support if it is not to degenerate into an ungrounded commentary on the putative accomplishments of mathematics/physics or things "setting themselves to work" in art.

In contrast to speculative realism, New Realism draws on an elaborate epistemology. The sense in which this represents a reappropriation of German idealism's method of theory-building does not (as Maurizio Ferraris rightly observes) consist in surreptitiously factoring realism out of the equation. Rather, one ought to understand the projects of Kant, Fichte, Schelling, and Hegel as contributions to the question of how we should go about reconstructing empirical realism, both epistemologically and ontologically/metaphysically, such that it is compatible with our embeddedness in natural, social, logical-semantic, and ultimately *geistige* contexts. The reality we know is clearly so constituted that it does not actively oppose its being known. The alternative of inserting particulars beneath the threshold of knowability is not an appropriate means of rendering realism respectable. Rather, this maneuver is based on the ungrounded suspicion that the appearances we knowing creatures confront on a daily basis are spectral phenomena in the narrow space of correlationism. The only spectral phenomenon in this scenario is correlationism itself, which might perhaps present a danger worth taking seriously if it were somewhat clearer what exactly it is supposed to be. Yet this, as I have argued, would require the epistemology that speculative realism, at least for the time being, appears to lack.

Notes

1. A prior version of this chapter was originally published in German as "Tatsachen statt Fossilien. Neuer versus Spekulativer Realismus" in *Zeitschrift für Medien und Kulturforschung* 2016 (2):187–204. It is revised and expanded by the author and translated here by Alex Englander, with the kind permission of the *Zeitschrift für Medien und Kulturforschung*.
2. Quentin Meillassoux, *After Finitude*, trans. Ray Brassier (London: Continuum, 2010), 19.
3. Dan Zahavi, "The End of What? Phenomenology vs. Speculative Realism," *International Journal of Philosophical Studies* 24, no. 3 (2016): 289–309, 293.
4. Immanuel Kant, *Critique of Pure Reason*, trans. Paul Guyer and Allen Wood (Cambridge: Cambridge University Press, 1998), A 26/B 42, 177.
5. On the metaphor of mental access and the question of whether the image itself is already prejudiced in a skeptical direction, see Marcus Willaschek, *Der mentale Zugang zur Welt. Realismus, Skeptizismus und Intentionalität* (Frankfurt am Main: Vittorio Klostermann, 2015).
6. See the appendix "On the Inhabitants of the Planets" of Kant's *Universal Natural History and Theory of the Heavens or Essay on the Constitution and the Mechanical Origin of the Whole Universe According to Newtonian Principles*, in Immanuel Kant, *Scientific Writings* (Cambridge: Cambridge University Press, 2012), 294–308.
7. See especially Iain Hamilton Grant, *Philosophies of Nature after Schelling* (London/New York: Continuum, 2006).
8. Meillassoux, *After Finitude*, 10.
9. Kant, *Critique of Pure Reason*, A 227/B 280f.
10. On this issue, see my reflections in "What Kind of an Idealist (if any) Is Hegel?" forthcoming in: *Hegel Bulletin* 37, no. 2 (2016): 181–208.
11. Compare the critique developed in Ray Brassier, *Nihil Unbound. Enlightenment and Extinction* (Basingstoke/New York: Palgrave Macmillan, 2007), 49–56.
12. For a discussion with relevant citations, see Markus Gabriel, *Sinn und Existenz. Eine realistische Ontologie* (Frankfurt am Main: Suhrkamp, 2016), 98–122.
13. Meillassoux, *After Finitude*, 67–70.
14. Meillassoux, *After Finitude*, 1.
15. Markus Gabriel, "Neutraler Realismus," *Philosophisches Jahrbuch* 121, no. 2 (2014): 352–72.
16. Compare the similar considerations in Amie L. Thomasson, *Ontology Made Easy* (Oxford/New York: Oxford University Press, 2015).
17. Georg Wilhelm Friedrich Hegel, *Philosophy of Mind*, trans. W. Wallace and A. V. Miller (Oxford: Clarendon Press, 2007), 202.
18. Hegel, *Philosophy of Mind*, 202.
19. Hegel, *Philosophy of Mind*, 202.
20. Georg Wilhelm Friedrich Hegel, *Phenomenology of Spirit*, trans. Terry Pinkard (Cambridge: Cambridge University Press, 2018), 49.
21. Besides the works of Meillassoux and Brassier cited above, see too Graham Harman, *The Quadruple Object* (Winchester: Zero Books, 2011), and Graham Harman, *Towards Speculative Realism. Essays and Lectures* (Ropley: Zero Books, 2010).
22. See, for example, Maurizio Ferraris, *Realismo Positivo* (Turin: Rosenberg & Sellier, 2013).
23. For arguments against the anti-realist consequences drawn by Frege and Kant, see Gabriel, *Sinn und Existenz*, 97–140.

24 See too Maurizio Ferraris, "Was ist der Neue Realismus?" in *Der Neue Realismus*, ed. Markus Gabriel, 52–76 (Berlin: Suhrkamp, 2014).
25 See my discussion of the "contrast of objectivity" in Markus Gabriel, *The Limits of Epistemology* (Cambridge: Polity, 2019). This discussion owes a considerable debt to Anton F. Koch, *Versuch über Wahrheit und Zeit* (Paderborn: Mentis, 2006). On realism, see too the more recent, Anton F. Koch, *Hermeneutischer Realismus* (Tübingen: Mohr Siebeck, 2016).
26 On formal object theory, compare: Markus Gabriel, *Die Erkenntnis der Welt* (Freiburg i. Br.: Verlag Karl Alber, 2012), 237–44.
27 On this issue, see Gabriel, *Sinn und Existenz*, 256ff. and Markus Gabriel and Slavoj Žižek, *Mythology, Madness and Laughter. Subjectivity in German Idealism* (London/New York: Continuum, 2009), 81–94.
28 Meillassoux, *After Finitude*, 7.
29 Milton K. Munitz, *Existence and Logic* (New York: New York University Press, 1974), esp. 180–91.
30 See Markus Gabriel, *I Am Not a Brain: Philosophy of Mind for the 21st Century* (Cambridge: Polity, 2017), and Markus Gabriel, "Für einen nicht-naturalistischen Realismus," in *Seien wir realistisch. Neue Realismen und Dokumentarismen in Philosophie und Kunst*, ed. Magdalena Marszalek and Dieter Mersch, 59–88 (Zürich/Berlin: Diaphanes, 2016).
31 See Markus Gabriel, *Why the World Does Not Exist* (Cambridge: Polity, 2015), 27–35.
32 See Gabriel, *Why the World Does Not Exist*, 146–84 (and fn. 33 below). For a similar understanding in contemporary philosophy, see for example Thomas Nagel, *Secular Philosophy and the Religious Temperament. Essays 2002–2008* (Oxford: Oxford University Press, 2010).
33 See Crispin Wright's concept of width of "cosmological role" in Crispin Wright, *Truth and Objectivity* (Cambridge MA: Harvard University Press, 1994), 196ff.
34 Plato, *Sophist*, trans. Harold North Fowler (Cambridge, MA: Harvard University Press, 1921), 248c1f.
35 See Bruno Latour, *Politics of Nature: How to Bring the Sciences into Democracy*, trans. Catherine Porter (Cambridge, MA: Harvard University Press, 2004).
36 David Lewis, *On the Plurality of Worlds* (Cambridge/Malden MA: Blackwell, 1986), 1. David Lewis's vividly articulated metaphysics of Humean supervenience is nothing more than a misinterpretation of the truth conditions of our statements about the universe. In an oft-cited passage, he defines Humean Supervenience as "the doctrine that all there is to the world is a vast mosaic of local matters of particular fact, just one little thing and then another" (David Lewis, *Philosophical Papers* Vol. II [New York: Oxford University Press, 1986], ix).
37 On this well-known connection, see the lucid discussion, which includes relevant references, in Andreas Hüttemann, *Ursachen* (Berlin/Boston: de Gruyter, 2013), 15–40.
38 Meillassoux, *After Finitude*, 112–29. An especially forceful advocacy of a return to pre-critical philosophizing can be found in Tom Sparrow, *The End of Phenomenology. Metaphysics and the New Realism* (Edinburgh: Edinburgh University Press, 2014).

Cited Works

Brassier, Ray. *Nihil Unbound. Enlightenment and Extinction*. Basingstoke/New York: Palgrave Macmillan, 2007.

Ferraris, Maurizio. *Realismo Positivo*. Turin: Rosenberg & Sellier, 2013.
Ferraris, Maurizio. "Was ist der Neue Realismus?" In *Der Neue Realismus*, edited by Markus Gabriel, 52–76. Berlin: Suhrkamp, 2014.
Gabriel, Markus. *Die Erkenntnis der Welt*. Freiburg i. Br.: VerlagKarl Alber, 2012.
Gabriel, Markus. "Neutraler Realismus." *Philosophisches Jahrbuch* 121, no. 2 (2014): 352–72.
Gabriel, Markus. *Why the World Does Not Exist*. Cambridge: Polity, 2015.
Gabriel, Markus. *Sinn und Existenz. Eine realistische Ontologie*. Frankfurt am Main: Suhrkamp, 2016.
Gabriel, Markus. "Für einen nicht-naturalistischen Realismus." In *Seien wir realistisch. Neue Realismen und Dokumentarismen in Philosophie und Kunst*, edited by Magdalena Marszalek and Dieter Mersch, 59–88. Zürich/Berlin: Diaphanes, 2016.
Gabriel, Markus. *I Am Not a Brain: Philosophy of Mind for the 21st Century*. Cambridge: Polity, 2017.
Gabriel, Markus. *The Limits of Epistemology*. Cambridge: Polity, 2019.
Gabriel, Markus. "What Kind of an Idealist (if any) Is Hegel?" forthcoming in *Hegel Bulletin* 37, no. 2 (2016): 181–208.
Gabriel, Markus and Slavoj Žižek. *Mythology, Madness and Laughter. Subjectivity in German Idealism*. London/New York: Continuum, 2009.
Grant, Iain Hamilton. *Philosophies of Nature after Schelling*. London/New York: Continuum, 2006.
Harman, Graham. *Towards Speculative Realism. Essays and Lectures*. Ropley: Zero Books, 2010.
Harman, Graham. *The Quadruple Object*. Winchester: Zero Books, 2011.
Hegel, Georg Wilhelm Friedrich. *Philosophy of Mind*. Translated by W. Wallace and A. V. Miller. Oxford: Oxford University Press, 2007.
Hegel, Georg Wilhelm Friedrich. *Phenomenology of Spirit*. Translated by Terry Pinkard. Cambridge: Cambridge University Press, 2018.
Hüttemann, Andreas. *Ursachen*. Berlin/Boston: de Gruyter, 2013.
Kant, Immanuel. *Critique of Pure Reason*. Translated by Paul Guyer and Allen Wood. Cambridge: Cambridge University Press, 1998.
Kant, Immanuel. *Universal Natural History and Theory of the Heavens or Essay on the Constitution and the Mechanical Origin of the Whole Universe according to Newtonian Principles*, in: Immanuel Kant, *Scientific Writings*. Cambridge: Cambridge University Press, 2012.
Koch, Anton F. *Versuch über Wahrheit und Zeit*. Paderborn: Mentis, 2006.
Koch, Anton F. *Hermeneutischer Realismus*. Tübingen: Mohr Siebeck, 2016.
Latour, Bruno. *Politics of Nature: How to Bring the Sciences into Democracy*. Translated by Catherine Porter. Cambridge, MA: Harvard University Press, 2004.
Lewis, David. *On the Plurality of Worlds*. Cambridge/Malden, MA: Blackwell, 1986.
Lewis, David. *Philosophical Papers*. Vol. II. New York: Oxford University Press, 1986.
Meillassoux, Quentin. *After Finitude*. Translated by Ray Brassier. London: Continuum, 2010.
Munitz, Milton K. *Existence and Logic*. New York: New York University Press, 1974.
Nagel, Thomas. *Secular Philosophy and the Religious Temperament. Essays 2002-2008*. Oxford: Oxford University Press, 2010.
Plato. *Sophist*. Translated by Harold North Fowler. Cambridge, MA: Harvard University Press, 1921.

Sparrow, Tom. *The End of Phenomenology. Metaphysics and the New Realism*. Edinburgh: Edinburgh University Press, 2014.
Thomasson, Amie L. *Ontology Made Easy*. Oxford/New York: Oxford University Press, 2015.
Willaschek, Marcus. *Der mentale Zugang zur Welt. Realismus, Skeptizismus und Intentionalität*. Frankfurt am Main: Vittorio Klostermann, 2015.
Wright, Crispin. *Truth and Objectivity*. Cambridge, MA: Harvard University Press, 1994.
Zahavi, Dan. "The End of What? Phenomenology vs. Speculative Realism." *International Journal of Philosophical Studies* 24, no. 3 (2016): 289–309.

Chapter 4

PRODUCTION OF REAL PRESENCE: WHAT PRESENCE CANNOT CONVEY

Benjamin Boysen

Hans Ulrich Gumbrecht's book, *Production of Presence: What Meaning Cannot Convey* (2004), has proven to be and remains highly influential in the humanities, especially in the art world and in cultural and literary studies. In this chapter, I argue that the book and its key concept, "presence," are beset by inconsistencies, self-contradictions, and theoretical misunderstandings (especially of Heidegger). Moreover, rather than the critique of metaphysics announced by the author, Gumbrecht's quest for sensuous immediacy is demonstrably a quest for transcendental spirituality and quasi-religious meaningfulness, displaying a passionate longing to overcome modern secularization and expressing a nostalgic yearning for spirituality and union with the cosmos. The author, in effect, contradicts his announced program for the book and his call for an epistemological change in the humanities turns out to be less profound and innovative than he seems to believe, though more in keeping with present-day retrograde reveries about an enchanted premodern world.

"But Is This Not, Finally, a Religious Experience?"

With *Production of Presence*, Hans Ulrich Gumbrecht makes a passionate plea for the notion of "presence" in the humanities—a plea that found an enthusiastic resonance within academia. In a wide-ranging critique of modern Western culture ranging from the Renaissance to today, Gumbrecht identifies Descartes's dualistic separation between *res cogitans* and *res extensa* as the deplorable climax of an intellectual tendency that subsequently culminated in the apotheosis of the mind as the only valid instrument of producing knowledge. Descartes's dualism gave rise to an ensuing split between subject and object, which, Gumbrecht argues, meant that the humanities has neglected affective and sense-based experience and in turn disregarded spatio-sensual modes of relating to cultural phenomena. For Gumbrecht, "presence" counteracts the tradition of Cartesian dualism by deemphasizing conventional notions of meaning in favor of an experiential appeal to the senses.

The story of Gumbrecht's thoughts on presence is arguably representative of the contemporary interest in materiality that characterizes the emergent new materialisms. In recent decades, cultural studies, art studies, and literature have articulated a general feeling of worldlessness and a consequent longing for reality. Gumbrecht seems to be congenial with critical aspects of these new materialisms inasmuch as they constitute a turn toward or call for a renewed spiritualization of the world. And, like the new materialisms, Gumbrecht's apparent interest in materiality seems to cloak a vague and ill-defined spiritualism,[1] which is why he seems justified in asking rhetorically: "But is this not, finally, a religious experience?"[2]

Good (Premodern) Signs and Bad (Modern) Signs

Like the main currents within the material turn and the new materialisms, Gumbrecht's *Production of Presence* voices a discontent with the prison house of language, mediacy, categorial, and schematic thinking—in sum, the semiotic dimension—and asserts a yearning for a more immediate access to and engagement with the nonlinguistic world.

Gumbrecht argues that the advent of modernity and its attendant emphasis on scientific rationalism and liberalism meant that a Realistic world-picture was replaced by a Nominalist one, which, in effect, implies that what he calls "presence culture" was succeeded by "meaning culture." Unlike the Nominalism of modern "meaning cultures," "presence cultures" embody an understanding of the sign "close to the Aristotelian sign definition [...] where a sign is a coupling between a substance (something that requires space) and a form (something that makes it possible for the substance to be perceived)."[3]

In Aristotle's theory of hylomorphism—which is not strictly a semiotics, but an ontology conceiving being or substance (οὐσία) as a compound of matter (ὕλη) and form (μορφή)—mental impressions are *likenesses* of actual things. According to Gumbrecht, this Realistic sign concept neatly avoids the duality "between the purely spiritual and the purely material for the two sides of what is brought together in the sign." Aristotle's hylomorphism implies an ideal metaphysical correspondence and unity between matter and our mental impressions of them that is secured by the semiotic convergence taking place in the forms. In other words, existent material corresponds with us via forms, as matter is *a priori* shaped in an intelligible form immediately accessible to us. Or, to put it differently: our mental impressions and the forms of substance are "formulated" in the same language, and the imprint or stamp of the forms on matter implies that there exists a correspondence and unity between humans and the world by which both mirror each other ideally.

In effect, Gumbrecht argues that "presence-culture" is paradigmatically and emphatically exemplified by the allegorical Realist world-picture of the Middle

Ages, that is, the medieval Christian-Aristotelian sign theory, according to which all creation is a sign of the Creator. According to this understanding, mental ideas are not limited to the mind but find an echo in things and vice versa. Therefore, it makes perfect sense when Gumbrecht adds that such a sign-concept—typical of presence cultures—denotes a "world where stones keep on coming closer and where truth can be substance [...] a world where [...] humans want to relate to the surrounding cosmology by inscribing themselves [...] into the rhythms of the cosmos."[4]

This deep, immediate unity with the world in which the cosmos is pre-shaped in a humanely recognizable manner is undone by Nominalism that, according to Gumbrecht, advances a dualism like the one proposed by Descartes. Indeed, what Descartes is for modern ontology, Saussure is for modern linguistics—and more broadly, the humanities. In both Saussure and Descartes, the ideal unity between the signifier and the signified, or between the human mind and the world, is broken apart. Modern "meaning cultures" are thus dominated by a dualist debasement of the material and the signifier. Gumbrecht explains that "a sign in a meaning culture needs to have precisely the metaphysical structure that Ferdinand de Saussure contends is the universal condition of the sign: it is the coupling of a material signifier with a purely spiritual signified (or 'meaning')." Descartes's dualist metaphysics, Gumbrecht claims, reappears in Saussure's semiotic theory of the linguistic sign; and inasmuch as Saussure exercised a strong influence on the humanities in the twentieth century, it should come as no surprise that he effected a hermeneutic hegemony according to which "the 'purely material' signifier ceases to be an object of attention as soon as its 'underlying' meaning has been identified."[5]

However, it is false to claim that Saussure's sign is composed of a binary duality between *a purely material signifier* and *a purely spiritual signified*. In fact, Saussure insists on the direct opposite: "This two-sided unity [between the signifier and the signified] has often been compared to the unity of the human person, composed of a body and a soul. *The comparison is hardly satisfactory.*"[6] Saussure is careful to stress that the signifier and the signified are inseparable and that they presuppose each other like "a sheet of paper" where "one cannot cut the front without cutting the back at the same time."[7] Unlike Descartes's *res extensa* and *res cogitans*, for example, one simply cannot exist in the absence of the other. Hence, Saussure in no way dualistically opposes *a material signifier against a purely spiritual signified*, for *both* are mental and psychological entities:

> The linguistic sign unites, not a thing and a name, but a concept and a sound-image. *The latter is not the material sound, a purely physical thing, but the psychological imprint of the sound, the impression that it makes on our senses.* The sound-image is sensory, and if I happen to call it "material," it is only in that sense, and by way of opposing it to the other term of the association, the concept, which is generally more abstract.

In short, the linguistic sign constituted by the unity of a signifier and a signified is "then a two-sided psychological entity."[8]

What the autonomy of the linguistic sign implies, according to Saussure, is that language (and its constituent parts) is "*a form and not a substance*."[9] Neither the signifier nor the signified has a substance. Since in language there are "only differences *without positive terms*," this means that whether "we take the signified or the signifier, language has neither ideas nor sounds that existed before the linguistic system."[10]

With no prenatal ideas and no materiality, Saussure's signs have no intrinsic determination, but function through their relative position in a system. And since the "bond between the signifier and signified is arbitrary," meaning that "*the linguistic sign is arbitrary*,"[11] we are obviously extremely far from Gumbrecht's endorsement of the Aristotelian and medieval sign definition. Not because Saussure's semiotics is dualistic, as Gumbrecht claims, but because in this Nominalism, defined by negativity, difference, and arbitrariness, there is neither a deep metaphysical and positive determinancy nor any fundamental unity with any inner or outer world outside language.

Presence and the "Desire for Immediacy"

Gumbrecht declares in his preface that his concept of presence is intended to accede to "the desire for [...] immediacy."[12] The concept of "presence" therefore also bears witness to a yearning to abrogate human mediacy and what Gumbrecht labels "meaning." Meaning is defined no differently than its normal, conventional usage; yet, Gumbrecht seems to associate it with signs, because attributing "a meaning to a thing that is present" equals forming "an idea of what this thing may be in relation to us."[13] The problem with the sign and meaning is that we never get the thing itself, which is not only mediated by the process of representation but also by the subject (i.e., the interpretant) for whom it represents something and is interpreted accordingly. Moreover, meaning and signs are, according to Gumbrecht, directly opposed to things and presence, for whenever meaning is attributed to a sensuous thing, "we seem to attenuate, inevitably, the impact that this thing can have on our bodies and our senses."[14]

Gumbrecht continues to stress that presence effects "*exclusively* appeal to the senses."[15] Notwithstanding the repeated assurances of the opposite, Gumbrecht does effectively posit the difference between "presence" and "meaning" in terms of an opposition. Indeed, he markedly spells out how he is "emphasizing so much this *noncomplementarity* in the relationship between presence effects and meaning effects."[16]

Now, Gumbrecht adds that presence effects "have nothing to do with *Einfühlung*, that is, with imagining what is going on in another person's psyche."[17] In compliance with a scientistic and positivistic attitude endeavoring, for example, to unlock the secret of George Elliot's *Middlemarch* by doing a CAT brain scanning of someone reading it, Gumbrecht behavioristically reduces the content of an aesthetic experience to nothing "more than a specifically high level in the functioning of some of our general cognitive, emotional, and perhaps even physical faculties."[18] Presence calls for an attitude only focusing on what the senses receive.

4. Production of Real Presence

I propose that the problems with this way of defining "presence" become clear if we measure Gumbrecht's phenomenalistic definition against Heideggerian phenomenology. To do so is somewhat ironic, for Gumbrecht claims that it would be difficult "to imagine his own work without the philosophy of Heidegger,"[19] and he professes a close philosophical affinity with Heidegger's existentialist thinking.[20] However, not only has Gumbrecht grossly misunderstood key Heideggerian concepts (as will be shown in more detail in the subchapter "Gumbrecht's mésalliance with Heidegger"), but, as it turns out, explaining what Heidegger states in his thinking is *equal* to providing the most scathing critique of Gumbrecht's theoretical agenda.

According to Heidegger, when actively engaged in practical operations, activities, or producing, human existence (*Dasein*) has no conscious experience of the things in use as independent and distinct objects. When engaged in hammering, the craftsman has no conscious recognition of the hammer, the nails, or the workbench, as one would have if one passively stood back and looked at them. However, not only are the hammer, nails, and workbench absorbed in the active engagement; so, in a sense, is the craftsman, as he becomes wrapped up in his activity in such a way that he has no awareness of himself as a subject opposed to objects. This does not mean, as a strictly theoretical position might have you think, that this active absorption in the work precludes any awareness at all, but rather that this existentially primordial awareness, "circumspection" (*Umsicht*), does not follow the subject-object model of consciousness. Heidegger's phenomenology thus claims that, in the experience of the ongoing tasks characteristic of the human way of existing, there are no subjects and no objects—only concerned and caring activity. In sum, Heidegger denies that the concepts of subject and object characterize our most basic way of encountering entities. Heidegger thus reverses the traditional dichotomy between the theoretical attitude of passive contemplation (θεωρία) against an active involvement (πρᾶξις).

Returning to Gumbrecht, the irony here is that his concept of "presence" plainly falls victim to Heidegger's critique of the traditional subject-object dichotomy. For when Gumbrecht is careful to explicate "presence" as a phenomenon to which a human being does not contribute—for the human is only passively overwhelmed by an exterior presence that absorbs and assimilates it from the outside—the subject-object model of consciousness resurfaces with a vengeance.

Unilaterally stressing that the purely sensuously given exists in abstract isolation from the synthetic union with the subjective not only presupposes the undesired subject-object dichotomy, it also—at least according to Heidegger's critique— reaffirms one of the fundamental presuppositions of scientific rationality and objectivity. According to Heidegger, the idea that pure and immediate perception is fully adequate to the sense-stimulus constitutes the hidden dogma and ontological prejudice that inform Western scientism. Thus, Gumbrecht's ideal of doing away with the subjective contribution in favor of pure passive intuition or perception à la Hume or Locke is actually at the heart of the theoretical standpoint which has always advanced a self-forgetfulness that admits only a pure, nonsubjective θεωρία, i.e., a "gaze" or "contemplation."

Is "Meaning" Not "Meaningful"?

Gumbrecht identifies the concept of "meaning" with metaphysics, and metaphysics is understood as the attitude that "gives a higher value to the meaning of phenomena than to their material presence" and which points "to a worldview that always wants to go 'beyond' (or 'below') that which is 'physical.'" However, in a peculiar and highly curious move, Gumbrecht explicitly states that, as concerns the meaning of "metaphysics," he disregards "religion" and "transcendence"—thus leaving us with a rather fractured notion of metaphysics not pertaining to religion or transcendence.[21] So, when emptied of its traditional and lexical meaning, what does the concept of "metaphysics" entail for Gumbrecht? Quite simply: the semiotic. For as he says in an aside toward the end of the book, "an exclusively semiotic [...] concept of the sign" is "in my terminology, exclusively metaphysical."[22] Metaphysics is semiotics—though yet again, the semiotic systems of religious and transcendental thinking and narratives are deliberately excluded.

In addition, Gumbrecht insists that his book aims at contributing to "the traditional 'critique of metaphysics'": "[W]hat I try to develop here is inevitably part of this very tradition in Western philosophy."[23] Claiming to exercise a critique of metaphysics in which religion and transcendence are protected seems very perplexing—a critique of metaphysics without metaphysics. Something does not add up here. Why is it—in the words of the author—necessary to use these basic philosophical notions "in an unfamiliar way"?[24] And why does Gumbrecht inscribe himself into a philosophical tradition critical of metaphysics whilst discarding its basic tenets? Inscribing oneself within a traditional *"critique" of metaphysics* is, it must be noted, a strong intellectual gesture; moreover, counting oneself as *part of this very tradition in Western philosophy* entails a considerable imbursement of intellectual authority and ethos. Despite the urgency of Gumbrecht's stance, nevertheless, his predicament remains. However much he seeks to narrow his definition of metaphysics, it is hardly justifiable to present the tenets of the Eucharist, mysticism, revelation, epiphanies, theophany and religious dogma, rituals of magic, the search for the mystery from an unknown source, and the quest for a transcendental unity with the world as part of a long philosophical tradition critical of metaphysics.[25]

The contradictions involved in these maneuvers, in which "meaning" is defined as metaphysical, become clear when we look at what Gumbrecht means by the idea of "meaningfulness." Talking of the "presence effect" that the Japanese No theater might exercise on the spectator, Gumbrecht explains: "Perhaps you even begin to feel the composure that allows you to let things come, and perhaps you cease to ask what these things mean—because they seem just present and *meaningful*."[26] The ensuing opposition between "meaning" and "meaningfulness" gives a strong hint that, for Gumbrecht, the problem with "meaning" seems not so much to be that it is metaphysical, but rather that it is *not*. In other words, the problem with "meaning" is that it is not "meaningful" enough, that is, it is not sufficiently *full of meaning*. "Meaning" does not offer a satisfactory sense of meaning*fulness*, i.e., a sense of the world or the things of the world as intrinsically imbued with meaning.

"Meaning" is "meaningless," for by stripping it of its former magic, unity, mystery, transcendence, and religious content, modernity has confined meaning to the space of secularism. Things and the cosmos are now only merely present in their independent and alien being-different. They are merely present in their separate and self-standing otherness. Gumbrecht's topsy-turvy "critique of metaphysics" is therefore a critique of the disappearance of metaphysics in the wake of modernity, that is to say, a critique of secularism and Weberian disenchantment (*Entzauberung*) of the things of the world.[27] The absent meaning of "meaning" thus seems to be the lack of an anthropomorphized world picture akin to an interpretation of the world as Creation intrinsically bestowed with meaning by a (divine) Creator (as we shall see in the next subchapter).

To recapitulate: meaning is what is not physical; it is centered on human subjectivity and involves mediation and signs. Although it relates to the spiritual, mental, and what reaches beyond the worldly and earthly, religious experience and the transcendent are—for unexplained (though nonetheless not entirely unclear) reasons—left out of the equation here. Finally, by definition, meaning implies what is different from itself, and impure.

Is "Presence" the Same as "Real Presence"?

At this moment, we have a dichotomy between meaning/metaphysics and presence. But what happens to the remainder of religion and transcendence excluded from the category of metaphysics? Being uprooted from their traditional domain, religion and transcendence are now transferred to the opposed category of "presence," where they become paradigmatic and exemplary of what Gumbrecht means by presence as physical, sensuous, immanent, and unmediated.

In the chapter "Metaphysics: A Brief Prehistory of What Is Now Changing," the dichotomy between "presence" and "meaning" is expanded by the evocation of an epochal dichotomy between a Realist medieval culture of unity and a Nominalist modern culture of distance and difference. According to Gumbrecht, medieval "presence culture" gives primary importance to the body, whereas modern "meaning culture" is characterized by Cartesian subjectivity and dualism. For the author, the Realist "presence culture" is nowhere better exemplified than in the medieval Eucharist, which consequently becomes the paradigmatic example of what "presence" implies. Gumbrecht claims that—unlike subsequent Protestant views of the Eucharist, which allegorically and symbolically "redefined the presence of Christ's body and blood into an evocation of Christ's body and blood as 'meanings'"—the medieval Catholic Eucharist embodied a "ritual through which the 'real' Last Supper and, above all, Christ's body and Christ's blood could 'really' be made present again."[28] The deictic gesture of the ritual—*hoc est enim corpus meum* (for this is my body)—means not only that the body and blood of Christ are tangible in the transubstantiated bread and wine here and now, but also that historical distance is obliterated as the Last Supper is not merely commemorated, but is taking place here and now in a time *synchronous* with that of Jesus and the Apostles on the evening before the crucifixion.

The Catholic and the Protestant Eucharists that exemplify the divide between a "meaning" and a "presence" culture are furthermore representative of two opposed conceptions of the sign. In the Nominalist sign theory characteristic of modern "meaning culture," "signs at least potentially leave the substances that they evoke at a temporal and spatial distance."[29] Conversely, the Realist sign theory typical of medieval "presence culture" advances "the Aristotelian concept of the sign" that "brings together a substance (i.e., that which is present because it demands a space) and a form (i.e., that through which a substance becomes perceptible)."[30] This is all true and fair. However, the premodern conceptual Realism of the Middle Ages does not square very well with Gumbrecht's definition of presence effects (cited above) as that which "exclusively appeal to the senses."[31] For is it really true that the Eucharist equals presence as defined by Gumbrecht—as what "is 'present' to us (very much in the sense of the Latin form *prae-esse*)" and what "is in front of us, in reach of and tangible for our bodies"?[32] Does the Eucharist really offer a sensuous immediacy of something merely present, something that, in Gumbrecht's own words, is in no way metaphysically "going 'beyond' (or 'below') that which is 'physical'"?[33]

One suspects that Gumbrecht is disingenuous when he expresses surprise at "the suspicion (or was it rather meant to sound like praise?) that [he] had turned into a religious 'thinker.'" And, when he counters this suspicion by assuring that his "desire to reconnect with the things of the world" is "as strictly immanentist as one could possibly imagine,"[34] he is far from convincing. For again, are the Eucharist, mysticism, magic, epiphanies, and the yearning for the "mystery from an unknown source" along with the desire of "*being in sync with the things of the world*" really the most strictly immanentist phenomena that one can possibly conceive?[35]

To take one prominent medieval scholar amongst others of the same mind, Umberto Eco, in *Art and Beauty in the Middle Ages*, defines the medieval world picture as essentially "pan-semiotic," which means that the whole world and all the things in it serve as signs or mirrors of God.[36] In the Middle Ages, the world was typically interpreted *per speculum creaturarum*, i.e., as a perfect system of signs mirroring the Creator, God himself. Understanding was to take its point of departure from an immanent way of perceiving things which, taken together, constituted a hierarchical system of slumbering signs (*signa*) completely dependent on God. Particulars did not enjoy an autonomous, individual existence, but were rather *signa* and *exempla* of the divine *exemplar*. Heidegger thus argues that medieval thinking anthropomorphized the world and so cast a veil over it. For what happens in the Middle Ages, according to Heidegger, is that "on the basis of a religious faith, namely, the biblical faith, the totality of all beings is represented in advance as something created, which here means made."[37]

In sum, Gumbrecht defines his notion of "presence" as the phenomenalistically immediate and as what, in contrast to "meaning," exclusively appeals to the senses. However, he exemplifies this notion with the metaphysico-theological conception of "real presence," according to which things are not only what they seem immediately because God has incarnated himself in them and thus imbued them with a deeper metaphysical meaning. What is presented as a materialist and physically oriented theory betrays itself as it proves on closer inspection to be a quasi-premodern spirituality rejecting modernity. "Presence" becomes an alibi for "real presence."

Gumbrecht's Mésalliance with Heidegger

Gumbrecht claims that Heidegger's philosophical project has been indispensable for his own work and he considers his own position quite close to Heidegger's.[38] Indeed, Heidegger's presence is strongly felt in his book, and Gumbrecht obviously shares the diagnosis of the current endpoint of the metaphysical history in which the subject-object paradigm has led Western culture to an extreme state of alienation. Heidegger's call for a composed stance of quiet waiting likewise makes the ontological fatalism of his late thinking quite appealing to Gumbrecht. So, in the context of a discussion of his fascination with theology and the yearning for "something 'beyond' those beings […] or entities that make up our everyday world […] and for an 'unknown source,'"[39] Gumbrecht tellingly evokes Heidegger's (in)famous Spiegel interview from 1966 (posthumously published in 1976), where the thinker darkly declared that "only a God can save us."[40] Since no other thinker went "further in criticizing and revising the metaphysical world-view than Martin Heidegger,"[41] and as Gumbrecht has metaphysics play "the role of a scapegoat" in his own book,[42] it should be clear why the latter considers Heidegger a brother in arms.

But, as shown earlier in "Presence and the 'desire for immediacy,'" Gumbrecht's understanding of "presence" and "meaning" fails to overcome the subject-object dichotomy that Heidegger strove to dismantle. And, as we saw, Gumbrecht's accentuation of "presence" as a sensuous and spatial immediacy runs against Heidegger's critique of Occidental ontotheology. Moreover, Gumbrecht shares in the Occidental forgetfulness of Being (*Seinsvergessenheit*) that follows from thinking of Being in terms of "presence," i.e., as the spatially and nontemporal presence of an immediate entity in front of us. Heidegger's critique thus states that Being (*das Sein*) has mistakenly been conceived in the manner of beings or entities (*das Seiende*). Now, to make matters worse for Gumbrecht, he furthermore not only misconstrues basic philosophical concepts of Heidegger, but the concepts he evokes (*In-der-Welt-sein* and *das Sein*) to strengthen and validate his own notion of "presence" speak directly against his own case.

In Heidegger's characterization of human existence as Being-in-the-world, Gumbrecht sees a strong affirmation of how we are part of the physical world and not ontologically separate from it, as the concept designates "an existence that is always already in a substantial and therefore in a spatial contact with the world."[43] Thus, Gumbrecht explains that "a feeling of our being-in-the-world" during an aesthetic experience amounts to a feeling of "being part of the physical world."[44] What Heidegger did with this concept was to bring "human self-reference back in touch with the things of the world,"⁴⁵ which is why "Being-in-the-world is a concept perfectly fit to a type of reflection and analysis that tries to recover the component of presence in our relation with the things of the world."⁴⁶ Therefore, Being-in-the-world is a concept speaking in favor of Gumbrecht's notion of "presence," as it stresses how we are interconnected and one with the physical and spatial world of things. Being-in-the-world is a concept that elucidates how we are "always already in [...] spatial [...] contact with the world."⁴⁷

When, however, Gumbrecht understands Heidegger's Being-in-the-world as testimony that humans are constituent objects of the physical world as one object among others in a relationship characterized by substantiality and immediacy, he is simply incorrect. As mentioned above, what Heidegger criticizes is precisely the traditional, substantialist interpretation of Being that defines human existence as an object present in its immediacy. Being-in-the-world is, conversely, meant to challenge a series of traditional philosophical assumptions: assumptions dictating that the entities that surround us in the world are objects characterized by substantiality, sensuous materiality, extension, and so on. According to Heidegger, this is a fundamental mistake, for perception is not immediate but is rather mediated in a pragmatically lived context in which things are always seen *as* something for us (the so-called As-Structure, *Als-Struktur*).⁴⁸ So, what we are dealing with in our lived world is not the sheer presence of something, what Heidegger calls presence-at-hand (*Vorhandenheit*), but entities that show themselves on the basis of an understanding of their being as equipment (*Zeug*) available in their mode of readiness-to-hand (*Zuhandenheit*). As we are first and foremost *engaged* with things, we primarily encounter them as "something-in-order-to"⁴⁹ and pure perception is thus deemed a "deficient" mode of engaged perception.⁵⁰ Heidegger turns the usual order of priority upside-down, since things have meaning as signs *first* and may only *afterwards*, in a very convoluted manner, be approached in their pure perceptive presence abstracted from everything else (i.e., from their "world" in the Heideggerian sense).

There is nothing substantialist in Heidegger's concept of things. He even claims that "[t]aken strictly, there 'is' no such thing as an equipment."⁵¹ For belonging to the "As-Structure" of intentional experience that makes up Being-in-the-world, the thing must be understood as "Being-a-sign-for."⁵² This intervention marks "a *universal kind of relation*, so that the sign-structure itself provides an ontological clue for 'characterizing' any entity whatsoever." In other words, Heidegger stresses how things are always perceived and understood with reference to *us* (*Dasein*). Hence, the thing (as Being-a-sign-for) is characterized by significance or meaning (*Bedeutsamkeit* or *Sinn*). Therefore, the transcendence of *Dasein* that allows us to have a world in the first place originates in the circumstance where "in the Being-in-the-world of *Dasein* itself—a supply of 'signs' is presented."⁵³

In the Heideggerian sense, the world is not an entity or any sum or totality of entities; it does not denote the earth or the physical universe, and "being-in" does not entail spatial containment in something (and therefore, the world is in no way to be confused with the totality of the "things of the world," as Gumbrecht wrongly claims). The world is the sum of a large-scale holistic network of interconnected relational significance (*die Verweisungsganzheit*), that is, "worldhood as that referential totality which constitutes significance."⁵⁴ So, what Heidegger means by the concept of "world" is nothing external, but a structure of *Dasein*'s being, and this is, furthermore, how we must understand the seemingly solipsistic and paradoxical statement that there would be no world without human *Dasein*.⁵⁵ For the statement is, in fact, both logical and natural inasmuch as the "world" is "not a way of characterizing those entities which *Dasein* essentially is *not*; rather, it is a characteristic of *Dasein* itself."⁵⁶

Associating Being-in-the-world with the *things of the world, the physical world*, and with a *spatial contact with the world*, Gumbrecht is as far off the mark as he can be. Furthermore, the assumption that Being-in-the-world is *perfectly fit* to elucidate his project with, and concept of, "presence" turns out to be ill-founded since he defines "presence" in terms of what *exclusively appeals to the senses, is in front of us, in reach of and tangible for our bodies*, and holds that "presence" is ideally *immediate* and uncontaminated by *meaning, understanding*, and the production of signs. In what might seem an ironic anticipation of Gumbrecht's quest for phenomenal immediacy, Heidegger is careful to stress that the type of reflection and analysis in which a "Being-just-present-at-hand (*Nur-vorhandensein*) comes to the fore" actually brings about and presupposes a world deprivation.⁵⁷ The path shown by Gumbrecht to recuperate what he perceives to be a current "loss of world"⁵⁸ would thus, according to Heidegger, conversely amount to nothing but, yes, a world-deprivation (*Entweltlichung*).

Turning to the other Heideggerian key concept of Being (*Sein*), Gumbrecht declares that it is "the most inspiring philosophical resource available for a further development of reflection on presence" since "there cannot be any doubt that this concept is very close to the concept of 'presence.'"⁵⁹ Being is not "something spiritual or something conceptual. Being is not a meaning. Being belongs to the dimension of things [...] it has substance [...] and unlike anything purely spiritual [...], it occupies space."⁶⁰ Being simply is there, has "a substance, an articulation in space,"⁶¹ which denotes "primordial material qualities" as a "thing independent of its integration into any semantic network."⁶² At this point, Gumbrecht presents Heidegger's concept of Being as follows: "Being is tangible things, seen independently of their culturally specific situations."⁶³ So, in its "preconceptual thingness,"⁶⁴ Being is construed as almost identical to Gumbrecht's "presence" and is directly opposed to the corresponding concept of "meaning."

Again, on closer inspection, Gumbrecht's idea of "presence" is most certainly *not* contained in Heidegger's notion of Being, which rather speaks directly against it.

Now, since Heidegger states in *The Origin of the Work of Art* that an artwork is a happening of truth disclosing Being, and since he says (as quoted by Gumbrecht) that "[a]rt works universally display a thingly character, albeit in a wholly distinct way," Gumbrecht takes this as evidence that Being is "something that has the character of a thing."⁶⁵ Heidegger, however, also insists that "the artwork is something else over and above the thingly element,"⁶⁶ for "the work is at bottom something else and not a thing at all."⁶⁷ As concerns the thing-like nature of the artwork, the essence of the artwork is not to display the materialistic character of any *particular* thing, but the *universal* nature of things and their material: "The work, therefore, is not the reproduction of some particular entity that happens to be present at any given time; it is, on the contrary, the reproduction of the thing's general essence."[68] Therefore, in contrast to Gumbrecht, Heidegger underscores that "[a]s long as we supposed that the reality of the work lay primarily in its thingly substructure we were going astray,"[69] for the reality of the artwork is to erect a world. In this manner, Heidegger is very careful to distance the emergence of truth in the artwork from anything like tangible things with material qualities and a substance. For in the artwork the "*world worlds* and is more fully in being than the tangible and perceptible realm in which we believe ourselves to be at home."[70]

What happens in the artwork is the erection of a world that discloses Being, which *cannot* be reduced to or confused with any tangible and perceptible things of the world. To do so (which is what Gumbrecht suggests that we do) would, in the Heideggerian optic, be tantamount to simply repeating the traditional metaphysical gesture oblivious of Being—as it, too, would fail to draw the crucial distinction between Being (*Sein*) and beings (*das Seiende*). The truth and disclosure of Being in the artwork are rather rooted in an uncanny (*unheimlich*) transcendence of beings. This transcendence or clearing (*Licthung*), which "is in a greater degree than are beings," is rooted in something that itself is not a thing or thing-like but constitutes the precondition for the givenness of any things, namely "the Nothing."[71]

Gumbrecht interprets Heidegger's Nothing as "a dimension where all cultural distinctions are absent,"[72] that is, as "presence," meaning that Nothing designates things immediately present with no "meaning" attached to them. The exact opposite is the case, however, for Nothing and Being are two sides of the same coin: Being is Nothing in that it is no-thing and not to be confused with any things or entities. Nothing is nothing substantial, physical, or anything existing independently of *Dasein*. The Nothing is a concept that, as it denotes the transcendence of *Dasein*, hints how *Dasein*—by holding itself out into the Nothing, as Heidegger has it—places itself beyond beings and entities, thereby allowing us to behold them as we lean away from them and into the Nothing: "Being and the nothing do belong together [...] because being itself is essentially finite and manifests itself only in the transcendence of a *Dasein* that is held out into the nothing."[73]

It might be objected that Heidegger's famous turn (*die Kehre*) changes all that, but if anything, the turn radicalizes the showdown with any transcendental and metaphysical attempt at substantiating Being. In other words, what is radicalized by the turn is the critique of the substantialist tendency in metaphysics to inquire about entities and never about Being, since it only conceives of Being (as Gumbrecht does, too) in terms of beings.[74] The human being (*Dasein*) never abdicates its part and Heidegger never becomes a substantialist thinker. However, the human being is not a lord of beings, but is now understood as a shepherd of Being.[75] Being is neither *Dasein* nor things, but the transcendence allowing for an understanding of the being of beings—an understanding or revealed quality that can only be played out in *Dasein*. Being is what allows for *Dasein* to relate to beings and entities, and is thus, in a sense, the difference between the two. The intelligibility and understanding of Being continue to constitute the central character of *Dasein*, and the disclosedness of Being is something that can only take place in connection with *Dasein*. As man is the shepherd of Being and designates the place where dwells Being, Heidegger stresses in his late thinking that "language is the house of being." And seeing that "language [...] is propriated by being and pervaded by being,"[76] Heidegger accentuates that "Being comes, clearing itself, to language. It is perpetually under way to language."[77]

The turn is, moreover, marked by a changed perspective on historicity. Where in *Being and Time*, *Dasein* was thought capable of projecting its own possibilities and thus choosing its own individual destiny, this process is now perceived as too subjectivistic. Instead of a sovereign player, *Dasein* is now a participant in what Heidegger characterizes as *die Geschichte des Seins* or *Seinsgeschichte*. Being is *Geschichte* or *Geschick* as a historical fate (*Schicksal*) being sent (*schicken*). *Dasein* does not choose its history of Being, which has been forwarded by Being itself. In other words, Being is not static or synchronous, but changes: in the Middle Ages everything, as we saw above, was being thought as the Creation of the Creator (God), while after the "death of God" in modernity under the reign of a calculative rationality, we perceive everything as a resource to be exploited with reference to technological usefulness and benefit. These occurrences did not follow from a subjective activity or endeavor on the part of any *Dasein* but were the result of an event in Being itself, which cannot be fathomed or substantiated further. Now, the question of Being thus arises from the perspective of history and time rather than from *Dasein*.

In sum, Gumbrecht dismally fails to take Heidegger seriously when the latter insists that "[t]hat which genuinely is, is in no way this or that particular being."[78]

Concluding Remarks: The Dream to "Sleep Forever"

As suggested in this chapter, Gumbrecht's concept of "presence" is in noteworthy alignment with other theories within the new materialisms, which tend overwhelmingly to repudiate the conditions that modernity demands with respect to *secularism*, *finitude*, and *autonomy*. In Gumbrecht's case, the rejection of these tenets of modernity is comprised in the longing for the arrival of an absolute presence annulling temporality and historicity. In his rendition of the Eucharist, we saw how finite history was transcended in the synchronicity of an infinite history executed in the mysterious real presence. In other words, the concept of "presence" invokes not only something merely present and tangibly at hand *hic et nunc*, but also, and more importantly, something transhistorical that metaphysically suspends the finite experience of time. "Presence" thus denotes synchronicity (as in the Eucharist) and signifies an abrogation of historicity.

In such a paradigm, we must efface ourselves from the equation and cancel human reality. In other words, the problems of finitude and autonomy must be abrogated in the dissolution of history and human reality. As such, the immediacy and infinitude experienced in presence and making present seem to depend on a dissolution of human subjectivity. Gumbrecht is, in a sense, surprisingly candid about this, saying that the dream of "presence" would amount to the "redemption from the permanent obligation to move and to change" and from "'historical' changes."[79] In fact, he explains how he often daydreams of being "in a state of just 'being there,' that is, existing as a life form that would simply occupy space without doing much else,"[80] adding that most days he wishes that he "could, literally, sleep forever."

Gumbrecht's dream of an eternal and unchanging presence to oneself in perfect union with the cosmos points to an absolute happiness in the sense of a present presence with no future or past and with no privation, insecurity, desire, or fear. Gumbrecht's presence project takes its point of departure from the "intensity of wanting to be and of being there, unpermeated by effects of distance."[81] The dream of cancelling time and historicity is hardly new, as it embodies the core of a persistent dream in Western theology and metaphysics of a paradisiacal *in*finite and *a*temporal state. As it says in Revelation with reference to the coming paradise, "there should be time no longer."[82]

The desire to cancel human temporality, finitude, and historicity goes hand in hand with the desire for immediacy and a reality Immanuel Kant says we have no ability to inhabit, since human sensation has no direct access to phenomena unmediated and not synthesized by the a priori categories of the mind. The fulfillment of the desire driving Gumbrecht's quest for presence requires the absence or cancellation of subjectivity. Desiring to be a tree, to sleep forever, or to be dead to the world implies a wish to escape an embarrassing and agonizing feeling of merely being human by taking refuge in the time of the child, as it were. A no-time in which there is no conception of birth or death, in which one would be merely present and not yet inserted into history; one would not have a world in the full sense of the word. When asleep, one is not only unconscious of oneself; one is also dead to the world from which one is sealed off. The yearning for an absolute presence with oneself and the world seems to demand states in which one is not only absent to oneself, but also to the world.

If Heidegger was right in claiming that the only way to come to grips with "the essential homelessness of human beings" is by recuperating the ontological dimension of Being,[83] then sensual and spiritual immediacy will be the wrong place to look or hope to erect a "home." Heidegger's phenomenological analysis of Being-in-the-world and his subsequent central positioning of the mediating As-Structure show that humans will find no existential dwelling in dreaming of a world without us, i.e., in a nonmediated and sensual "world" divested of human historicity and cultural interpretation and mediation. In contrast to what I have elsewhere characterized as a contemporary *semiophobia*,[84] the only way of creating an abode for ourselves as *human* beings is to be mindful of ourselves as speaking and interpreting beings (for a stone or a tree or a God, things probably look differently), simply because "language is the home of the essence of the human being."[85] Hannah Arendt, I believe, offers an unassuming and clear answer to why this is so: "The sheer naming of things, the creation of words, is the human way of *appropriating* and, as it were, disalienating the world into which, after all, each of us is born as a newcomer and a stranger."[86]

As Gumbrecht's book *Production of Presence* convincingly demonstrates, and as can be seen from the current *Zeitgeist* of which it is representative, it is only, it seems, by undoing and contradicting ourselves (existentially, discursively, and argumentatively) that we can turn back time to undo modernity and achieve pure immediacy that satisfies the desire for a re-enchantment and unification with the world. Merely closing our eyes in wishful thinking is hardly an appropriate response to our current challenges. A more sober and meticulous rethinking of the challenges, consequences, and promises of modernity would be a better place to start.

Notes

1. For the critique of new materialism and object-oriented ontology as a premodern and dogmatic metaphysics or spiritualism, see Slavoj Žižek, *Absolute Recoil: Towards a New Foundation of Dialectic Materialism* (London: Verso, 2015), 5–15; Andrew Cole, "The Call of Things: A Critique of Object-Oriented Ontologies," *The Minnesota Review* 80 (2013): 106–18; and my "The Embarrassment of Being Human: A Critique of New Materialism and Object-Oriented Ontology," *Orbis Litterarum* 73, no. 3 (2018): 225–42.
2. Hans Ulrich Gumbrecht, *Production of Presence: What Meaning Cannot Convey* (Stanford, CA: Stanford University Press, 2004), 151.
3. Gumbrecht, *Production of Presence*, 81–2.
4. Gumbrecht, *Production of Presence*, 82.
5. Gumbrecht, *Production of Presence*, 81.
6. Ferdinand Saussure, *Course in General Linguistics*, trans. Wade Baskin (New York: McGraw-Hill Book Company, 1966), 103; my emphasis.
7. Saussure, *Course*, 113.
8. Saussure, *Course*, 66; my emphasis.
9. Saussure, *Course*, 122; emphasis in the original.
10. Saussure, *Course*, 120; emphasis in the original.
11. Saussure, *Course*, 67; emphasis in the original.
12. Gumbrecht, *Production of Presence*, xiv.
13. Gumbrecht, *Production of Presence*, 82.
14. Gumbrecht, *Production of Presence*, xiv.
15. Gumbrecht, *Production of Presence*, xv; my emphasis.
16. Gumbrecht, *Production of Presence*, 108; my emphasis.
17. Gumbrecht, *Production of Presence*, xv.
18. Gumbrecht, *Production of Presence*, 98.
19. Gumbrecht, *Production of Presence*, xvi.
20. See, for example, Gumbrecht, *Production of Presence*, xvi and 149.
21. Gumbrecht, *Production of Presence*, xiv.
22. Gumbrecht, *Production of Presence*, 110.
23. Gumbrecht, *Production of Presence*, 157n1.
24. Gumbrecht, *Production of Presence*, xiii.

25 See Gumbrecht, *Production of Presence*, 28–30 (the Eucharist), 88 (mysticism), 80–1 (revelation), 111–13 (epiphanies), 29–30 (theophany and religious dogma), 82–3 (rituals of magic), 149 (the search for the mystery from an unknown source), and 117 (the quest for a transcendental unity with the world).
26 Gumbrecht, *Production of Presence*, 151; my emphasis.
27 For Gumbrecht's analysis and critical comments upon the Western process of secularization and disenchantment of the world (in the sense of Max Weber), see *Our Broad Present: Time and Contemporary Culture* (Chicago: Chicago University Press, 2014), xiv, 40, and 46 ff.
28 Gumbrecht, *Production of Presence*, 29 and 28.
29 Gumbrecht, *Production of Presence*, 30.
30 Gumbrecht, *Production of Presence*, 29.
31 Gumbrecht, *Production of Presence*, xv.
32 Gumbrecht, *Production of Presence*, 17.
33 Gumbrecht, *Production of Presence*, xiv.
34 Gumbrecht, *Production of Presence*, 145.
35 Gumbrecht, *Production of Presence*, 149 and 117; emphasis in the original.
36 See Umberto Eco, *Art and Beauty in the Middle Ages*, trans. Hugh Bredin (Yale: Yale University Press, 2002).
37 Martin Heidegger, *Poetry, Language, Thought*, trans. Albert Hofstadter (New York: HarperCollins, 2001), 29.
38 See Gumbrecht, *Production of Presence*, xvi and 149.
39 Gumbrecht, *Production of Presence*, 148–9.
40 See Gumbrecht, *Production of Presence*, 172n25.
41 Gumbrecht, *Production of Presence*, 46.
42 Gumbrecht, *Production of Presence*, xiv.
43 Gumbrecht, *Production of Presence*, 66.
44 Gumbrecht, *Production of Presence*, 116.
45 Gumbrecht, *Production of Presence*, 46.
46 Gumbrecht, *Production of Presence*, 66.
47 Gumbrecht, *Production of Presence*, 71.
48 Martin Heidegger, *Being and Time*, trans. John Macquarrie and Edward Robinson (Oxford: Blackwell, 2001), § 32.
49 Heidegger, *Being and Time*, 97.
50 Heidegger, *Being and Time*, 138.
51 Heidegger, *Being and Time*, 97.
52 Heidegger, *Being and Time*, 107.
53 Heidegger, *Being and Time*, 108.
54 Heidegger, *Being and Time*, 160.
55 See Heidegger, *Being and Time*, 417.
56 Heidegger, *Being and Time*, 92; emphasis in the original.
57 Heidegger, *Being and Time*, 106.
58 Gumbrecht, *Production of Presence*, 49.
59 Gumbrecht, *Production of Presence*, 19 and 77.
60 Gumbrecht, *Production of Presence*, 68.
61 Gumbrecht, *Production of Presence*, 69.
62 Gumbrecht, *Production of Presence*, 74.
63 Gumbrecht, *Production of Presence*, 76.
64 Gumbrecht, *Production of Presence*, 118.

65 Gumbrecht, *Production of Presence*, 68.
66 Heidegger, *Poetry, Language, Thought*, 19.
67 Heidegger, *Poetry, Language, Thought*, 20.
68 Heidegger, *Poetry, Language, Thought*, 36.
69 Heidegger, *Poetry, Language, Thought*, 37.
70 Heidegger, *Poetry, Language, Thought*, 43; emphasis in the original.
71 Heidegger, *Poetry, Language, Thought*, 51.
72 Gumbrecht, *Production of Presence*, 72.
73 Martin Heidegger, *Pathmarks*, trans. William McNeill (New York: Cambridge University Press, 1998), 94–5.
74 See Heidegger, *Pathmarks*, 256.
75 See Heidegger, *Pathmarks*, 260.
76 Heidegger, *Pathmarks*, 254.
77 Heidegger, *Pathmarks*, 274.
78 Martin Heidegger, *The Question Concerning Technology and Other Essays*, trans. William Lovitt (New York: Harper & Rov, 1977), 44.
79 Gumbrecht, *Production of Presence*, 138.
80 Gumbrecht, *Production of Presence*, 134.
81 Gumbrecht, *Production of Presence*, 136.
82 *Revelation* 10:6 (King James version).
83 Heidegger, *Pathmarks*, 260.
84 For the concept of *semiophobia*, see my article, "The Embarrassment of Being Human," 225–42.
85 Heidegger, *Pathmarks*, 274.
86 Hannah Arendt, *The Life of the Mind* (New York: Harcourt Brace Jovanovich, 1978), II, 100.

Cited Works

Arendt, Hannah. *The Life of the Mind*. New York: Harcourt Brace Jovanovich, 1978.
Boysen, Benjamin. "The Embarrassment of Being Human: A Critique of New Materialism and Object-Oriented Ontology." *Orbis Litterarum* 73, no. 3 (2018): 225–42.
Cole, Andrew. "The Call of Things: A Critique of Object-Oriented Ontologies." *The Minnesota Review* 80 (2013): 106–18.
Eco, Umberto. *Art and Beauty in the Middle Ages*. Translated by Hugh Bredin. Yale: Yale University Press, 2002.
Gumbrecht, Hans Ulrich. *Production of Presence: What Meaning Cannot Convey*. Stanford, CA: Stanford University Press, 2004.
Gumbrecht, Hans Ulrich. *Our Broad Present: and Contemporary Culture*. Chicago: Chicago University Press, 2014.
Heidegger, Martin. *Sein und Zeit*. Tübingen: Max Niemeyer Verlag, 1967.
Heidegger, Martin. *The Question Concerning Technology and Other Essays*. Translated by William Lovitt. New York: Harper & Rov, 1977.
Heidegger, Martin. *Letter on Humanism. Pathmarks*, edited by William McNeill. Cambridge: Cambridge University Press, 1998.
Heidegger, Martin. *Pathmarks*. Translated by William McNeill. New York: Cambridge University Press, 1998.

Heidegger, Martin. *Art. Poetry, Language, Thought*. Translated by Albert Hofstadter. New York: HarperCollins, 2001.

Heidegger, Martin. *Being and Time*. Translated by John Macquarrie and Edward Robinson. Oxford: Blackwell, 2001.

Saussure, Ferdinand. *Course in General Linguistics*. Translated by Wade Baskin. New York: McGraw-Hill Book Company, 1966.

Žižek, Slavoj. *Absolute Recoil: Towards a New Foundation of Dialectic Materialism*. London: Verso, 2015.

Chapter 5

INTERPRETING THE FACTS: NIETZSCHE AND THE NEW REALISTS

Hans Ruin

In their jointly authored book from 2017, *The Rise of Realism*, Manuel DeLanda and Graham Harman, develop their respective viewpoints in the form of a dialogue. To both of them, realism amounts to a "the belief in a mind-independent reality."[1] For DeLanda this realism should be "materialist," whereas Harman prefers a "speculative realism" that is not restricted to materialism. But their shared sense of a mission is to contribute to what they see as a realist turn in continental philosophy, even though the realization of their respective programs points in different directions, as do their intellectual backgrounds. Whereas DeLanda takes his inspiration from Deleuze, Harman comes from phenomenology and Heidegger, whose existential ontology he seeks to dissociate from its idealist background in Husserl and Kant. In *Après la finitude* from 2006 Quentin Meillasoux argued that much of previous philosophy, from Kant to Husserl and Heidegger and their followers, were caught in "correlationism," a collective term for the position that all reality is mediated through subjectivity and language.[2] In its place, he expressed the desire to reach the "great outdoor" (*le grand dehors*). In the German philosophical context, the new current has been represented most audibly by Markus Gabriel, who has also declared himself to be an adherent of a "new realism" that seeks to challenge the constructivism and relativism of post-Kantian philosophy. Gabriel often refers to Maurizio Ferraris, whose *Manifesto for a New Realism* was published in English in 2012. In Gabriel's book from 2013 *Warum es die Welt nicht gibt*, postmodern thinking and critique is said to have led to a radical "constructivism" that denies that there are solid facts in the first place.[3] Nevertheless, it is not in explicit polemic against Kant or the different neo-Kantianisms—among them phenomenology—that Gabriel develops his position. His "new" philosophical program is neither a naturalism nor a materialism, but it situates itself instead in the extension of a certain understanding of phenomenology, focusing on "fields of meaning" and "givenness" rather than on transcendental subjectivity and its constructions/correlations. The same lineage can be traced in Ferraris, whose background is hermeneutic philosophy and deconstruction.

Rather than seeing current New Realisms/materialisms as a new take on the analytical-continental divide, it can best be understood as an internal debate within the larger continental philosophical tradition. To some extent it recalls the debates from the early twentieth century, between the more "realist" and the more "transcendental" interpretations of Husserl's original breakthrough, where Heidegger leaned toward the former, without entirely abandoning the transcendental-idealist motive in philosophy. From some of the leading representatives of phenomenology, the critique against this suggested new realist/materialist turn has been harsh. In a widely circulated text "The End of What? Speculative Realism vs. Phenomenology" from 2016, Dan Zahavi targets several of its leading representatives, notably Tom Sparrow, Graham Harman, Ray Brassier, and Quentin Meillasoux, for presenting what he sees as philosophically superficial, inconsistent and ultimately nonoriginal position on the question of the real in phenomenology.[4] Since they fail to take into account the genuine nature of the transcendental, they are unable to properly address the topic on a par with how it is treated within phenomenology. For Zahavi, it is precisely the correlationist understanding of how our knowledge is finite and perspectival that gives a more adequate account of the epistemic situation, rather than the presumptuous promise to have reached a reality beyond all mediation.[5] In a response in return to Zahavi's article, Harman—in the introduction to the aforementioned book—refers to him disparagingly as the "phenomenological gatekeeper of my generation."[6]

From within the core group of phenomenological-hermeneutical researchers there has also been attempts to bridge this intellectual chasm, notably in the group around Günter Figal, who in his book *Gegenständlichkeit* from 2006 also argued for a re-orientation of hermeneutic philosophy toward a *something*—an *etwas*— as the experience of an irreducible thing-hood.[7] In this work, he too highlighted what he saw as a tendency in earlier phenomenological-hermeneutic thinking to, as it were, lose hold of the real. If we affirm that "all is interpretation" there is ultimately nothing of which it can be an interpretation.[8] Unlike Meillasoux, Figal's ultimate purpose was never to undermine the tradition of phenomenological-hermeneutical thinking, but rather to redirect its focus, partly through a critical rehearsal of what he takes to be a prevailing subjectivism also in the work of Heidegger. In 2014 two researchers connected to Figal, Diego D'Angelo and Nicola Mircovic, edited a special issue of the journal *Meta*, around precisely the theme of "New Realism and Phenomenology," with articles from several of the leading representatives of this movement.[9] In their preface they refer to the necessity of establishing the relation between these two domains, i.e., phenomenology and different "theories of the real."[10] In his own contribution to the issue, Figal stresses that realism can only be fulfilled as a phenomenological realism, i.e., a realism that recognizes how reality *appears* to a spectator.[11]

More recently the research group around Jocelyn Benoist and the Husserl archive in Paris, also brought together a similar volume, but with a larger historical scope on *Réalismes anciens et nouveaux*, that was also triggered by the same movement toward re-establishing the real. In the preface to that book, Benoist notes that for long philosophical realism had been viewed simply as the "stupid or impossible position," but that its current re-emergence has forced phenomenologically minded philosopher to become more explicit in how they understand the meaning of the real.¹² For his own part, he prefers to see philosophy as a critique of claims to have reached the real. The purpose, however, can never be to disregard the real, but to articulate a "critical realism." Partly aligning himself with Maurizio Ferraris's criticism of an exaggerated constructivist tendency, Benoist marks his distance toward the position that there are "not facts, but only interpretations."¹³ But in an attempt to balance the scales, he also marks a skepticism toward those versions of neo-realism that could be qualified as "neo-conservatists, which consists only in the defense of the right of the object in the face of the risk of its subjectivation."¹⁴ In his own contribution to the Benoist volume, Ferraris is more outspoken on his felt need to distance himself from the hermeneutic Turin school and its "weak" thought. In place of what he takes to be the "false" claim that there are "only interpretations and no facts," he too affirms the existence of both facts, objects and individuals.¹⁵

Throughout these debates, there is one thinker who occupies a curiously present-absent position, and that is Nietzsche. When the postmodernist position presumably run amok is recalled, it is almost always with reference to this one formulation: there are no facts, only interpretations. Often, as in several of the examples above, this idea is simply taken to stand for a generic radical constructivism that the realists are critical toward, and it is not even mentioned that it comes from Nietzsche. But even when it is recognized to originate from Nietzsche, its context is rarely actualized or discussed. The famous line belongs to an entry in the late notebooks from 1887 and was first published as section 481 in the Förster-Nietzsche/Köselitz compilation *Der Wille zur Macht*. In this entry Nietzsche speaks out "against Positivism," as a name for a position that clings to what it takes to be the "facts" (*Tatsachen*), stating instead that "facts is precisely what there is not, only interpretations."¹⁶ But after having thus disparaged the idea of stable and objective facts, he invites a voice of a potential critic or interlocutor who says: "Everything is subjective."¹⁷ But to this remark he responds: "but even this is interpretation."¹⁸ In other words, the very idea of subjectivity, as a distinct and identifiable dimension or position, is also a construction. The staged dialogue is then followed by the famous lines:

> In so far as the word "knowledge" has any meaning, the world is knowable; but it is interpretable otherwise, it has no meaning behind it, but countless meanings.
> "Perspectivism".¹⁹

And the short section then ends with the additional remark that all interpretations issues from our "drives" (Triebe) and their desire to rule and regulate. How should we understand this passage? It points to the complex issue of what to make of Nietzsche's so-called perspectivism. This is a large scholarly topic in its own right, all the aspects of which we cannot try to rehearse here. But in view of the fact that this particular statement has obtained an almost canonically antithetical position within large segments of the contemporary neo-realist/

materialist camp of thinkers, its meaning and place in Nietzsche's work deserve our particular attention in the context of a critical survey of this movement. For this purpose, I will focus on two prominent voices among the new realist thinkers, Günter Figal and Maurizio Ferraris. Whereas many people who refer to Nietzsche's statement today do not even recognize it as a citation from him, Figal and Ferraris are unique in that they have both engaged seriously with Nietzsche as scholars. Their respective understanding of Nietzsche and of his legacy in modern philosophy can therefore throw light on the inner dynamic and motivation of the realist turn, as well as offer a platform from which to critically discuss and assess its philosophical significance and rationale.

1.

In his book *Gegenständlichkeit* (*Objectness*) Figal has a brief discussion of Nietzsche's views on interpretation in the context of his own overall effort to orient hermeneutics in a more "realist" direction. Based on a reading of the early essay on "On truth and lie in extramoral sense" he describes Nietzsche as having a *metaphorical* understanding of language and reality, where every manifestation will always amount to a refiguration of an ultimately inaccessible something. From this theory of the metaphorical nature of experience, Nietzsche is then said to have later developed the idea of how there are "only interpretations" as different manifestations of a generic "will to power."[20] But, Figal concludes, when the theory of the interpretative character of experience reaches all the way to making everything an interpretation, and not an interpretation of *something*, then it can no longer be said to constitute an interpretation.

The situation is similar in the case of Ferraris. His problem with Nietzsche and his legacy is not something auxiliary to his overall orientation; instead, it is situated at the center of this philosophical restaging of himself as a proponent of a new realism. In his *Manifesto of New Realism*, first published in Italian in 2012 (with the English version from 2014), he begins by analyzing the emergence of postmodern thinking through Lyotard's book on *The Postmodern Condition* from 1977 about the collapse of grand narratives and the realization that truth can be evil and illusion good. However, the "core of the matter," Ferraris continues, "is not so much the assertion that 'God is dead' (as Hegel claimed before Nietzsche) but rather in the sentence 'there are no facts, only interpretations', because the real world ended up being a tale."[21] In a footnote to this passage he quotes the entire entry from the *Nachlass*. But he does not interpret it. It is as if it were not in need of further interpretation, since it has already—as he writes—"showed its true meaning," which is that "the argument of the strongest is always the best."[22] And as a paramount illustration to this idea he points to the triumph of the illusory world of "media-populism" (read: Berlusconi, and nowadays it would also be: Trump).[23]

Thus, Nietzsche's totalizing of the concept of interpretation is here depicted as leading to a philosophical and political abyss, where everything is drawn into a metaphysics of a distinction-less will to power, for which there is no longer an exterior. Neither Figal nor Ferraris refer explicitly to Heidegger in their confrontations with Nietzsche and his philosophical legacy in these passages. Yet their critical conclusions largely resemble those reached by Heidegger already in his extensive interpretations from the 1930s and 1940s that were later published as the two-volume work *Nietzsche* in 1961. Heidegger's basic idea is that Nietzsche fails to move beyond metaphysical thinking by positing a will to power as the ultimate nature and source of being. Just like Figal and Ferraris later, he starts his lectures in a promising mood, turning to Nietzsche as a possible philosophical accomplice, only to gradually develop a suspicion that eventually leads him to part ways from the predecessor in the second volume. If Nietzsche is first projected as a critic that can help him break out of the cage of inherited metaphysics, the concept of an all-encompassing will to power is ultimately said to confirm his captivity in subjectivism and a forgetfulness of being. This leads Heidegger to argue for a need to move beyond the horizon of Nietzsche's thinking altogether, toward a deeper sense of the exposure and openness of experience in an overcoming of anthropocentric humanism.

Even though the resonance of Heidegger's critical confrontation with Nietzsche's subjectivism and will to power can be heard in both Figal's and Ferraris's attempts to forge a post-hermeneutic philosophy that is presumably more faithful to the thing-ness and exteriority of being, this background is not addressed as such. Figal indicates that his own trajectory marks a development also with respect to his closest predecessors Heidegger and Gadamer, and it is clear that he is driven by a desire to expand and renew this hermeneutic lineage to which he belongs. In Ferraris's case, the situation with Heidegger's Nietzsche becomes more complicated. His departure from an earlier commitment to a version of Nietzschean hermeneutics is triggered by his political frustration over the rise of what he sees as a fascist version of postmodern philosophy, and thus to a political legacy in which both Nietzsche and Heidegger in their different ways are implicated. The fact that his own criticism of Nietzsche in some parts overlaps with that of Heidegger in the thirties then—presumably—becomes a difficult fact to fit into his overall picture.

Early in his career, Ferraris published an introduction to Nietzsche and the reception of his philosophy in modern thought.[24] The book, which was first published in 1989, is a short but knowledgeable presentation of the main points of Nietzsche's thinking, in the context of a biography of his life and writings together with a survey of the reception and later impact of his philosophy. When reviewing his influence Ferraris spends a good section on the critique from the left, notably Lukács, who saw in Nietzsche a proponent of irrationalism and a precursor and inspiration to the mid-war fascist movements. He notes that the cultural prestige of Lukács contributed initially to "censoring" the interest in Nietzsche from the left, to which he presumably counts himself.[25] But against Lukács's simplified image of Nietzsche as only an extension of a romantic anti-rationalism leading up to Hitler, the young Ferraris instead points to his influence on Adorno's and Horkheimer's *Dialectics of Enlightenment*. And he expresses sympathy with Thomas Mann's famous post-war essay "Nietzsche in the light of our experience" in its defense of a non- or post-political aesthetical reading of his works.

He then summarizes the most important representative of French left-liberal neo-Nietzscheans, notably Deleuze, Derrida, Ricœur, and Foucualt, who in Nietzsche saw a de-mythologizing suspicious critic of metaphysics. In regard to hermeneutic thinking he notes Gadamer's (Heideggerian) criticism of the doctrine of a will to power. He detects two trajectories in the attempt to relate Nietzsche to hermeneutics, one that sees him as a radical post-hermeneutic thinker that permits us to move beyond both Heidegger and Gadamer, represented by Derrida and Foucault. The other is represented by his teacher Vattimo, who sought to combine Nietzsche and hermeneutic thought in bypassing the criticism of Heidegger, ending up in an image of his thought as a form of aesthetic play with a metaphysical truth in which it no longer believes.[26]

Among these modern Nietzscheans it is only in response to Foucault that Ferraris voices an explicit criticism. Foucault's version of genealogy depicts all stages of human development as just shifting interpretations against an underlying mute wall of power.[27] Ultimately it thus becomes another version of previous idealistic systems, through which the world as we know and experience appears as the production of a trans-historical agent. In the version of Derrida, Ferraris writes, Nietzsche comes forth more as a performer and master of style, beyond the distinction of truth and falsity.

In this largely sympathetic compilation of different readings and interpretations Ferraris does not present any clear summary statement. While experimenting with different ways of reading the Nietzschean text and its reception in later thinkers, he signals a desire to move beyond both the essentializing of power and the naïve belief in an original meaning. But when he reissues the book twenty years later, in 2009, he adds a postscript. Its title—"The philosophy of Nietzsche 'in the light of my experience'"—recalls Thomas Mann's post-war confrontation with his own earlier Nietzscheanism.[28] Here Ferraris declares that even though the main line of his interpretations remains intact, the two decades that have passed have changed his judgment, and most importantly when it comes to the *political* implications of Nietzsche's thought. Up until the publication of his earlier interpretation he had been convinced of the guilt of Elisabeth-Förster Nietzsche for making her brother into a proto-nazi. But following a deeper engagement with the original material from the *Nachlass*, in combination with the collapse of the contemporary Italian political landscape, he has come to see how Nietzsche's discrediting of equality, justice, reason, and violence did indeed prepare the way for the destruction to come. It is as if what Lukács had been saying from his vantage point in the twenties had been more right all the time, concerning "what infernal cocktail could be created from these kind of affirmations."[29] Through the idea of a will to power Nietzsche is now said to have prepared not only Auschwitz, but also Dresden, Hiroshima, and Guantanamo.

When it comes to the post-war leftist interpretations of Nietzsche, that dominated postmodern thought (and of which Ferraris himself had been a part), he now sees it as leading to an extremism and aestheticism that point to the undermining of democracy and rule of law. Comparing himself to Mann in the immediate post-war situation, Ferraris summarizes his own love-affair with

Nietzsche, from the first reading of Deleuze's book in the seventies through the work of Foucault. But now the Nietzschean infatuation of his generation appears in a new light after the fall of the wall. Instead of a new freedom it gave birth to the rise of "mediatic populism." Anticipating the introduction to his *Manifesto* from a few years later, he sees this new political landscape as the triumph of some of Nietzsche's basic ideas, "the dream of fame, a politics of spectacle with grandiose gestures, and most of all the practical application of the principle according to which 'there are no facts, only interpretations.'"[30]

He now sees Nietzsche's celebration of force, ruthlessness, and amorality, through such figures as Cesare Borgia, Napoleon, and Alexander, as signs of a "protracted adolescence." For his own part he wants to move beyond the intoxication with Nietzsche of the seventies, and reach for a more disenchanted comprehension. Complementing the earlier biography, he draws a quick line from the early precocious works on tragedy to the later writings that display a more grim and even desperate tone that he traces to Nietzsche's increasing loneliness after the break with Wagner and the previous group of friends, and also the crisis with Lou Salomé. All of this leads up to *Zarathustra*, where he dresses up as a religious prophet. The later thinking Ferraris summarizes through the formula of the will to power. Here there is no happiness, no utility, and no morality; instead, everything is reduced to power. And unlike Schopenhauer this is not a philosophy of resignation, but of affirmation of precisely the active principle of power. Nietzsche's own prophecy, that a time will come when there will be academic chairs devoted to the teaching of *Zarathustra*, in Ferraris's view, was realized with Nazi Germany. We cannot, he declares, hide from this conclusion. The fact that Nietzsche was not an anti-semite, and that he was even anti-German, does not change it, since Hitler was the most consistent of Nietzscheans through his pure affirmation of the struggle for power at all costs.[31] The last pages of this contorted and abjective confession stress the paradoxes of Nietzsche's life, the many masks under which he appeared. For his own part, Ferraris declares that he has made peace with him and that he still reads him, even though it is unclear for what philosophical purpose.

Unlike the earlier book, to which the afterword is appended, this is a poor and careless reading of Nietzsche. It is lacking not only in distinctions and nuances, but also in facts. As such it marks a downgrading of the scholarly level in relation to the text from twenty years earlier to which it is attached. But the fact that it is a superficial and sweeping account of Nietzsche and his legacy does not make it less interesting for us in the present context, on the contrary. Its emotional response to his work and to its earlier impact on the author himself shows just how much that is at stake here. The afterword is the manifestation of a personal crisis, which is also a philosophical and political crisis of a whole generation, emerging from within a genuine and authentic frustration over the inability of progressive intellectuals to counter the rise of a manipulative and ruthless political populism. It bears witness of a deep feeling of disappointment with the postmodernist critique of the seventies and eighties. Its titillating promises of a new post-metaphysical culture of frivolous intellectual play are now instead seen as having led up to the dead-end of an irresponsible estheticism and a nihilistic philosophy of power with no means to counter the more ruthless profiteers of the same philosophical spirit.

If we want to understand the rise of realism in contemporary philosophy over the last decades, it is important to see and correctly evaluate this political-philosophical dimension of its motivation. And more specifically it is important to see the role and position played by Nietzsche, both as the most charismatic predecessor to a radical constructivism and as a philosopher with a troubling political legacy. However, in trying to sort out these questions, we should be cautious not to accept at face value the partly ideologically motivated rejections of his thinking among neo-realist thinkers. Instead of accepting their critical conclusions as philosophical facts, we should tread more carefully and explore them as ideologically motivated and historically situated interpretations. When it comes to Figal and Ferraris, there is actually more to learn from their own earlier hermeneutic readings of Nietzsche than from their later realist critiques of his position.

In the case of Ferraris, he discusses Nietzsche also in his wide-ranging *History of Hermeneutics*, originally published in Italian in 1988, a year before the monograph on Nietzsche.[32] There he quotes the same passage cited above from the *Nachlass* with the critique of positivism, commenting: "Here Nietzsche goes much beyond historicism and positivism. His critique of the objectification of method and of the fetischization of the given does not stop at returning to subjectivity its epistemological role, as with the classical theory of knowledge. Even the subject is the result of an interpretation, 'something stuck on afterwards.'"[33] There is no ultimate tribunal of historical reason that can serve as a correlate to the actual interpretations. Instead they are seen as energetic expressions of a self-evolving life in a foregrounding of interest over knowledge. But instead of criticizing the consequences of this position he then goes on to cite a late essay by Dilthey from 1907 in which the latter recognized the greatness of Nietzsche as a kindred hermeneutic spirit. This is followed by a summary of Heidegger's reading, that first raised Nietzsche to the level of a metaphysical thinker on a par with Plato and Aristotle, only to finally see him as "fulfilling the history of metaphysics as history of the will to power of a subject who wants to exert its his instrumental power over objects."[34] But with this drastic rejection, Heidegger is said to have "subjected Nietzsche's thought to a despotic hermeneutical torsion."[35] Thus the analysis positions itself, just as in the *Introduction*, midways, in a more neutral reading of Nietzsche that highlights the originality of his approach to the hermeneutic problem, while also marking a distance vis-à-vis Heidegger's final disparaging judgment.

2.

If we turn to Figal's *Introduction* to Nietzsche's thinking published in 1998, he too is more conciliatory vis-à-vis Nietzsche's aspirations at this earlier stage of his own philosophical trajectory.[36] In the book he brings together a rich source material from Nietzsche's writings, notably from *The Gay Science*, that better conveys the uniquely challenging way in which he sought to navigate the strait between idealism and realism. He describes not just how Nietzsche stands for a subjectivism/interpretationism, but how he also encompasses a radical realist/materialist position. He highlights section 374 in the Fifth book of *The Gay Science*, with the title "Our new 'infinite'" (*Unseres neues 'Unendliches*). Here Nietzsche presents and discusses the possibility that "all existence essentially is interpretation."[37] But here he also adds that even if this were the case, it could never be decided once and for all, since it would require that we could step out of our own interpretation and examine ourselves from an objective outside. We have reached a point of intellectual maturity, he writes, where we are called to recognize that it could be the case that the world contains endless different perspectives, even different ways of experiencing space and time. But this view—and this is really the key formulation—does not imply that we are bound by and enclosed within our own subjective perspective. Instead it means that the world has become *larger*, indeed that it has become *"infinite"*. Before this prospect of an infinitely distributed and diffracted world we may experience a "Shudder" (*Schauder*), he writes, tempting us to posit it as another configuration of *the divine*. But why rush to make this larger world into something divine? Even "divinity" is an interpretation. From these formulations, it is clear that the "perspectivism" conveyed by Nietzsche, whatever its ultimate metaphysical implications may be, does not prevent or rule out a genuine access to the world, but that it instead invites a larger and more complex sense of world, in which subjectivity and mediation are also included.

The same thought is explored in the adjacent entry (*Gay Science*, §372) that explicitly addresses the question "Why we are no idealists." Here Nietzsche begins by noting that in earlier times philosophers feared the senses, while today they all seem to embrace sensualism of various kinds. And whereas the ancient philosophers avoided the senses because they perceived them as a threat to their ascetic controlled comportment, modern thinkers are instead increasingly characterized by a suspicion vis-à-vis ideas and idealisms, which is then seen as somehow draining them of their life and blood. Apparently aligning himself with this new turn to sensualism, he portrays idealism as something "unhealthy," which he finds an example of in the writings of Spinoza, whose philosophy is depicted as lacking every "drop of blood."[38] If we only read this far, we are inclined to draw the conclusion that here Nietzsche is rejecting (Platonic) idealism in favor of a purely energetic philosophy of life and sensuality. But there is a further twist to this entry that displays the complexity and subtlety of his approach. Even though Nietzsche does take the idealists to trial for having attempted to shield themselves from an overabundant life by means of conceptual abstractions, he also recognizes that at least in Plato there was also something else at work. In Plato we should see not only a reactive escape from a sensuous life, but a prudence and restraint as in fact a response to an "abundant" and even "dangerous health."[39] And with the last lines of the section the scales are reversed, when he asks, in a sentence that ends with two empty spaces: "Perhaps we moderns are not healthy enough to be in need of Plato's idealism? And we are not afraid of the senses because – –."[40]

The empty space leaves the reader to answer the question: why indeed could it be that we no longer fear the senses as older-day idealists presumably did? Why do we no longer experience the need of idealism as Plato did? What makes this question so intriguing is that it can be read as partly also directed toward himself and a caricature image of his own thinking as just an anti-idealist philosophy of life pure and simple. What the question implies is that since we moderns are so immersed in a watered-down idealism inherited from a long legacy of Apollonian-rational culture we have somehow lost our deeper understanding of its original motivation, which was the necessity to balance a more original and destructive Dionysian existence. It is the idea from *Die Geburt der Tragödie* in a new shape, according to which the Apollonian rational sphere was always also a counter-force, a way for an otherwise groundless existence to maintain a sense of individuality and clarity.

The ancient origin of idealism and its conceptual inventions would then have its roots in an effort to master an otherwise potentially overpowering sense of life, and to establish order within chaos. We, as a thoroughly Apollonian culture, stand at the other end of this historical trajectory. When we affirm the senses and the real—as in our realisms and materialisms—criticizing presumably worn-out, bloodless, and world-denying idealisms, we also reveal how we have reached the point where the real can be posited as the liberating other of the abstract, conceptual, and rational. When contemporary positivists affirm the sensual, the worldly, and the solid facts, and when the new realists direct their hopes toward a "great outdoor," they also expose their own version of idealism in the form of an *idealization of the real*.

The broader philosophical challenge thus indicated by Nietzsche is to balance these temptations, not by retreating to earlier versions of idealism, nor by affirming naively its opposite, as if we had now miraculously discovered how to reach outside and beyond thought and subjectivity simply by committing ourselves to a concept of the "positive," "real," or "objective." When read alongside one another these two sections present us with a sophisticated and concentrated analysis of how idealism and realism/objectivism do not necessarily represent contrary positions. Just as idealism can come from a stronger experience of being exposed to reality, conventional realism/objectivism can hide an idealization that it silently and simultaneously takes for granted.

Against the background of such a reading, we can understand better how Nietzsche can reject idealism while also presenting himself as a critic of positivism and realism. This is the case when it appears as philosophical position claiming self-confidently to have acquired a secure access to what really is. In this context, section 57 from *The Gay Science* adds an important dimension to the discussion. Just as in the critical remark on the positivists from the *Nachlass*, this section takes aim at the naiveté of the modern objectivist-realist position. The text addresses itself directly "To the realists" (*An die Realisten*), and it begins with an ironic interjection:

> You sober people who feel well armed against passions and phantasies and would like to turn your emptiness into a matter of pride and an ornament: you

call yourselves realists and hint that the world really is the way it appears to you. As if reality stood unveiled before you only and you yourselves were perhaps the best part of it [...].⁴¹

The address makes fun of the pretension to be a sober observer, as opposed to the others who are presumably intoxicated by idealism, religion, or superstition. But just as earlier idealisms tend to conceal the passion that they themselves are trying to control with the help of idealizations, so also the realism of the moderns is depicted as concealing the passionless passion that animates its own continued quest for the ultimate reality. On the next line he continues:

But in your unveiled state are you not still very passionate and dark creatures compared to fish, and still far too similar to an artist in love? And what is "reality" for an artist in love? You are still burdened with those estimates of things that have their origin in the passions and loves of former centuries. Your sobriety still contains a secret and inextinguishable drunkenness. Your love of "reality" for example—oh, that is a primeval "love" [...].⁴²

The implication of this combined criticism is that every attempt to posit oneself as having achieved the final and unconditional access to reality will have to suppress its own subjectivity, its "descent," its "past," its "training," its entire "humanity and animality."⁴³

In the final line of this condensed argument, Nietzsche displays the subtlety of his reasoning, bringing the question of the hidden pathos of realism to yet another level. Here he first affirms: "There is no 'reality' for us—not for you either my sober friends." But whereas the access to the absolute is thus denied to both, he is able to place himself in the double exposure of someone who is trying his best to see through this intoxication while recognizing the ultimately impossibility of this task. And in this paradoxical attempt to display the nonreality of reality, he recognizes his kinship with the people for whom this intoxication is not an issue, since they already believe themselves to be free from it. Therefore he can conclude: "[W]e are not nearly as different as you think, and perhaps our good will to transcend intoxication is as respectable as your faith that you are altogether incapable of intoxication."⁴⁴ With this final reflection he opens the door to a reflexive reconciliation between the two positions. The recognition of how the real is always mediated will see itself as the more sophisticated position in relation to the presumptuous claim to simply access the real (the "stupid" position in the words of Benoist quoted at the outset). But in the end this truth in and of a continuous mediation can contain something of the innocence of the realist position, through its very claim to know mediation. There is intoxication and desire but also prudence on both sides, but this is something that can only be seen and experienced as such from the hyper-reflexive approach to which Nietzsche's playful dialectics invites its readers.

Nietzsche has seen the inevitability of mediation and the non-accessibility of the ultimately "real." He has seen how the world is given perspectively, through a mediated subjective awareness, that is at once psychological, temporal, historical, and linguistic. He has also seen through the presumptuousness of the claim to surpass this situation simply by declaring that there is indeed a reality out there. It takes little effort to say that one has access to the *real* world as opposed to only a mediated/interpreted world. The very notions of mediation and interpretation imply that there is *something* that is mediated or interpreted. But stating this obvious fact does not in itself lead closer to its implied reality. Inversely, an academic form of idealism—be it Kantian or Husserlian—that relies on its mastery of the means, conceptual schemata, or intentional structures through which the unknown world in itself is presumably mediated, can likewise conceal a theoretical hubris. Whereas a conventional realism displays an innocent desire for the absolute, a conventional idealism conceals its desire to control in advance the fundamental unpredictability of the real.

3.

When social constructivism becomes complacent, when hermeneutic thinking evolves into an irresponsible historicism, and when philosophy at large loses its connection to the living reality in response to which it always needs to ground its voice and motivation anew, it needs to be shaken and awakened. This is especially the case in troubling times where the struggle for justice, freedom, and intellectual honesty requires engaged intellectuals. To the extent that the new realism/materialism constitute a response to such a heightened sense of the ethical-political urgency of our time it could perhaps be heard as such a wake-up call. But often it appears only as the rhetorical re-staging of a well-rehearsed position from the past, in its claim to access the real over and against its interpretation and mediation, simply in virtue of its claim to do so. The gesture whereby one claims to know and have access the real beyond all interpretation will then signal a refusal of interpretation that mostly just amounts to bad interpretations. The conventional and careless use of the famous expression from Nietzsche's *Nachlass* is a case in point. By taking it out of context and making it into a cipher for the position that one is opposing, these critics ultimately expose themselves as bad readers of the text. Already in his writings from the 1880s, notably in the *Gay Science*, Nietzsche himself had diagnosed the affective layers of these debates around the status of real and its accessibility.

In his book *Gegenständlichkeit*, Figal mentions Nietzsche, alongside Wittgenstein, Husserl, and Heidegger, as having contributed to the dissolution of reality in a flux of competing interpretations and language games, and of failing to account for the objectivity of the object. Also in Ferraris's attempts to break free from the wheel of subjectivism and endless mediation, Nietzsche is the recurrent culprit of a philosophy that has turned a blind eye to the reality of the real. In Ferraris's case we saw how this was largely motivated by his political frustration with the rise of a manipulative media-populism. But even when recognizing the dismal impact of the fascist reception of Nietzsche's writings in the mid-war period, the connection between his critical interventions and the rise in more recent times of such figures as Berlusconi and Trump remains conjectural. But as a result of their frustration with both the epistemological and political-ideological pitfalls of the presumed subjectivism of Nietzsche's position these philosophers follow Heidegger's path in ultimately depicting him as a symptom of forgetfulness of being and reality. For the attentive reader, however, who is prepared to continue to engage with and interpret the text, there is more to be found. There is a larger world—a "new infinity"—perhaps even a new *reality*. In a poem entitled "Toward new seas," that Nietzsche included in a section to the *Gay Science* that he named "Songs of Prince Vogelfrei," he writes:

Thither—I *want*; so doing
trust myself now and my grip
Open lies in the sea my Genoese ship.[45]

Notes

1. Manuel DeLanda and Graham Harman, *The Rise of Realism* (Cambridge: Polity Press, 2017), 2. An earlier and shorter version of the present text was first published as "Looking into the Open—Nietzsche and the New Quest for the Real," in *Die Gegenständlichkeit der Welt. Festschrift für Günter Figal zum 70. Geburtstag*, ed. A. Egel et al. (Tübingen: Mohr Siebeck, 2019).
2. Quentin Meillassoux, *Après la finitude* (Paris: Seuil, 2006). See also Harman's book *Quentin Meillasoux and Philosophy in the Making* (Edinburgh: Edinburg University Press, 2011) in the series "Speculative realism" edited by Harman himself. The origin of this particular branch of the more general turn toward realist/materialist thinking was a conference organized at Goldsmith's College in 2007, by Harman and others. Another influential book from the same group and generation of philosophers, arguing for an even more radical anti-correlationist position, was Ray Brassier's *Nihil Unbound: Enlightenment and Extinction* (Basingstoke: Palgrave, 2007).
3. Markus Gabriel, *Warum es die Welt nicht gibt* (Berlin: Ullstein, 2013). Gabriel specifically mentions a meeting with Ferraris in the summer of 2011 as the moment that to him personally signaled a "new realistic" age.
4. Dan Zahavi, "The End of What? Speculative Realism vs. Phenomenology," *International Journal of Philosophical Studies* 24, no. 3 (2016): 289–309.
5. Zahavi, "The End of What? Speculative Realism vs. Phenomenology," 292.
6. DeLanda and Harman, *The Rise of Realism*, 1.
7. Günter Figal, *Gegenständlichkeit* (Tübingen: Mohr Siebeck, 2006). In English as *Objectivity: The Hermeneutical and Philosophy*, trans. Th. George (Albany: State University of New York Press, 2010).
8. Figal, *Gegenständlichkeit*, 62.
9. Diego D'Angelo and Nikola Mirkovic, ed., *Meta: Research in Hermeneutics, Phenomenology, and Practical Philosophy*, Special issue *New Realism and Phenomenology* (2014).
10. Diego D'Angelo and Nikola Mirkovic, "Neuer Realismus und Phänomenologie. Einleitung der Herausgeber," in *Meta: Research in Hermeneutics, Phenomenology, and Practical Philosophy*, ed. Diego D'Angelo and Nikola Mirkovic, Special issue *New Realism and Phenomenology* (2014), 7–14: 14.
11. Günther Figal, "Phenomenological Realism. Programmatic Considerations," *Meta: Research in Hermeneutics, Phenomenology, and Practical Philosophy*, ed. Diego D'Angelo and Nikola Mirkovic, Special issue *New Realism and Phenomenology* (2014), 15–20: 20.

12 Jocelyn Benoist, ed., *Réalismes anciens et nouveaux* (Paris: Vrin, 2018), 7.
13 Benoist, *Réalismes anciens et nouveaux*, 13: "pas de faits, mais que des interpretations."
14 Benoist, *Réalismes anciens et nouveaux*, 15: "néo-conservateurs, qui consistent simplement à defender les droits de l'objet face au risque de son éventuelle subjectivation."
15 Benoist, *Réalismes anciens et nouveaux*, 76.
16 For the English version of this passage, see W. Kaufmann's translation in Friedrich Nietzsche, *The Will to Power* (New York: Vintage, 1968), 267. In the *Kritische Studienausgabe* it is found in the *Nachlass* volume 12 (Berlin: de Gruyter, 1988), 315, as entry no. 12:7[60].
17 Nietzsche, *The Will to Power*, 267.
18 Nietzsche, *The Will to Power*, 267.
19 Nietzsche, *The Will to Power*, 267.
20 Nietzsche, *The Will to Power*, 62.
21 Maurizio Ferraris, *Manifesto of New Realism* (Albany: SUNY Press, 2015), 2f.
22 Ferraris, *Manifesto for a New Realism*, 2f.
23 Ferraris, *Manifesto for a New Realism*, 2f.
24 Maurizio Ferraris, *Nietzsche et la filosofia del novecento* (Milano: Bompiano, 2009).
25 Ferraris, *Nietzsche et la filosofia del novecento*, 113 passim.
26 Ferraris, *Nietzsche et la filosofia del novecento*, 134.
27 Ferraris, *Nietzsche et la filosofia del novecento*, 140.
28 Ferraris, *Nietzsche et la filosofia del novecento*, 167–79: "La filosofia di Nietzsche 'alla luce della mia esperienzia.'"
29 Ferraris, *Nietzsche et la filosofia del novecento*, 168.
30 Ferraris, *Nietzsche et la filosofia del novecento*, 171: "il sogno della fama, di una politica spettaculo con grandi tirature, e sopratutto costituisce l'attuazione pratica del suo principo secondo cui 'non ci sono fatti, solo interpretazioni.'"
31 Ferraris, *Nietzsche et la filosofia del novecento*, 177.
32 Maurizio Ferraris, *History of Hermeneutics*, trans. L. Somigli (Atlantic Highlands, N.J.: Humanities Press, 1996).
33 Ferraris, *History of Hermeneutics*, 130.
34 Ferraris, *History of Hermeneutics*, 134.
35 Ferraris, *History of Hermeneutics*, 134.
36 Günter Figal, *Nietzsche. Eine Philosophische Einführung* (Stuttgart: Reclam, 1998).
37 Friedrich Nietzsche, *Die Fröhliche Wissenschaft* (*Kritische Studienausgabe* 3) (Berlin: de Gruyter, 1988), 626.
38 Nietzsche, *Die Fröhliche Wissenschaft*, 624.
39 Nietzsche, *Die Fröhliche Wissenschaft*, 624.
40 Nietzsche, *Die Fröhliche Wissenschaft*, 624.
41 Nietzsche, *Die Fröhliche Wissenschaft*, 421.
42 Nietzsche, *Die Fröhliche Wissenschaft*, 421.
43 Nietzsche, *Die Fröhliche Wissenschaft*, 422.
44 Nietzsche, *Die Fröhliche Wissenschaft*, 422: "wir sind einander lange nicht so fremd, als ihr meint, und vielleicht ist unser guter Wille, über die Trunkenheit hinausgekommen, ebenso achtbar als euer Glaube, der Trunkenheit überhaupt unfähig zu sein."
45 Friedrich Nietzsche, *Die fröhliche Wissenschaft* (Leipzig: Verlag von E. W. Fritzsch, 1887), 347; my translation:

"Dorthin—*will* ich; und ich traue
Mir fortan und meinem Griff.
Offen liegt das Meer, in's Blaue
Treibt mein Genueser Schiff."

Cited Works

D'Angelo, Diego and Nikola Mirkovic, ed. *Meta: Research in Hermeneutics, Phenomenology, and Practical Philosophy*, Special issue *New Realism and Phenomenology*, (2014).
D'Angelo, Diego and Nikola Mirkovic. "Neuer Realismus und Phänomenologie. Einleitung der Herausgeber." In *Meta: Research in Hermeneutics, Phenomenology, and Practical Philosophy*, edited by Diego D'Angelo and Nikola Mirkovic. Special issue *New Realism and Phenomenology*, (2014): 7–14.
Benoist, Jocelyn, ed., *Réalismes anciens et nouveaux*. Paris: Vrin, 2018.
Brassier, Ray. *Nihil Unbound: Enlightenment and Extinction*. Basingstoke: Palgrave, 2007.
DeLanda, Manuel and Graham Harman. *The Rise of Realism*. Cambridge: Polity Press, 2017.
Figal, Günther. "Phenomenological Realism. Programmatic Considerations." In *Meta: Research in Hermeneutics, Phenomenology, and Practical Philosophy*, edited by Diego D'Angelo and Nikola Mirkovic. Special issue *New Realism and Phenomenology*, 15–20, 2014.
Ferraris, Maurizio. *History of Hermeneutics*. Translated by L. Somigli. Atlantic Highlands, NJ: Humanities Press, 1996.
Ferraris, Maurizio. *Nietzsche et la filosofia del novecento*. Milano: Bompiano, 2009.
Ferraris, Maurizio. *Manifesto of New Realism*. Albany: SUNY Press, 2015.
Figal, Günter. *Nietzsche. Eine Philosophische Einführung*. Stuttgart: Reclam, 1998.
Figal, Günter. *Gegenständlichkeit*. Tübingen: Mohr Siebeck, 2006.
Figal, Günter. *Objectivity: The Hermeneutical and Philosophy*. Translated by Th. George. Albany: State University of New York Press, 2010.
Gabriel, Markus. *Warum es die Welt nicht gibt*. Berlin: Ullstein, 2013.
Harman, Graham. *Quentin Meillassoux and Philosophy in the Making*. Edinburgh: Edinburg University Press, 2011.
Meillassoux, Quentin. *Après la finitude*. Paris: Seuil, 2006.
Nietzsche, Friedrich. *Die fröhliche Wissenschaft*. Leipzig: Verlag von E. W. Fritzsch, 1887.
Nietzsche, Friedrich. *The Will to Power*. Translated by W. Kaufmann. New York: Vintage, 1968.
Nietzsche, Friedrich. *Die Fröhliche Wissenschaft* (*Kritische Studienausgabe*. Vol. 3). Berlin: de Gruyter, 1988.
Nietzsche, Friedrich. *Nachlass* (*Kritische Studienausgabe*. Vol. 12). Berlin: de Gruyter, 1988.
Ruin, Hans. "Looking into the Open—Nietzsche and the New Quest for the Real." In *Die Gegenständlichkeit der Welt. Festschrift für Günter Figal zum 70. Geburtstag*, edited by Antonia Egel, David Espinet, Tobias Keiling, and Bernhard Zimmermann, 97–106. Tübingen: Mohr Siebeck, 2019.
Zahavi, Dan. "The End of What? Speculative Realism vs. Phenomenology." *International Journal of Philosophical Studies* 24, no. 3 (2016): 289–309.

Chapter 6

MODERN THROUGH AND THROUGH: LATOUR'S QUASI-OBJECT AS A MODERN MIX-UP

Jesper Lundsfryd Rasmussen

Like probably no other theory of a contemporary scientist, social or otherwise, the studies of scientific enquiry and modernity initiated by Bruno Latour in the early 1990s continue to fascinate and influence theories within the humanities and social sciences concerned with nature, society, and the problems that we as a political and scientific community face today. This is particularly the case amongst adherents of the new materialisms. Central figures, such as Jane Bennett, Karan Barad, and Graham Harman, have on several occasions and in various degrees expressed their agreement with and methodological dependence on Latour's discontent with and diagnosis of modernity.[1] Latour delivers his critique of the modern project in the form of a *new metaphysics* which he ultimately determines as pre- or nonmodern. By challenging the narrative about the modern project and its absolute distinction between subject and object, Latour not only offers his readers a critical examination of the imperatives and implications of modernity but ultimately intends to demask the modern worldview and, in so doing, replace it altogether with a nonmodern ontology. Hence, as will be demonstrated below, Latour effectually substitutes critique as well as modernity with a theory of being in which he construes everything as hybrid actants, i.e., acting entities comprised of a subject pole and an object pole.

While different factions within the new materialisms disagree whether Latour's notion of being adequately captures the basic structure of reality, they share his goal of repudiating the modern project as a meaningful framework for gaining knowledge about reality. With the acceptance of this goal, the new materialists seem to have likewise accepted the means of pursuing a new monistic theory of being and substituting it for a modern worldview, which they not only deem inadequate, but dangerous. Hence, Bennett constructs her theory of *vibrant matter* in direct continuance of Latour's ontology of actants,[2] and Barad largely embraces Latour's theory of actants in her *agential realism*.[3] In a more critical vein, Harman acknowledges Latour's theory of actants "as the founder of a *secular occasionalism*,"[4] which anticipates his own version of occasionalism, namely object-oriented ontology, and which Harman deems "superior"[5] to the conceptual framework of Quentin Meillassoux. Despite his disapproval of Latour's *actor-network theory* that, according to Harman, completely reduces every object to its effects and relations with other things in a network, Harman maintains a strong notion of the "secret inner life"[6] of objects, only diverging from Latour's actants due to the inexhaustibility of their relational potential. Indeed, Harman sometimes constructs his concept of an object by extrapolating that which he takes to be the Kantian relation between human cognition and a thing-in-itself to every entity: "What Kant failed to note is that since any relation fails to exhaust its *relata*, every inanimate object is a thing-in-itself for every other as well."[7] In other words, the problem with Kant's position, Harman argues, "is that the human-world relation takes priority over all others. [...] And more importantly, nowhere does Kant pay serious attention to relations between these things-in-themselves."[8]

Setting aside Harman's dubious interpretation of Kant's concept of the thing-in-itself and the bewildering conditions under which this structure could ever be realized, Harman's notion of an object is rather straightforward: an object always exhausts its relations as a withdrawn *substratum*, never completely affected by its relations with other objects. Consequently, according to Harman, the human-world relation is also just a relation between two objects and, as such, merely an instance of a general structure that applies to all of reality.[9] As has been briefly suggested, even the critical varieties of the new materialisms thus seem to rely on the same type of solution to the inadequacies and problems of modernity proposed by Latour—namely, to substitute what they consider the flawed worldview of modernity with an ultimately panpsychist ontology.

Given the substantial attention that Bruno Latour's work has received from adherents of the new materialisms, it may seem rather puzzling that critical examinations of Latour's significance to these trends are largely absent from discussions of the movement.[10] This chapter aims to redress this deficit by paying special attention to the construction and constituents of Latour's self-proclaimed nonmodern worldview. While it cannot address the question of Latour's use and import within the new materialisms in detail, the chapter sets itself the task of undertaking the first steps toward such a scrutiny. First, I will briefly sketch Latour's overall project of a rejection of modernity in *We Have Never Been Modern*. Second, I will examine the details of Latour's theory of the so-called *quasi-objects* in his examination of the debates between Thomas Hobbes and Robert Boyle. Third, a brief excursus to Hobbes's concept of freedom and Boyle's concept of matter will serve as the backdrop of my thesis that Latour, owing to the construction of his position from modern notions of subjectivity and objectivity and against his intention to champion a nonmodern worldview, never departs from modernity, but transforms it into an obscure variant of modern metaphysics.

Substantial and important critique of Latour's project as a position that is bordering nonsense has been raised,[11] especially regarding the constructivist position developed by Latour and Steve Woolgar in *Laboratory Life: The Social Construction of Scientific Facts* (1979).[12] Recently, Latour and the new materialists have also received critical attention from a Marxist point of view that rejects Latour's metaphysical position as a dangerous confirmation of the status quo incapable of political change.¹³ However, focusing almost exclusively on undesired political consequences of a theory amounts at best to a rather one-sided critique and risks overlooking the wider significance of the theory in question.¹⁴ Ultimately, a theory's practical consequences are a poor measure of its falseness or truthfulness. Contrary to such attempts, I aim to unfold the significance of Latour's issue with modernity and its import according to his own position.

The Modern Project

In his book, *We Have Never Been Modern*, Latour undertakes the task of establishing an anthropology of the modern world. Such an endeavor is, Latour bemoans, beset with grave hindrances from its very outset, owing to the origins and methodological constraints of anthropology. According to Latour, anthropology presupposes a specific type of object that he terms *nature-culture*. Nature-culture is an object constituted by "the seamless fabric"¹⁵ of that which we, under normal circumstances, would divide analytically into categories belonging to either nature or culture, respectively. For example, "even the most rationalist ethnographer is perfectly capable of bringing together in a single monograph the myths, ethnosciences, genealogies, political forms, techniques, religions, epics and rites of the people she is studying."¹⁶ Ultimately, anthropology is limited to the study of a certain class of objects in which "you will not find a single trait that is not simultaneously real, social and narrated."¹⁷ In order to be studied anthropologically, objects must belong to this category of *hybrids*, i.e., objects comprising sociocultural as well as natural components that cannot be studied in isolation without distorting the entity that they constitute.

The problem arises, Latour argues, when modern cultures such as our own are to be studied, because modernity is defined by its adherence to an absolute dichotomy between the subjective and the objective, the human and the nonhuman, culture and nature. Modernity is fundamentally characterized by two *practices*: On the one hand, it "creates mixtures between entirely new types of beings, hybrids of nature and culture."¹⁸ Latour labels this practice of modernity *translation*, a practice that signifies *networks*. On the other hand, a pronounced modern practice consists in *purification* or a *critical stance*, a practice which "creates two entirely distinct ontological zones: that of human beings" and "that of nonhumans."¹⁹ This division allows Latour to conceive of modernity as the *self-conviction* that the two practices can be isolated and, thus, kept absolutely apart from each other: "So long as we consider these two practices of translation and purification separately, we are truly modern—that is, we willingly subscribe to the critical project, even though that project is developed only through the proliferation of hybrids down below."²⁰ To be truly modern, according to Latour, thus comes down to the claim that the subject and the object are incommensurable and, furthermore, the rejection of any attempt to unite culture and nature.²¹ As soon as we realize the inherent relation between networks and critique, translation and purification, we not only stop being "wholly modern" but also "stop having been modern."²² In other words, the intermingling of subject and object, of culture and nature, constitutes no new event in the course of history. Instead, it serves only to emphasize a process that has always taken place.

Due to Latour's claim that anthropological examination presupposes the entanglement of culture and nature, a modern attitude would therefore render any anthropological examination of modern practice impossible, which collides with the fact that proper anthropological work of such practices has been carried out. Contrary to the modern conviction, the analytical distinction of modernity is exactly that which we cannot uphold any longer, according to Latour. It is, Latour proclaims, "possible to do an anthropological analysis of the modern world—but then the very definition of the modern world has to be altered."[23]

Indeed, this fact is what Latour undertakes to emphasize in *We Have Never Been Modern* by offering an anthropological analysis of the modern constitution. To this end, he endeavors to establish the following three claims: (1) that the critical stance (that is, purification) enables translation (that is, the creation of hybrids); (2) that the premoderns undermined their own proliferation through their exclusive focus on networks and hybrids; (3) facing the fact that we neither are nor have ever been modern, we "have to slow down, reorient and regulate the proliferation of monsters by representing their existence officially."[24] Whereas the first two claims are diagnostic in character and form the basis of his central thesis that modernity never took place, the third claim is prognostic and addresses the future changes needed for an adequate understanding of the world. For the present purpose, the second claim shall be set aside to assess the meaning and implication of Latour's rejection of modernity.

To be fair, Latour nowhere denies that we *thought* we were modern and, hence, acted *as if* we could absolutely hold nature and culture apart. He rather undertakes the attempt to expose that both practices continued to exert their effects in the period that we normally consider to be modern. In the next section, the notion of modernity, which Latour's denies, will thus serve as a folio for his notion of his nonmodern replacement. The next step is to examine Latour's exposition of the historical context in which he, on the one hand, locates the origin of modernity and the claim of an absolute distinction between subject and object, and, on the other, intends to exhibit the continuing processes of purification and translation. According to Latour, the most convincing way of uncovering the interdependence of purification and translation is by "studying scientists and politicians in tandem."[25] Following Steven Shapin and Simon Schaffer's study of the interplay between science and politics in the seventeenth century, Latour takes as his starting point the debates between Robert Boyle and Thomas Hobbes.[26] This exemplary case of scientific-political interaction functions as his main evidence for the claim that purification enables and proliferates translation and, as will be argued, as the basis for his own theory of quasi-objects. Closer scrutiny of his analysis of Boyle and Hobbes will thus shed light on Latour's own views on culture, nature, and the quasi-object. This approach corresponds with the one taken by Latour, who emphasizes the modern constitution precisely on basis of the discussion between Boyle and Hobbes—a debate which must be followed closely, if we wish to gain insight into the real ontological structure of worldly processes.²⁷ As will become clear, the theoretical elements of Hobbes and Boyle ultimately serve as the inventory out of which Latour models his own view.

The Interplay of Politics and Science: Boyle, Hobbes, and the Quasi-Object

Latour's pragmatic approach to the question of modernity necessitates his focus on processes that are *ipso facto* social processes themselves, i.e., practices in a broad sense. From this perspective, it hardly comes as a surprise that his terminology draws on political theoretical vocabulary that stems from the practices under investigation. Paradigmatically, he conceives of his object, modernity, as founded on a *constitution*:

> Just as the constitution of jurists defines the rights and duties of citizens and the State, the working of justice and the transfer of power, so this Constitution [...] defines humans and nonhumans, their properties and their relations, their abilities and their groupings.²⁸

This constitution, however, is achieved by the means of a set of practices that we, in a modern world, think of as substantially different—namely, science and politics. In the room between the realm of science, represented by Boyle, and that of politics, represented by Hobbes, Latour wants to draw attention to an emerging object named a *hybrid*, *quasi-object*, or *quasi-subject* that, in effect, resides in both realms. If he is right, the presence of hybrids thus disproves the existence of the modern constitution. In reality, we would not be able to keep apart the processes of purification and translation because every attempt, for instance, to isolate purification from translation itself amounts to a translation, i.e., the creation of a new object.

These processes are that which Latour attempts to make evident from his study of Boyle and Hobbes. Under the headings "Boyle and His Objects"²⁹ and "Hobbes and His Subjects"³⁰ he utilizes Shapin and Schaffer to exhibit "how Boyle and Hobbes fought to invent a science, a context, and a demarcation between the two."³¹ *How* they achieve this demarcation, i.e., a purificatory process in Latour's terminology, is invoked to display his thesis that this was only possible on the basis of a translational process which remained active before, under, and after the demarcation. In this process, Latour sees not only that "Boyle has a science and a political theory; Hobbes has a political theory and a science," but also that "by good fortune, they [Boyle and Hobbes] agree on almost everything. They want a king, a Parliament, a docile and unified Church, and they are fervent subscribers to mechanistic philosophy."³² Instead of keeping one side on a close distance from the other, their disagreements about experimental processes (particularly, the process of creating a vacuum inside an air pump) ultimately come down to "what can be expected from experimentation, from scientific reasoning, [and] from political argument."³³

Boyle chose a "method of argument—that of opinion—that was held in contempt by the oldest scholastic tradition."[34] Rather than exemplifying a rational approach (*episteme*), Boyle's methods resemble doxa—he "relied on a parajuridical metaphor: credible, trustworthy, well-to-do witnesses gathered at the scene of the action can attest to the existence of a fact, the matter of fact."[35] By constructing a setting in which a group of people could bear witness to certain events, in this case the events visible within an air pump made of glass, onlookers in the laboratory would be able to give evidence concerning their observations, e.g., the death of living beings contained in the vacuum and so on. Surprisingly, this framework suggests that scientific processes occur according to similar procedures involved in one of society's highest institutions: the court. In this way, the scientist can control and construct facts that "will never be modified, whatever may happen elsewhere in theory, metaphysics, religion, politics or logic."[36] By virtue of his politically inspired empirical method, Boyle thus successfully secures scientific fact.

Hobbes, on the other hand, secured the State through a scientific theory designed to reject Boyle's method. Contrary to Boyle, Hobbes preferred a "method of argument" known from the sciences, namely "mathematical demonstration."[37] To secure peace and prevent a civil war, he invoked a mechanical theory of nature that rendered the existence of any supernatural being, which could be used to question sovereign authority, obsolete. And such a threat was posed, Latour claims, by Boyle's vacuum: "Inert and mechanical matter is as essential to civil peace as a purely symbolic interpretation of the Bible. In both cases, it behoves us to avoid at all costs the possibility that the factions may invoke a higher Entity—Nature or God—which the Sovereign does not fully control."[38]

Hence, Hobbes's and Boyle's debate about the existence of a vacuum created inside an air pump comes down to a disagreement about the import and legitimacy of opinion and scientific fact. To achieve their goals, they both sought refuge in a mix of science and politics:

> All the elements are now in place for the confrontation between Hobbes and Boyle. After Hobbes has reduced and reunified the Body Politic, along comes the Royal Society to divide everything up again: some gentlemen proclaim the right to have an independent opinion, in a closed space, the laboratory, over which the State has no control. And when these troublemakers find themselves in agreement, it is not on the basis of a mathematical demonstration that everyone would be compelled to accept, but on the basis of experiments observed by the deceptive senses, experiments that remain inexplicable and inconclusive. Worse still, this new coterie chooses to concentrate its work on an air pump that once again produces immaterial bodies, the vacuum—as if Hobbes had not had enough trouble getting rid of phantoms and spirits![39]

While Hobbes denies the vacuum on political grounds, demanding of Boyle *demonstrations* of the falseness of his own theory, Boyle responds by elaborating his constructs and, consequently, produces more nuanced witnesses.[40] Setting the correctness of this interpretation of the dispute between Hobbes and Boyle aside, Latour's real goal becomes evident. In this dispute Latour believes to have displayed the

> invention of a new actor recognized by the new Constitution: inert bodies, incapable of will and bias but capable of showing, signing, writing, and scribbling on laboratory instruments before trustworthy witnesses. These nonhumans, lacking souls but endowed with meaning, are even more reliable than ordinary mortals.[41]

And now Latour can draw his conclusions for the modern constitution and the so-called four guarantees of the moderns, which, however, do not concern us further, here. Instead, I will simply list these guarantees briefly and turn to Latour's notion of hybrids in more detail. The first guarantee states that "even though we construct Nature, Nature is as if we did not construct it"; the second states that "even though we do not construct Society, Society is as if we did construct it"; the third states that "Nature and Society must remain absolutely distinct: the work of purification must remain absolutely distinct from the work of mediation"[42]; the fourth guarantee rids nature as well as society of divine presence.[43]

The treatment of hybrids within this paradigm springs from the inability of this modern constitution to include the legions of emergent hybrids, which Latour exemplifies with the air pump: "Where are we to put these hybrids? Are they human? Human because they are our work. Are they natural? Natural because they are not our doing. Are they local or global? Both."[44]

Every hybrid is thus a product of the dimensions of the constitution, i.e., purification and translation: "The moderns have always been using both dimensions in practice […], but they have never been explicit about the relation between the two sets of practices."[45] Moreover, these hybrids constitute a mix of an object pole (nature) and a subject pole (society):

> Quasi-objects are in between and below the two poles. […] Quasi-objects are much more social, much more fabricated, much more collective than the "hard" pats of nature, but they are in no way the arbitrary receptacles of a full-fledged society. On the other hand they are much more real, nonhuman and objective than those shapeless screens on which society—for unknown reasons—needed to be "projected."[46]

Consequently, there are no objects or entities in the span of the two practices that represent one and only one pole but only hybrids of purification and mediation, all containing subjective-objective or objective-subjective properties. Accordingly, the doings of these *actants* "must be pieced together and put to work in shadowing quasi-objects or networks."[47] In other words, the quasi-objects demand a description in terms of what they *do* in the network, thereby simulating in a nonconscious way purposeful human action. To understand their actions in terms of a free will inherent to these objects would, however, misconstrue Latour's point. Quasi-objects cannot be said to have a capacity to *choose* between different objects or scenarios; their effects are actions in the sense of a purposeful activity, rooted in a field of such actants. Their actions are the manifestation of a goal-directed behavior, a *telos*, which they execute of themselves, i.e., autonomously, in the absence of oppositely directed action and in cooperation with other quasi-objects within the network. Hence, they exhibit meaning in and by themselves through their multiple relations with other quasi-objects and, thus, contribute to worldly processes on the same footing as human actions. In this sense, Latour is not defending the thesis that all entities share the conscious features of the human being, which would amount to reducing them to the subject pole: "We are indeed different from others, but we must not situate the differences where the now-closed question of relativism had located them. As collectives, we are all brothers. Except in the matter of dimension, which is itself caused by small differences in the distribution of entities, we can recognize a continuous gradient between premoderns and nonmoderns."[48] Rather, Latour maintains the position that all entities act according to the same schema or structure, which unites subjective as well as objective properties in such a way that their actions can be understood to be spontaneous in the absence of obstructions. Consequently, no object, be it human or nonhuman, can be stripped of its natural and social properties and effects. This fact needs to be acknowledged, Latour claims, through representatives or spokespersons that bring the voices, the meanings of quasi-objects into political life.[49] This fact is also evident from Latour's discussion of how quasi-objects are produced in processes of differentiation, i.e., purification:

> But the machine for creating differences is triggered by the refusal to conceptualize quasi-objects, because this very refusal leads to the uncontrollable proliferation of a certain type of being: the object, constructor of the social, expelled from the social world, attributed to a transcendent world that is, however, not divine—a world that produces, in contrast, a floating subject, bearer of law and morality. Boyle's air pump, Pasteur's microbes, Archimedes' pulleys, are such objects. These new nonhumans possess miraculous properties because they are at one and the same time both social and asocial, producers of natures and constructors of subjects. They are the tricksters of comparative anthropology.[50]

In short, quasi-objects cannot be reduced to efficient causality, but act, trick, and, by so doing, produce subjects and objects, laws, and morality in a field of essentially similar actants.

A Modern Mix-Up

Latour thus defends a view where the opposition between the human being and its practices on the one hand and nature or actuality (*Wirklichkeit*) on the other is neglected. In such a paradigm, any *other* in relation to the human being has disappeared. Remaining in Latour's worldview are only artifacts, visible in the genitive constructions considered above (Boyle's air pump). In the literal sense, the object (*obicere*)⁵¹ of the human is completely left out of the equation as itself a proliferation based on the practices of purification and translation:

> Are you not fed up at finding yourselves forever locked into language alone, or imprisoned in social representations alone, as so many social scientists would like you to be? We want to gain access to things themselves, not only to their phenomena. The real is not remote; rather, it is accessible in all the objects mobilized throughout the world. Doesn't external reality abound right here among us? [...] The collectives we live in are more active, more productive, more socialized than the tiresome things-in-themselves led us to expect. [...] Our collectives are more real, more naturalized, more discursive than the tiresome humans-amongthemselves led us to expect. [...] Real as Nature, narrated as Discourse, collective as Society, existential as Being: such are the quasi-objects that the moderns have caused to proliferate. As such it behoves us to pursue them, while we simply become once more what we have never ceased to be: amoderns.⁵²

Quite surprisingly, in a process that he himself may qualify as a purification, Latour overlooks the differentiation between reality as the product of human or natural processes and actuality as the other of human practices. Moreover, the *sole* focus on practices is itself a very modern methodological approach, owing its origins to modern ethnography, anthropology, and sociology.⁵³ As will become clear in the following section, this is only but one instance of Latour's modern mix-up. Thus, it turns out that, even according to his own paradigm of modernity, Latour is himself neither postmodern nor pre- or amodern but quite straightforwardly modern.

A closer look at the properties of quasi-objects themselves uncovers a conspicuous mix of elements, all owing their origins to specific notions and positions of the modern epoch. The quasi-objects *produce*, Latour argues with his example of Boyle's air pump and Hobbes's plenum theory of materialism. They exhibit *purposeful actions* exempt of any *will*. Such statements of behavior could be taken as a sign of Latour's inheritance from the scholastic tradition, wherein the difference between purposeful behavior between nonhuman and human agents was often explained with reference to nonconscious and conscious actions, and thus confirm his amodern ambitions. In *Di Principiis Naturae*, Thomas Aquinas could, for example, refer to the teleological striving of natural agents (nonhumans) as actions occurring without foreknowledge of their ends, contrary to voluntary (human) actions that are like natural striving but presuppose a knowledge of their ends, which, by the means of the will, determine the actions themselves. According to Aquinas, whereas the ends of nonhuman agents are simply determined by the actions themselves, human beings determine their ends voluntarily through knowledge.⁵⁴ This conception is, however, evidently not the case with Latour's hybrids that, including human beings, know of no *volition* or *deliberation*, divine or otherwise. Quite to the contrary, they are more adequately understood as peculiar constructs of modern mechanistic materialisms.

Hobbesian Subjects and Boylean Objects United

Even though the early moderns upheld some traits of their scholastic opponents, such as the concept of substance, two novel notions entered the stage with the modern discourse: namely, the notion of the free will and a new form of mechanistic materialism.[55]

On the one hand, the early moderns pursued a new concept of matter, founded in various degrees upon new developments in mathematical analysis. One of the results of this endeavor was the mechanical concept of matter, which, amongst others, Boyle championed. Specifically, Boyle developed a theory of matter consisting of atoms with emerging chemical properties. Contrary to other mechanical theories of matter, Boyle determined these emergent properties as *relational* in character. Hence, according to Boyle, the emergence of these fundamental properties relies upon the proximity of other objects that permit these qualities to materialize. In the absence of such a presence, the properties are simply dispositions.[56]

On the other hand, the early moderns aimed to develop a concept of freedom of the will that would fit this new worldview. Specifically, Hobbes integrated this project into his political theory. One of the main opponents of Hobbes's theory of the will was John Bramhall, a proponent of the scholastic tradition from Francisco Suárez not that different from Thomas Aquinas. Suárez held, as did Aquinas, that free will rests on both a natural law, i.e., the moral law, and a theory of human ability to choose rationally and freely amongst more than one action. Whereas the moral law serves the function of establishing a foundation for right and wrong and thereby dictating obligations for beings capable of willing this law, the psychological dispositions of freedom and rationality secure the voluntary element necessary for a moral theory of the human being.[57] Without reason and the free will to deliberate action, the human being would not be blameworthy and, consequently, would not be a moral being at all. With the advent of the new mechanical theories of matter, these metaphysical theories of freedom were heavily challenged.

Constructing his political philosophy of the state, Hobbes introduced two notions of free will that serve to legitimate his theory of the Leviathan. Rejecting the existence of a voluntary faculty in the human being bound by the principles of his metaphysics, Hobbes conceived of freedom in terms of *non-commitment* as well as *non-obstruction*. In the first sense, an action is free if the choice is not bound or limited by preceding commitments. If the human being is bound by former obligations, such as the divine natural law of the scholastics, it cannot be said to be free, which it is, at least in some cases.[58] Moreover, for Hobbes, a free action is one that is not obstructed by external and natural impediments. If no external thing prevents me from an act of my choosing, then I am, Hobbes argued, free, regardless of my internal psychological state, including inhibitory fears or anxieties.[59]

Looking back at Latour's theory of the quasi-object, his inheritance of Hobbesian and Boylean features—what might also be described as modern elements—seems likelier than an inheritance of premodern influences. Latour's ontology is, of course, neither Hobbesian nor Boylean, but rather an odd mixture of notions shared across the vocabularies of moderns such as Hobbes and Boyle.[60] Along with Hobbes and Boyle, he rejects a metaphysical account of a human will that can freely choose between different ends. More importantly, however, he posits an ontology of intertwined objects, the quasi-objects, whose multiple relations produce never-ending realms of new quasi-objects. This, obviously, cannot be reduced to Boyle's emergent properties, because Latour's relational ontology posits the emergence not of properties, but of whole new objects. However, as emergent creatures, these quasi-objects are products of societal and natural relations.[61]

On top of this relational ontology, Latour infuses a purposeful striving into the actions of his quasi-objects which easily could be misconstrued as scholastic. Contrary to the scholastic tradition, the purposeful behavior of a quasi-object does not seem to obey any natural laws or advertise any form of determinism. Conversely, such objects exhibit quite accidental behavior. Given the absence of any obstructions, such as other hybrids, quasi-objects are rather bestowed with a will to act and engage in the creation of new and unexpected quasi-objects. They are not steered by the inner voice of a sailor directing a boat, but rather acting out their dispositions in a given field where they accidently happen to be situated.[62] If they are inclined to go in a certain direction rather than another, they simply do so—provided they are not obstructed. This behavior is the outcome of their subjective component. Hence, their will and behavior resemble a negative concept of the free will championed by the likes of Hobbes.

Against the backdrop of Hobbes and Boyle, Latour's quasi-objects thus turn out exactly as that which he constructs them to be: hybrids of a subjective pole and an objective pole, both of which he inconspicuously models on his objects of study, i.e., politics and science. Modernity or, in Latour's terminology, the modern constitution thus dishes up the courses that Latour eagerly, and without further hesitations, devours.[63]

Conclusion

On the face of it, Latour departs from modern discourse and, at a distance from the ruins of the modern project, erects a wholly new metaphysics. Due to its anti-mechanistic components and antimodern attitude, an ontology like Latour's would of course be intolerable to Hobbes as well as to Boyle. Nevertheless, this feature alone makes Latour's ontology neither premodern nor amodern. In fact, Latour is profoundly modern; he only believes he is not. Instead of having discovered a new foundation for metaphysics, Latour raised his new building out of the ruins of the old. He relies heavily on modern categories such as a negative concept of freedom, the constitutional theory of the state, and an absolute notion of matter as spontaneous and emergent. As such, Latour's substitution of the modern worldview with a pre- or amodern one is more caught up in the modern inventory than he seems willing to accept or even to realize. Indeed, closer scrutiny reveals that his alleged rejection of modernity looks more like a modern mix-up than a critique.[64]

This severe confusion does not, however, require us to stop taking Latour's work seriously. On the contrary, it forces us to study him and the intense attention which his work receives even more closely. The allure of discarding modernity and embracing the world as a network of hybrid forms ultimately gives voice to a recent disappointment with the modern project. As an inherently modern expression of an age-old craving for actuality (*Wirklichkeit*), Latour shows himself to be a seismograph of our times and the yet unsettled promise of modernity's potential. That he fails to take stock of his own modern inheritance and, so to speak, personifies a rather childlike instrument of measurement only makes him a more conspicuous voice of our times.[65]

Notes

1. See Jane Bennett, *The Enchantment of Modern Life: Attachments, Crossings, and Ethics* (Princeton, NJ: Princeton University Press, 2001); Jane Bennett, "Modernity and Its Critics," in *Oxford Handbook of Political Science*, ed. Robert E. Goodin (Oxford/New York: Oxford University Press, 2009); Karen Barad, *Meeting the Universe Halfway: Quantum Physics and the Entanglement of Matter and Meaning* (Durham: Duke University Press, 2007), 58–9; Graham Harman, *Prince of Network: Bruno Latour and Metaphysics* (Melbourne, Australia: re.press, 2009); Graham Harman, "In the Late Afternoon of Modernism: An Interview with Graham Harman," Bad at Sports, Caroline Picard, accessed August 5, 2020, available at http://badatsports.com/2016/in-the-late-afternoon-of-modernism-an-interview-with-graham-harman. For a somewhat more critical approach to Latour's thesis on modernity, see also Timothy Morton, *Dark Ecology: For a Logic of Future Coexistence* (New York: Columbia University Press, 2016), 63, and Timothy Morton, *Hyperobjects: Philosophy and Ecology after the End of the World* (Minneapolis/London: University of Minnesota Press, 2013), 19.
2. See Jane Bennett, *Vibrant Matter: A Political Ecology of Things* (Durham, NC: Duke University Press, 2010), viii–ix.
3. See Barad, *Meeting the Universe Halfway*, 41–2 and 141–2. Keeping in mind Donna Haraway's explicit indebtedness to Latour, Barad's attempt to differentiate her agential realism from Latour's theory through her indebtedness to Haraway seems futile. See for example Donna J. Haraway, *When Species Meet* (Minneapolis/London: University of Minnesota Press, 2008), 250.
4. Graham Harman, *Object-Oriented Ontology: A New Theory of Everything* (London: Pelican Books, 2017), 166.
5. Graham Harman, "The Only Exit from Modern Philosophy," *Open Philosophy* 3 (2020): 133.
6. Graham Harman, *The Quadruple Object* (Winchester/Washington: Zero Books, 2011), 121. For Harman's reservations about Latour, see for example Harman, *The Quadruple Object*, 12.
7. Graham Harman, *Immaterialism: Objects and Social Theory* (Malden, MA: Polity Press, 2016), 29.
8. Harman, *The Quadruple Object*, 45.
9. One may wonder, if Harman's view does not align better with an extrapolated position of the British empiricist John Locke, who, unlike Kant, construed the pure substance

or substratum of things and cause of human ideas as "a Supposition of he knows not what support of such Qualities, which are capable of producing simple *Ideas* in us" (John Lock, *An Essay Concerning the Human Understanding* [Oxford/New York: Oxford University Press, 2008], 179). Whereas the thing-in-itself for Kant is no thing and, consequently, cannot be thought in plural, Locke defends largely the view on substance as the unknowable but actual and necessary bearer of knowable accidents, a position that Harman believes himself to have located in Kant.

10 Naturally, Latour's position has been problematized and criticized and his significance for the new materialisms has not gone unnoticed. For example, Sarah Ellenzweig and John Zammito critically highlight the role of Latour and his commitment to the notion of active matter in their introduction to *The New Politics of Materialism* (2017). See Sarah Ellenzweig and John H. Zammito, "Introduction: New Materialism: Looking Forward, Looking Back," in *The New Politics of Materialism: History, Philosophy, Science*, ed. Sarah Ellenzweig and John H. Zammito (New York City: Routledge, 2017). However, the implications of Latour's claims and theory have yet to be examined on their own terms.

11 See Paul R. Gross and Norman Levitt, *Higher Superstition: The Academic Left and Its Quarrels with Science* (Baltimore: Johns Hopkins University Press, 1997) and Massimo Pigliucci, *Nonsense on Stilts: How to Tell Science from Bunk* (Chicago/London: The University of Chicago Press, 2010), 255f.

12 Bruno Latour and Steve Woolgar, *Laboratory Life: The Social Construction of Scientific Facts* (Beverly Hills: Sage Publications, 1979). For some of the most influential criticisms, see Ian Hacking, *The Social Construction of What?* (Cambridge, MA/London: Harvard University Press, 1999).

13 See Andreas Malm, *The Progress of this Storm: Nature and Society in a Warming World* (London/New York: Verso, 2017).

14 As he offers an alternative metaphysical account of nature and culture, albeit a very brief one, Malm seems to acknowledge this point. His claim that "historical materialism is a substance monist property dualism" (Malm, *The Progress of This Storm*, 59) as well as his rather pragmatic adherence to such a variant of property dualism do, however, fall out rather accidental to his critique that, thus, remains politically motivated.

15 Bruno Latour, *We Have Never Been Modern* (Cambridge, MA: Harvard University Press, 1993), 7.

16 Latour, *We Have Never Been Modern*, 7.

17 Latour, *We Have Never Been Modern*, 7.

18 Latour, *We Have Never Been Modern*, 10.

19 Latour, *We Have Never Been Modern*, 10f.

20 Latour, *We Have Never Been Modern*, 11.

21 A concern regarding Latour's definition of modernity deserves mentioning here. Besides noting the fact that he fails to mention even the most basic literature on the study of modernity in his own work on this subject, one could simply deny that Latour captures the nature of modernity with his definition—one that undoubtedly appears rather peculiar. Indeed, his identification of modernity with the acceptance of a *consideration* of or *belief* in the possibility of keeping two ontological realms apart immediately transforms the discussion of modernity into an epistemological (i.e., about mental capabilities) or a sociological (i.e., about human practices) question. This transformation makes the entire discussion depend on human capabilities. Formulated in these terms, the question of modernity is a lost cause, rejected from the

very outset. More traditional notions of modernity tend, instead, to define modernity in terms of a worldview, i.e., metaphysics. See, for example, Charles Taylor, *A Secular Age* (Cambridge, MA/London: The Belknap Press, 2007), 1–4, or Hans Blumenberg, *Legitimität der Neuzeit* (Frankfurt am Main: Suhrkamp, 1966).

22 Latour, *We Have Never Been Modern*, 11.
23 Latour, *We Have Never Been Modern*, 7.
24 Latour, *We Have Never Been Modern*, 12.
25 Latour, *We Have Never Been Modern*, 15
26 See Steven Shapin and Simon Schaffer, *Leviathan and the Air-Pump: Hobbes, Boyle, and the Experimental* (Princeton, NJ: Princeton University Press, 1985). As my interest concerns Latour's quasi-objects, I omit giving an account of differences between Latour's treatment of Boyle and Hobbes and Shapin and Schaffer's, on which he almost exclusively draws.
27 See Latour, *We Have Never Been Modern*, 46–7.
28 Latour, *We Have Never Been Modern*, 15. To be fair, Latour wants to distinguish these kinds of constitutions from political ones. To what extent he achieves this goal is questionable, insofar as he simply asserts that he wishes to make this distinction in the quotation's omitted passage. The main difference seems to lie in the process of establishing such constitutions and in the entities capable of contributing to them, which is the reason behind his infamous claim about the needed redistribution of agency and the parliament of things. See Latour, *We Have Never Been Modern*, 144. Interestingly, he continues to draw heavily on the constitutional theory of Hobbes in his later works that resurrect the necessity of a new political Leviathan in the guise of ancient Greek mythology, i.e., the Earth Goddess Gaia. See, respectively, Bruno Latour, *The Politics of Nature. How to Bring the Sciences into Democracy*, trans. Catherine Porter (Cambridge, MA: Harvard University Press, 2004), especially 221–8, and *Facing Gaia: Eight Lectures on the New Climatic Regime*, trans. Catherine Porter (Cambridge/Medford, MA: Polity Press, 2017). Also in this respect, he stays well within the theoretical framework and tradition normally conceived as modern.
29 Latour, *We Have Never Been Modern*, 15.
30 Latour, *We Have Never Been Modern*, 18.
31 Latour, *We Have Never Been Modern*, 16.
32 Latour, *We Have Never Been Modern*, 17.
33 Latour, *We Have Never Been Modern*, 17.
34 Latour, *We Have Never Been Modern*, 17f.
35 Latour, *We Have Never Been Modern*, 18.
36 Latour, *We Have Never Been Modern*, 18.
37 Latour, *We Have Never Been Modern*, 19.
38 Latour, *We Have Never Been Modern*, 19.
39 Latour, *We Have Never Been Modern*, 20. Cf. Latour, *We Have Never Been Modern*, 22.
40 Latour, *We Have Never Been Modern*, 22.
41 Latour, *We Have Never Been Modern*, 23. Indeed, the adequacy of Latour's interpretation of the dispute between Hobbes and Boyle has been questioned. See, for example, Margaret C. Jacob, "Reflections on Bruno Latour's Version of the Seventeenth Century," in *A House Build on Sand: Exposing Postmodernist Myths about Science*, ed. Noretta Koertge (Oxford: Oxford University Press, 2006), 240–54.
42 Latour, *We Have Never Been Modern*, 32.
43 Latour, *We Have Never Been Modern*, 33.

44 Latour, *We Have Never Been Modern*, 50.
45 Latour, *We Have Never Been Modern*, 51.
46 Latour, *We Have Never Been Modern*, 55.
47 Latour, *We Have Never Been Modern*, 67. See also Bruno Latour, *Reassembling the Social: An Introduction to Actor-Network-Theory* (Oxford: Oxford University Press, 2005) and *An Inquiry into Modes of Existence: An Anthropology of the Moderns*, trans. Catherine Porter (Cambridge, MA: Harvard University Press, 2013).
48 Latour, *We Have Never Been Modern*, 114.
49 Latour, *We Have Never Been Modern*, 144.
50 Latour, *We Have Never Been Modern*, 112. At this point, Latour could object that I confuse his theory of an anthropology with ontology or metaphysics. Latour himself, however, emphasizes that his theory of quasi-objects remains within metaphysics or infra-physics. See Latour, *We Have Never Been Modern*, 128.
51 The Latin *ob-icere* literally translates "against-thrown."
52 Latour, *We Have Never Been Modern*, 90. One could only wish that Latour had taken Kant's liminal concept of *das Ding an sich* more seriously and refrained from imagining it in plural (thing-in-it-self, not things-in-themselves). This mistake seems to be a shared feature of the new materialisms. See, for example, Lodberg and Lautrup's contribution to this volume. There are no things-in-themselves, Kant argues, precisely because the thing-in-itself is no thing, and, consequently, cannot be differentiated in any way, the least of which in multiple substances.
53 See, for example, Thomas Kuhn's *The Structure of Scientific Revolutions* (Chicago: The University of Chicago Press, 1962) or John H. Zammito's study on the discoveries and studies of non-European cultures in early anthropology (*Kant, Herder, and the Birth of Anthropology* [Chicago: The University of Chicago Press, 2002]). On a more skeptical note, Latour's attempt to overcome the dualist beliefs of modernity quite fatally fails to take stock of the many nuances of modern metaphysics. René Descartes, for example, explicitly defended the oneness of the soul and body, which he took to be forming a unity (*unum*), just as numerous variants of materialism proliferated forms of hylomorphism in the early modern period. See, respectively, René Descartes, *Meditationes de prima philosophia/Meditations on First Philosophy* (Cambridge: Cambridge University Press, 2013), here 112, and Sarah Ellenzweig and John Zammito, ed., *The New Politics of Materialism: History, Philosophy, Science* (London/New York: Routledge, 2017).
54 Thomas Aquinas, *Sancti Thomae Aquinatis, Doctoris Angelici, Opera* omnia, tome XLIII (Rome: Ex Typographia Polyglotta S. C. de Propaganda Fide, 1976), cap. 3.
55 A nuanced exposition of the philosophies of Hobbes and Boyle exceeds the limits of this article. By highlighting Hobbes's and Boyle's positions, which Latour utilizes for his own account of the new constitution, I aim to draw attention to the modern features of his theory, rather than arguing for Latour as a representative of Hobbes or Boyle.
56 See Robert Boyle, *The Works of Robert Boyle. Vol. 5: The Origin of Forms and Qualities and Other Publications of 1665-7* (London: Pickering & Chatto, 1999). For a discussion, see especially Marina Paola Banchetti-Robino, *The Chemical Philosophy of Robert Boyle: Mechanicism, Chymical Atoms, and Emergence* (Oxford: Oxford University Press, 2020), 112.
57 See Thomas Pink, "Hobbes on Liberty, Action and Free Will," in *The Oxford Handbook of Hobbes*, ed. A. P. Martinich and K. Hoekstra (Oxford: Oxford University Press, 2016), 14f.

58 See Philip Pettit, "Liberty and Leviathan," *Politics, Philosophy & Economy* 4, no. 1 (2005): 133.
59 Pettit, "Liberty and Leviathan," 137-9.
60 By virtue of the Hobbesian vocabulary, which he increasingly employs, Latour may be more of a Hobbesian than a Boylean.
61 It is hard to estimate, but Latour's quasi-objects do not seem to be dispositional in the sense of being potentially there in an earlier stage of the network.
62 Likewise, Descartes denied the conception of an inner steersman as a proper picture of the soul. See René Descartes, *Meditationes de Prima Philosophia*, 112.
63 This great appetite is apparently a faculty shared by many of the new materialists. See Christoph Asmuth, "'Ich suchte, und fiel stets tiefer in das Labyrinth' Fichte und der Faden der Ariadne," *Revista de Estud(i)os sobre Fichte* 13, no. 2017 (2016): 1-12, esp. 2. The rather questionable use and reliance on positions from the history of philosophy and science amongst adherents of the new materialisms have likewise been critically noticed. See, for example, Dan Zahavi, "The End of What? Phenomenology vs. speculative realism," *International Journal of Philosophical Studies* 24, no. 3 (2016): 289-309, and Jan Faye and Rasmus Jaksland, "Barad, Bohr, and Quantum Mechanics," *Synthese* 199 (2021): 8231-55.
64 Latour may have partially come to this realization, as he published a self-critical article on critique in 2004. See Bruno Latour, "Why Has Critique Run out of Steam? From Matters of Fact to Matters of Concern," *Critical Inquiry* 30 (2004): 225-48. Nonetheless, he continues to adhere to his theory of quasi-objects and his rejection of modernity.
65 This chapter was made possible through the support of the Independent Research Fund Denmark (case no. 0127-00026B).

Cited Works

Banchetti-Robino, Marina Paola. *The Chemical Philosophy of Robert Boyle: Mechanicism, Chymical Atoms, and Emergence*. Oxford: Oxford University Press, 2020.

Barad, Karen. *Meeting the Universe Halfway: Quantum Physics and the Entanglement of Matter and Meaning*. Durham: Duke University Press, 2007.

Bennett, Jane. *The Enchantment of Modern Life: Attachments, Crossings, and Ethics*. Princeton, NJ: Princeton University Press, 2001.

Bennett, Jane. "Modernity and Its Critics." In *Oxford Handbook of Political Science*, edited by Robert E. Goodin, 211-24. Oxford/New York: Oxford University Press, 2009.

Bennett, Jane. *Vibrant Matter: A Political Ecology of Things*. Durham, NC: Duke University Press, 2010.

Blumenberg, Hans. *Die Legitimität der Neuzeit*. Frankfurt am Main: Suhrkamp, 1966.

Boyle, Robert. *The Works of Robert Boyle. Vol. 5: The Origin of Forms and Qualities and Other Publications of 1665-7*, edited by Michael Hunter and Edward B. Davies. London: Pickering & Chatto, 1999.

Descartes, René. *Meditationes de Prima Philosophia/Meditations on First Philosophy*. Cambridge: Cambridge University Press, 2013.

Ellenzweig, Sarah and John H. Zammito. "Introduction: New Materialism: Looking Forward, Looking Back." In *The New Politics of Materialism: History, Philosophy, Science*, edited by Sarah Ellenzweig and John H. Zammito, 1-15. New York: Routledge, 2017.

Ellenzweig, Sarah and John Zammito, ed. *The New Politics of Materialism: History, Philosophy, Science*. London/New York: Routledge, 2017.

Faye, Jan and Rasmus Jaksland. "Barad, Bohr, and Quantum Mechanics." *Synthese* 199 (2021): 8231–55.

Gross, Paul R. and Norman Levitt. *Higher Superstition: The Academic Left and Its Quarrels with Science*. Baltimore: Johns Hopkins University Press, 1997.

Hacking, Ian. *The Social Construction of What?* Cambridge, MA/London: Harvard University Press, 1999.

Harman, Graham. *The Quadruple Object*. Winchester/Washington: Zero Books, 2011.

Harman, Graham. *Immaterialism: Objects and Social Theory*. Malden, MA: Polity Press, 2016.

Harman, Graham. *Object-Oriented Ontology: A New Theory of Everything*. London: Pelican Books, 2017.

Harman, Graham. "The Only Exit from Modern Philosophy." *Open Philosophy* 3 (2020): 132–46.

Harman, Graham. "In the Late Afternoon of Modernism: An Interview with Graham Harman." By Caroline Picard. *Bad at Sports* (August 2, 2016). Available at http://badatsports.com/2016/in-the-late-afternoon-of-modernism-an-interview-with-graham-harman/. Accessed August 5, 2020.

Jacob, Margaret C. "Reflections on Bruno Latour's Version of the Seventeenth Century." In *A House Build on Sand: Exposing Postmodernist Myths about Science*, edited by Noretta Koertge, 240–54. Oxford: Oxford University Press, 2006.

Kuhn, Thomas. *The Structure of Scientific Revolutions*. Chicago: The University of Chicago Press, 1962.

Latour, Bruno. *We Have Never Been Modern*. Cambridge, MA: Harvard University Press, 1993.

Latour, Bruno. "Why Has Critique Run out of Steam? From Matters of Fact to Matters of Concern." *Critical Inquiry* 30 (2004): 225–48.

Latour, Bruno. *Reassembling the Social: An Introduction to Actor-Network-Theory*. Oxford: Oxford University Press, 2005.

Latour, Bruno. *An Inquiry into Modes of Existence: An Anthropology of the Moderns*. Translated by Catherine Porter. Cambridge, MA: Harvard University Press, 2013.

Latour, Bruno. *Facing Gaia. Eight Lectures on the New Climatic Regime*. Translated by Catherine Porter. Cambridge/Medford, MA: Polity Press, 2017.

Latour, Bruno and Steve Woolgar. *Laboratory Life: The Social Construction of Scientific Facts*. Beverly Hills: Sage Publications, 1979.

Locke, John. *An Essay Concerning the Human Understanding*. Oxford/New York: Oxford University Press, 2008.

Malm, Andreas. *The Progress of this Storm: Nature and Society in a Warming World*. London/New York: Verso, 2017.

Morton, Timothy. *Ecology without Nature: Rethinking Environmental Aesthetics*. Cambridge, MA/London: Harvard University Press, 2007.

Morton, Timothy. *Hyperobjects: Philosophy and Ecology after the End of the World*. Minneapolis/London: University of Minnesota Press, 2013.

Morton, Timothy. *Dark Ecology: For a Logic of Future Coexistence*. New York: Columbia University Press, 2016.

Pettit, Philip. "Liberty and Leviathan." *Politics, Philosophy & Economy* 4, no. 1 (2005): 131–51.

Pink, Thomas. "Hobbes on Liberty, Action and Free Will." In *The Oxford Handbook of Hobbes*, edited by A. P. Martinich and K. Hoekstra, 171–95. Oxford: Oxford University Press, 2016.

Pigliucci, Massimo. *Nonsense on Stilts: How to Tell Science from Bunk*. Chicago/London: The University of Chicago Press, 2010.

Shapin, Steven and Simon Schaffer. *Leviathan and the Air-Pump: Hobbes, Boyle, and the Experimental*. Princeton, NJ: Princeton University Press, 1985.

Taylor, Charles. *A Secular Age*. Cambridge, MA/London: The Belknap Press, 2007.

Thomas Aquinas. *Sancti Thomae Aquinatis, Doctoris Angelici, Opera omnia*. Tome XLIII. Rome: Ex Typographia Polyglotta S.C. de Propaganda Fide, 1976.

Zahavi, Dan. "The End of What? Phenomenology vs. Speculative Realism." *International Journal of Philosophical Studies* 24, no. 3 (2016): 289–309.

Zammito, John H. *Kant, Herder, and the Birth of Anthropology*. Chicago: The University of Chicago Press, 2002.

Chapter 7

ACKNOWLEDGING MATERIALITY WITHOUT FETISHIZING IT: SOME PITFALLS IN SPEAKING FOR MATTER

Alf Hornborg

Introduction

In order to be able to discuss the merits and shortcomings of a "material turn" in the humanities and social sciences, let us begin by agreeing that there is such a thing as materiality.[1] In the discussion that follows I use "materiality" to denote those aspects of reality that are physical or corporeal, i.e., exerting force (energy) or having mass and occupying space. Dictionary definitions of "matter" and "material" generally oppose these categories to "mind" or "spirit," i.e., "the seat of consciousness, thought, volition, and feeling" and "the vital animating essence" or "non-physical part of a person."[2] Common to the diverse proponents of a material turn is a critique of the traditional humanist focus on the mental or spiritual aspects of human existence and an aspiration to grant material aspects significance *on their own terms*. Also common to these efforts, of course, is the dilemma of representation: the intrinsic paradox of humans aspiring to give voice to nonhuman entities, whether living or nonliving. As we shall see, the ambition to abandon anthropocentrism risks leading to anthropomorphism and fetishism.[3]

The material/immaterial binary appears to have preoccupied human imagination throughout history and on all continents. To contemplate this fundamental duality of existence may be basic to the human condition. It is difficult to imagine humans *not* reflecting over the apparent disparity between consciousness and matter, or mind and body. Regardless of scale and complexity, the worldviews of people in various cultural contexts generally tend to deal in some way with the ubiquitous observation that mind and body may—and ultimately do—*part*. This is as true whether it is held that the mind or soul can survive the body or that it cannot. The corpse epitomizes materiality as an aspect of reality that can be analytically distinguished from consciousness.[4] This means that humans are compelled to somehow theorize the relation between sentience and the corporeal. They may conceive of the mind/body relation in very different ways, but their linguistic categories tend to recognize the analytical distinction between these two aspects of their existence.

My original reasons for wanting to understand the circumstances of the contemporary material turn derive from my struggles to argue that the discipline of economics ever since Victorian times has been deplorably inattentive to the material dimensions of world trade. Mainstream economics couches its concern with global exchange in the ultimately subjective terms of perceived "utility," consumer "preferences," and market "demand," while ignoring the objective quantities of physical resources—labor, land, materials, energy—that are embodied in the traded commodities. Money prices serve as a semiotic veil that both obscures and organizes material asymmetries under a surface of fictive reciprocity. To lift that veil and expose the materiality of world trade is an emancipatory project aiming at greater global justice.

Although generally perceived as "material"—as in the Marxist notion of infrastructure—the economy is ultimately organized by a system of *signs*. The currently hegemonic school of neoclassical economics is very far from "materialist" in the sense of laying "stress on the material aspect of objects."[5] It shares its idealist perspective with the traditions of humanities such as anthropology, philosophy, and art, which tend to emphasize systems of signs, meanings, and values conceived by humans. This preoccupation with ideas, which philosophers tend to trace back to Plato, is prevalent also in engineering. The essence of modern technology is predominantly understood as the *knowledge* represented by a blueprint, rather than on the physical articulation of the components of the machine. Paradoxically, this idealist understanding of technology as fundamentally a matter of technical know-how, ingenuity, and design also underlies the concept of "productive forces" as theorized in historical materialism.

While the general aspiration to escape from the idealist bias of the traditional humanities is understandable and commendable, the assumptions and objectives represented by concerns for the "new materiality" have frequently struck me as very far from emancipatory. In their efforts to attribute agency and even voice to abiotic objects, theorists of the material turn are prone to systematically blur not only the boundary between human and nonhuman but also the boundary between living and nonliving entities. To disregard this crucial distinction by attributing properties of living beings to nonliving things is to invite what Karl Marx recognized as fetishism. Such fetishism has afflicted several interrelated discourses on technology, material culture, and human-artifact relations in general.

Latour and the Animation of All Things

The most elaborate impetus toward the material turn derives from Science and Technology Studies (STS) and particularly the work of Bruno Latour. Latour's perspective on technological artifacts has bewildered his readers for decades, while persuading many that his counterintuitive challenges to social theory have some subtle and intriguing form of validity. In a series of books and articles beginning in the 1980s, he has offered a prolonged and serious argument for approaching artifacts as "actants" endowed with volition. In his book about Aramis—an intricately conceived, automated transport system designed for Paris that failed to materialize—Latour traces the complex processes leading up to its abortion.[6] His point is to shift our understanding of those processes from an exclusive concern with human strategies to an acknowledgment of the purported goals of the technology itself. As distilled on the book cover, he wants his readers to grasp that "technological innovation has needs and desires, especially a desire to be born." We are even told that Aramis has its own "point of view." In his preface, Latour indicates that he wants to "turn a technological object into the central character of a narrative" and to embrace the hitherto isolated "people who are interested in the souls of machines."[7] The social sciences are accustomed to dealing with "speaking subjects," he adds, but these subjects have "poor objects, our inferior brothers" attached to them at all points. "By opening up to include objects, the social bond would become less mysterious." Latour's radical empiricism refuses to be constrained by traditional assumptions of humanist sociology that privilege human beings as unique sources of agency, purposes, and perspectives. His empiricism also obviates any attempt at identifying macro-scale social patterns or structures propelled and reproduced by human purposes, such as capitalism or world-systems—indeed, one could argue, any attempt at social theory.

Latour's approach to Aramis is consistent with his programmatic critique of the "modern constitution," that is, the ontological distinction between nature and society.[8] Rather than approach physical forces and materials as an extra-social domain purified of social relations and representations, he asks us to acknowledge such forces and materials as equal partners in collaborative assemblages composed of both human and nonhuman "actants." Actants are defined as "*any thing* that does modify a state of affairs by making a difference."[9] This is a foundational premise of actor-network theory (ANT), a framework of propositions presented by Latour in a book with the appropriate title *Reassembling the Social*. In this book he dismisses traditional concepts of "society" or "social" as lacking a referent, preferring instead to speak of "collectives."

In rejecting distinctions between the agency of humans and the effects of objects, Latour's understanding of societal collectives ignores or dismisses the significance of purposive communication. He appears to impute no significance to specific human motivations or even consciousness. The implication should be that the material impact of an earthquake or volcanic eruption belongs to the same category of phenomena as actions instigated by language and legislation. Such a flattening of ontology implies that agency is simply a matter of having consequences and that there need be no purposiveness involved. What particularly disturbs humanists and traditional sociologists about ANT is that perceived *meanings*—that is, culture—appear to have no significant role in organizing human actions. To anthropologists and other social scientists accustomed to thinking that the use of complex symbolic systems is what defines human behavior—and what justifies the efforts of humanities and much social theory—Latour's disavowal of human exceptionalism is unacceptable.

Contra Latour, it can be argued that the categories "human society" and "social" indeed do have a referent: viz., all those aspects of the organization of matter and energy that are contingent on symbolic communication.[10] Communication and agency presuppose purpose, even when it is delegated by humans onto technological systems. Purpose ultimately derives from a living being. Nonliving phenomena like volcanoes and transport systems do not have purposes of their own; they cannot communicate or have desires, points of view, or souls. To claim that they do is to take metaphor literally—to confuse poetry and social theory.

Part of the reason why Latour's approach has gained so many followers is that it appears to solve the increasingly obvious problems of traditional nature/society dualism. But it does so in a highly unsatisfactory manner. It is not difficult to show that most real-world phenomena span across the nature/society divide, but this does not mean that we have reasons to abandon the categories of "nature" and "society." It would be misguided to believe that nature and society denote parts of reality that can be insulated from each other, but such an ontological distinction is very different from the *analytical* distinction that we must retain. Anthropogenic climate change, for instance, certainly has both natural and social aspects, but it does not give us reason to approach carbon cycles and capitalism with the same analytical toolbox.

As objects cannot participate in the processes of symbolic communication that define the social, it is incorrect to assert that "the project of ANT is simply to extend the list" of "who and what participates" as "full-blown actors" in society or that the inclusion of objects is "what explains [...] the huge asymmetries, the crushing exercise of power."[11] To acknowledge that the use of artifacts is what enables humans to integrate societies that are more extensive and complex than troops of baboons[12] is not to claim that those artifacts are the *instigators* of such social systems and asymmetries. Latour's apparent unwillingness to distinguish between the purposive agency of human subjects and the physical consequences of material objects suggests either a mechanical understanding of social processes—propelled not by acts of volition but by mindless momentum—or a metaphysical vitalism imputing desires and purposes to all things.

The latter interpretation most often comes to mind, as when Latour asks us to dissolve the distinction between "facts and fetishes."[13] His neologism "factish" is meant to persuade us that whatever we think we may know about our material environment is as fabricated and fetishized as the idols worshipped by premodern Africans encountered by Portuguese explorers in the sixteenth century.[14] The implication appears to be that any truth is as good as any other, as both "the truth of facts and the truth of minds" are products of "intense work of construction."[15] Latour explicitly confronts—as conceit—the Marxist project of *revealing* the societal truths obscured by the fetishism of money and commodities, implying that fetishism is prevalent even among "the Moderns," but does this mean that fetishism should not be challenged? He interprets scientific progress as the continuous replacement of obsolete "factish" idols with new ones,[16] but what can we gain—other than rhetorical flair—from representing the curing of illnesses or the exposure of social injustices as the installation of new *cults*?

Much of what I find misguided in Latour's deliberations may derive from his idiosyncratic use of the categories "subject" versus "object." He frequently claims that the subject/object distinction coincides with the society/nature distinction that is diagnostic of the much-maligned "modern constitution." He also argues that it can be replaced with the distinction between human and nonhuman. This series of homologies is concisely revealed in his announcement that "instead of making the distinction between subjects and objects, we shall speak of associations between humans and nonhumans; the term [association] thus includes both the old natural sciences and the old social sciences."[17] My objection is that none of these three distinctions coincide. The categories "nature" and "nonhumans" most certainly include a great diversity of sentient subjects, while "society"—as Latour himself has abundantly demonstrated—includes vast complexes of nonhuman objects. Latour writes that "'objects' and 'objectivity,' along with 'subjects' and 'subjectivity,' are polemical terms,"[18] which indicates that he uses the distinction only in its *political* sense—evoking a subject's power over an object—but as a dictionary will confirm the distinction can also denote an *ontological* difference distinguishing "a thinking or feeling entity; the conscious mind; the ego, esp. as opposed to anything external to the mind."[19] While in many contexts it may sound democratic to challenge the subject/object distinction in the political sense, to reject the validity of its ontological assertion is simply incorrect. In the latter sense, a piece of rock or metal is indisputably very different from a dog or a mouse, and the difference has huge implications for how we might theorize their possible ways of interacting with their environments.[20]

In his most recent books, Latour has turned his attention to the planetary processes of the Anthropocene.[21] The topic of global climate change provides a challenging arena for applying some of his most characteristic assertions, for instance, regarding the invalidity of society/nature and subject/object distinctions, the agency of nonliving things, and the fabrication of scientific facts. While anthropogenic global warming illustrates the interfusion of society and nature—defined as processes driven by the logic of symbolic versus nonsymbolic phenomena—it does not prompt us to dissolve this analytical distinction. Nor do the meteorological calamities of the Anthropocene turn the planet into a vengeful subject[22]—defined as "a thinking or feeling entity" (see dictionary definition above)—and humanity into its passive object. Moreover, Latour's firm conviction about the validity of Earth system science is difficult to reconcile with his decades of efforts to persuade us that scientific facts are to be regarded as contingent fabrications.

In Defense of Distinctions

Latour's impact on the humanities and social sciences has been formidable. More than anyone else, he has provided foundational concepts for the material turn. Many are following his example and demanding that we concede agency and voice to "nonhumans." But a fundamental question rarely answered is what to include in this category of "nonhumans." It is usually applied to any conceivable material entity, whether living or nonliving. Thus, for example, it may denote an amorphous mix of "microorganisms, animals, plants, machines, rivers, glaciers, oceans, chemical elements, and compounds."[23] The task of emancipating such a heterogeneous collection of entities inevitably strains our conventional vocabulary and worldview beyond what is conceivable. What would it mean to seriously accept assertions that even abiotic nonhumans—down to chemical elements—have properties previously reserved for humans: agency, participation in society, goals, desires, perspectives, rights, responsibility? What would the implications be for politics, legislation, and moral philosophy?

Some indications of where it would lead are provided by Jane Bennett's book *Vibrant Matter*, which wants us to acknowledge a "vital materiality" running through all matter.[24] In her preface, Bennett explicitly advocates the cultivation of anthropomorphism—at the expense of the anthropocentrism that she identifies among historical materialists focusing on the material constraints and contexts of human agency.[25] Drawing on a long line of philosophers from Spinoza to Deleuze, Bennett's agenda frequently approaches mysticism, as when she asserts that deep within inanimate things is "an *inexplicable* vitality or energy, a moment of independence from and resistance to us and other bodies: a kind of thing-power."[26] Her analysis of a major electrical blackout in North America in 2003, in attributing agency to the grid itself, appears to largely absolve humans from responsibility for the operation of their technologies. Referring to Latour, Bennett asserts that electricity itself was an "actant" contributing to the power failure. Rather than account for the blackout in terms of flaws in the design of the grid, which would ultimately implicate the fallibility of human engineers, she seriously seems to propose that the grid itself bears some of the responsibility. Her theory of vibrant matter, she writes, "presents individuals as simply incapable of bearing *full* responsibility for their effects."[27] "In a world of distributed agency," she continues, it is "virtuous" to hesitate about assigning singular blame to specific humans. The implications of her argument for our general approach to technological failures are as absurd as the infamous medieval trials where insects could be prosecuted for ruining harvests. It is one thing to acknowledge that responsibility for failure is more difficult to determine the more complex technologies are—or that a particular technology is ill-designed and needs to be recalled—but to propose that the artifacts bear part of the responsibility is a blatant case of fetishism.

The displacement of accountability from humans to objects is the most obvious ideological implication of Latour's actor-network theory and Bennett's brand of vitalism. The relinquishment of human responsibility goes hand in hand with the celebration of technology's agentive powers. It is not a coincidence that both Latour and Bennett[28] identify with the kind of "big and bold" investments in technology that are advocated by the ecomodernist *Breakthrough Institute*.[29] Yet, alongside technological hubris[30] Bennett paradoxically advocates ecological sensitivity. She proposes that recognition of a "vigorous materiality" would make humans more disposed to live sustainably and with a "more refined sensitivity" to an anthropomorphized nature that is no longer perceived as an "environment" but as "the-outside-that-is-inside-too." By giving up "the futile attempt to disentangle the human from the non-human," we would be able to "engage more civilly, strategically, and subtly" with non-humans.³¹ But this injunction addressed (exclusively) to humans seems contradictory. Are not the insights and capabilities on which such engagement is to be founded specifically *human*? Should not this acknowledgment in fact *reinforce* the distinction between humans and nonhumans?

The analytical boundaries that Latour and Bennett want to abolish are finally indispensable. For the anthropologist Eduardo Kohn, there is a significant distinction to be made between living and nonliving things. Drawing on his ethnographic fieldwork among the *runa* of lowland Ecuador, he admonishes post-humanists³² for flattening "important distinctions between humans and other kinds of beings, as well as those between selves and objects."³³ What distinguishes living from nonliving things is that the former use *signs* to "represent the world in some way or another."³⁴ In not recognizing nonhuman forms of semiotic representation, Kohn argues, post-humanists like Deleuze, Bennett, and Latour ultimately perpetuate the "Cartesian dualism" that fails to acknowledge modes of subjectivity that are intermediate to human mind and "unfeeling matter."³⁵ What humans and living nonhumans have in common is that they are *selves*. Selves have unique semiotic properties that distinguish them from objects such as artifacts. To treat nonhumans generically—"indiscriminately lumping together things and beings"—is to miss this. Objects can be sources of resistance, but not agency. To conflate resistance and agency "blinds us to the kinds of agency that do in fact exist beyond the human." Contra actor-network theorists like Latour and Bennett, Kohn concludes, "Selves, not things, qualify as agents. Resistance is not the same as agency. Nor, contra Bennett (2010), does materiality confer vitality."³⁶

What, then, is the difference between human and nonhuman beings? As C. S. Peirce long ago theorized and anthropologists have understood at least since Leslie White,³⁷ what makes humans exceptional is that special kind of sign that has a purely conventional relation to its referent, i.e., the *symbol*. As Kohn observes, "[s]ymbolic reference, that which makes humans unique, is an emergent dynamic that is nested within [the] broader semiosis of life from which it stems and on which it depends."³⁸ In other words, while semiosis distinguishes living from nonliving, symbolism distinguishes humans from nonhumans. Latour, Bennett, and other post-humanists appear to confer no significance to either of these distinctions, which should invalidate their flattening of ontologies implied by notions of "distributed agency." The distinction between symbolic and nonsymbolic aspects is what justifies the analytical distinction between society (or culture) and nature: phenomena classified as "social" are contingent on symbols—their configuration relies on processes of symbolic communication. To the extent that the global environmental dilemmas of the Anthropocene have a social component, this is an indication of the pervasive reverberations of human economies and technologies—phenomena founded on and imbued with symbolic systems—throughout the planetary biosphere.

The rejection of human exceptionalism and the vitalization of abiotic matter tend to go hand in hand among post-humanists. Proponents of both these kinds of claims tend to profess that their aim is to encourage more egalitarian and empathetic relations between humans and nonhumans. When focused on the relations between humans and other species, this appeal is understandable but inevitably asymmetric, given that it can clearly only be directed at humans (rather than, say, mosquitoes or ticks). When applied to abiotic material entities such as artifacts, it is even more decisively asymmetric.

The Naturalization of Technology

In offering a genealogy of post-humanism, Cary Wolfe traces its roots to the emergence of cybernetics in the late 1940s.[39] The interdisciplinary field of cybernetics blurred the boundary between living organisms and machines and between humans and nonhumans. Originally aimed at constructing military technologies—such as goal-seeking missiles—that imitate organisms, it focused on communicational processes in living and nonliving systems. The goal of cybernetics was to replicate life through technology, a project that has led to modern advances in robotics and artificial intelligence. The connection between cybernetics and the material turn is evident in what Wolfe calls the "locus classicus" of post-humanism: Donna Haraway's *A Cyborg Manifesto* (1985). As Haraway explains in her introduction to the manifesto, a "cyborg is a cybernetic organism, a hybrid of machine and organism, a creature of social reality as well as a creature of fiction."[40] Much of what Haraway has published is clearly intended to undermine human exceptionalism: she not only conveys the extent to which human life is mutually entangled with that of other species, but also argues that the human species is no more unique than other forms of life. In recent years, Haraway's influential challenges to conventional distinctions between humans and nonhumans have been applied to the global ecological predicament of the Anthropocene.[41] It is difficult to determine what the implications of her position are, not least with regards to accountability for ecological degradation.[42] At one point Haraway asserts that "[w]e are all responsible to and for shaping conditions for multispecies flourishing,"[43] but against the background of her constant insistence on dissolving boundaries between humans and nonhumans, we must ask to whom or *what* her appeal to responsibility is directed.

Haraway and Latour are foundational exponents of the material turn. Together with philosopher Don Ihde and physicist-cum-sociologist Andrew Pickering, they were both invited to contribute chapters and interviews to a collection called *Chasing Technoscience: Matrix for Materiality*.[44] In his introduction to the collection, Ihde suggests that it represents the convergence of two projects that had begun in 1979: Latour's sociology of science and his own philosophy of technology. Both approaches, he observes, have shown a special sensitivity to the role of the material dimension in scientific practice—a dimension that is often ignored by philosophers, sociologists, and anthropologists. Originally a biologist, Haraway explains to her interviewer how her notion of the cyborg was born:

> What interested me was the way of conceiving of us all as communication systems, whether we are animate or inanimate, whether we are animals or

plants, human beings or the planet herself, Gaia, or machines of various kinds. This common coin of theorizing existence, this common ontology of everything as communication-control-system was what interested me.[45]

For Haraway, the approach of cybernetics justified a blurring of the boundary between life and nonlife. For Gregory Bateson, the anthropologist-cum-biologist who is recognized as one of the founders of cybernetics, the challenge was to unravel the logic of communication in living systems, which provided more practically oriented cyberneticians with knowledge for designing information-processing technologies.[46] Such pervasive focus on the internal wiring of machines—that is, the *ideas* embodied in them—has precluded considerations of their material metabolism. Even the proponents of SCOT—the social construction of technology[47]—have neglected the fact that advanced technological systems, like organisms, rely on specific inputs of material substances, and at specific rates. While this clearly does not apply to simpler artifacts like speed bumps, door stops, or architectural design, it most certainly is the case for engines, computers, robots, and high-tech laboratories.

Technologies are indeed socially constructed, but this "social" includes the ratios at which material inputs are procured—generally through asymmetric resource flows organized by the world market. Societies and their technological systems have a metabolism—a *social* metabolism—that has very rarely concerned the sociologists, historians, and philosophers of technology. Even the cyberneticians and their post-humanist heirs have ignored the dependence of technological efficacy on the (asymmetric) structure of global resource flows. In this regard, the material turn spearheaded by Latour and Haraway has strangely disregarded the materiality of world trade, and its manifestations in the accumulation of technological infrastructure in core areas of the world-system. To fundamentally challenge the conventional distinction between the material and the social, we must recognize that the materiality of our artifacts is itself socially constituted. Rather than simply upgrade the role of materiality in society, as if it implied an "agency" equal to purposive action, we must understand the very stuff of technologies as products of social exchange. Artifacts do not just have social consequences stemming from their material properties—they owe their existence and material properties to social processes. The phenomenon of modern technology thus dissolves the boundary between the material and the social in a more profound way than generally imagined by proponents of the material turn.

Pickering's contribution to the above-mentioned volume illustrates two recurrent shortcomings of the material turn: it approaches biological evolution and the development of technology as continuous phenomena, and it completely disregards the global political economy—the intra-specific material flows— on which the emergence of advanced technologies is contingent. Jointly, these two flaws naturalize—and thus ideologically neutralize—what are *socionatural* instruments of exploitation.[48] Pickering refers to the cybernetician W. Ross Ashby's conviction that clocks and organisms are "simply at the extremes of a single scale" and to Deleuze and Guattari to argue that "self-organization" and other cybernetic concepts cover similar processes "over the entire range of the inanimate and the animate."[49] The aspiration of cybernetics to create artificial life has deflected our attention from the skewed political and distributive conditions of technological progress. Blurring the boundary between life and technological nonlife has blinded us to the widening economic gap between the victims and the beneficiaries of accumulation. As ideologies are prone to do, the image of technology as artificial life obscures social inequalities by representing them as natural.

Capitalist Modernity and Its Critics

The traditional distinction between nature and artifice goes back to Aristotle. In this tradition, technological artifacts have been understood as generated by the external intentions of their (human) makers, whereas living organisms are animated by inner purposes that derive from nature, not from humans. According to Martin Heidegger, it is the colonization of the Earth by technocratic modernity that makes it increasingly difficult to determine where the artificial starts and the natural ends. Modernity not only transforms nature and humans into instruments, but simultaneously *naturalizes* technology.[50] The ideological naturalization of technology can be traced from the *Naturphilosophie* of Schelling and other late-eighteenth-century German Romantics through Vernadsky and Teilhard to cybernetics, Lovelock's Gaia hypothesis, complexity theory, and the post-humanism of Latour and Haraway.[51] Common to these perspectives is the understanding of human technology as a creative expression of the inherent potential of nature itself. As Daniel Andersson observes, artificial intelligence and robotics illustrate how what Heidegger deplored as the instrumentalization of the human has morphed into the humanization of the instrument—that is, literal anthropomorphism.[52]

The "naturalization" of modern technology assumes many forms and is widespread among people in general. It obscures the obscene differences in wages and purchasing power that are a condition for the very existence of such technology, granting capitalism's central instruments of exploitation the ideological appearance of political neutrality and self-evident virtue. David Nye expresses what is no doubt a predominant attitude:

> Technology is not something that comes from outside us; it is not new; it is a fundamental human expression. It cannot easily be separated from social evolution, for the use of tools stretches back millennia [...] It is hard to imagine a culture that is pre-technological or a future that is post-technological.[53]

Such a continuity between premodern tools and modern technology was precisely what earlier philosophers of technology vehemently denied. Martin Heidegger, for instance, asserted that "modern technology [...] is, in contrast to the older handicraft technology, something completely different and therefore new."[54] As Ihde reminds us, the reaction of early philosophers of technology to the machinery of modernity was largely *negative*.[55] The shift in attitude—to recent discourse in which mention of "dystopian godfathers" such as Heidegger, Ellul, Mumford, and Marcuse has mostly disappeared[56]—is noteworthy. The fact that the dystopian apprehensions of technology articulated by Heidegger and others is becoming increasingly difficult to grasp for modern people may reflect the advance of a blind-spot akin to the proverbial blindness of fish to the water they swim in. If anything, this should increase our curiosity about what it was about modern technology that made the "dystopian godfathers" so uneasy.

In a chapter critically examining Heidegger's and Albert Borgmann's approaches to technology, Andrew Feenberg synthesizes some of their main concerns. Feenberg begins by observing that philosophers have traditionally been indifferent to the material world and now generally "feel safe in ignoring technology altogether."[57] He summarizes the "determinist premises of an earlier generation" in the field as follows:

> For these thinkers modernity continues to be characterized by a unique form of technical action and thought that threatens nontechnical values as it extends itself ever deeper into social life. [...] The results of this process are disastrous: the triumph of technological thinking, the domination of nature, and the shattering of community. On this account, modernity is fundamentally flawed.[58]

Drawing on Heidegger and Borgmann, Feenberg analyzes the modern phenomenon of technology in terms of how its instrumentalism—as both outlook and practice—implies a systematic decontextualization, reduction, autonomization, and strategic positioning of its various components. Whether humans or natural things, all the parts to be integrated in a technological system are alienated from their original contexts and stripped of their original diversity of relations and qualities so that only their technical usefulness remains. Once perceptually and practically reduced to autonomous objects valued only for their functional utility, humans and natural items are available for incorporation in abstract, predesigned production processes. Expressed in this way, Heidegger's and Borgmann's critiques of modern technology duplicate, within the technological sphere, the concerns of Marxist and substantivist economists about the logic of the market and more general sociological analyses of the condition of modernity.[59] Heidegger's concepts of "instrumentalization" and "enframing" clearly denote the same underlying societal logic that Marx and Polanyi denounced as commodification and the classical sociologists identified through a number of concepts synthesized by Anthony Giddens as processes of "disembedding."[60] The classical sociologists—including Marx, Durkheim, Weber, Simmel, and Tönnies—were all engaged in intense reflection over the radical transformations of European society during the emergence of what we today call modernity, and they clearly understood how closely connected these transformations were to the expansion of market exchange.

It is no doubt reasonable—and in line with what numerous critics of modernity have argued—to trace these convergences among classical philosophers of technology, economy, and society to the logic of general-purpose money. In transforming all humans and all things into interchangeable or "fungible" commodities—as "labor-power," "energy," "materials," and "resources" in general—the artifact of all-purpose money encourages humans to pursue transactions that inexorably generate the disembedding and repositioning processes that are foundational to modernity. The aggregate logic of general-purpose money is precisely what we know as capitalism, and its repercussions are as "instrumentalizing" for social relations as they are for our perception of nature. If such dystopian perspectives on society seem meaningless or pointless to modern people, it is no doubt because they can no longer *imagine* alternative ways of relating to other humans and nonhumans. The socially polarizing and ecologically destructive processes of capitalism are generated by the relentless algorithms emanating from the meme of all-purpose money—this infinitely powerful idea which makes all values commensurable and all things convertible into profit. It is deeply paradoxical that the post-humanists and neo-materialists, given their adamant assertions about the agency of abiotic things, have not focused their attention on this most potent of artifacts.

A major source of confusion among proponents of the material turn appears to be the fact that objects of material culture, like natural objects, are charged with meaning—for the humans who encounter them. Actor-network theorists tend to conceive of such meanings as features of the objects themselves, rather than as attributed to them by human agents. Latour writes:

> Signification is a property of all agents, in that they never cease to have agency; this is equally true of [Tolstoy's Marshal] Kutuzov, the Mississippi, the CRF receptor, and the gravity through which bodies "comprehend" and mutually "influence" one another. [...] In other words, existence and signification are synonyms. *As long as they are acting, agents signify*.[61]

Latour thus equates signification with agency. In his view, it seems, whenever an object is experienced as having some kind of meaning, it is *acting*. This clearly implies that, in the worldview of actor-network theory, existence is synonymous not only with signification, but with agency. To exist is to act. It would thus be impossible for an object *not* to act. But if existence is synonymous with agency, why not simply dispense with the concept of agency altogether? In the usage advocated by actor-network theory, the concept is completely redundant: it could not possibly discriminate between entities that do versus do not have agency. Among the many remarkable implications of Latour's equation should be concessions to astrologists regarding the agency of stars, to animists regarding that of geological formations, and to devout Catholics regarding crucifixes and relics.

Conclusions

Proponents of the material turn are justified in wanting to grant material aspects greater significance in accounts of social life than such aspects have previously been accorded. Traditional approaches in fields ranging from philosophy and anthropology to economics and engineering indeed tend to have an idealist bias. However, the new materialists have generally failed to integrate their emphasis on materiality with insights on the global, societal exchange relations that *condition* the physical constitution of artifacts. Prototypically, Bruno Latour's concern with the material agency of modern artifacts disavows any consideration of the social, asymmetric resource flows of which the artifacts are a manifestation—and on which their professed agency is contingent. The focus on individual artifacts thus deflects attention from the global political economy that has brought them into existence. This is fetishism in the classical Marxist sense. Rather than investigate and expose the pervasive human inclination toward fetishism—the obsessive manipulation of artifacts that obscures social relations by deflecting attention from them—the neo-materialists are in effect proposing that we ought to *embrace* fetishism.[62] If objects appear to have agency of their own, the new materialists argue, it is because they do. This is one of three principal ways in which the material turn may serve to ideologically buttress the capitalist world order.

A second sense in which the new materiality has ideological implications is its displacement of responsibility from humans to artifacts. As we have seen, the neo-materialist Jane Bennett explicitly asserts that her vitalist approach absolves humans from some of the accountability for the repercussions of the technological systems in which they are entangled. This is to disregard the extent to which technologies may be deliberately imbued with political interests.

A third way in which the material turn tends to depoliticize technology is by naturalizing it. This inclination has a genealogy as deep as industrialization itself, stretching back to eighteenth-century Romantics like Friedrich Schelling. In blurring the boundary between nature and artifice, post-humanists like Donna Haraway in effect defuse the feasibility of a political critique of modern technology. To classify a phenomenon as "natural" is to exonerate it from critique.

Paradoxically, the neo-materialist insight that artifacts powerfully contribute to the organization of human social relations has not been applied to the foundational role of general-purpose money in the capitalist world order over the past three centuries. In conjunction with the three above-mentioned ideological consequences of the material turn, this omission reinforces the conclusion that current concerns with the agency of nonliving things finally serve to avert critical attention from the insidious operation of global capitalism.

Notes

1   Parts of this chapter overlap with my article in *American Anthropologist* 123, no. 4 (2021): 753–66.
2   R. E. Allen, *The Concise Oxford Dictionary of Current English*, Eighth edition (Oxford: Clarendon Press, 1990), 753, 1173.
3   I use the word "fetishism" for the attribution to nonliving things of properties documented only in living beings, such as sentience and purposive agency.
4   Drawing on mortuary practices in ancient Egypt, Lynn Meskell discusses how mummies epitomize the ambiguous status of the corpse, suspended between subject and object, sign and thing, transitoriness and permanence. See Lynn Meskell,

"Objects in the Mirror Appear Closer than They Are," in *Materiality*, ed. Daniel Miller (Durham: Duke University Press, 2005). Referring to Meskell's chapter, Miller observes that humans may attempt to transcend the transient materiality of mortal existence *by means of* material monuments (e.g., pyramids) and the preservation of material forms (mummification) that paradoxically express the *im*material aspects of reality. Whether art, religion, or finance, Miller concludes, "[h]umanity constantly returns to vast projects devoted to immateriality," but finds that "immateriality can only be expressed through materiality" (Daniel Miller, "Materiality: An Introduction," in *Materiality*, ed. Daniel Miller [Durham: Duke University Press, 2005], 16 and 28).

5   Allen, *The Concise Oxford Dictionary*, 731.
6   Bruno Latour, *Aramis or the Love of Technology* (Cambridge, MA: Harvard University Press, 1996).
7   Latour, *Aramis*, vii–viii.
8   Bruno Latour, *We Have Never Been Modern* (Cambridge, MA: Harvard University Press, 1993).
9   Bruno Latour, *Reassembling the Social: An Introduction to Actor-Network-Theory* (Oxford: Oxford University Press, 2005), 71; emphasis in original.
10 The use of the word "social" for some nonhuman species of animals also implies communication, but using other types of signs than symbols. Cf. Alf Hornborg, "Artifacts Have Consequences, Not Agency," *European Journal of Social Theory* 20, no. 1 (2017): 95–110.
11 Latour, *Reassembling the Social*, 72.
12 Shirley S. Strum and Bruno Latour, "Redefining the Social Link: From Baboons to Humans," *Social Science Information* 26, no. 4 (1987): 783–802.
13 Bruno Latour, *On the Modern Cult of the Factish Gods* (Durham, NC: Duke University Press, 2010), 11.
14 Actually, the Portuguese word *feitico* also referred to the magical amulets used in fifteenth- and sixteenth-century Europe (Geert Mommersteeg, "Allah's Words as Amulet," *Etnofoor* 3, no. 1 [1990]: 63–76, 64).
15 Latour, *On the Modern Cult*, 21.
16 Latour, *On the Modern Cult*, 30–1.
17 Bruno Latour, *Politics of Nature: How to Bring the Sciences into Democracy* (Cambridge, MA: Harvard University Press, 2004), 237–8.
18 Latour, *Politics of Nature*, 246.
19 Allen, *The Concise Oxford Dictionary*, 1214.
20 As Gregory Bateson long ago reminded us, there is a crucial difference between the ways in which a rock and a dog will respond to being kicked. Whereas Bateson's emphasis was on the different sources of energy propelling the movement of the rock and the dog, we may just as well focus on their very different capacities for *chosing* a response—that is, agency. See Gregory Bateson, *Steps to an Ecology of Mind* (Frogmore: Paladin, 1972), 379 and 457.
21 Bruno Latour, *Facing Gaia: Eight Lectures on the New Climatic Regime* (Cambridge: Polity, 2017); Bruno Latour, *Down to Earth: Politics in the New Climatic Regime* (Cambridge: Polity, 2018).
22 Latour enthusiastically adopts James Lovelock's so-called Gaia hypothesis, according to which the biosphere functions like a gigantic organism.
23 Déborah Danowski and Eduardo Viveiros de Castro, *The Ends of the World* (Cambridge: Polity, 2017), 100.

24 Jane Bennett, *Vibrant Matter: A Political Ecology of Things* (Durham: Duke University Press, 2010).
25 Bennett, *Vibrant Matter*, xvi.
26 Bennett, *Vibrant Matter*, 18; emphasis added.
27 Bennett, *Vibrant Matter*, 37.
28 Bennett, *Vibrant Matter*, 153–4, n. 18.
29 John Asafu-Adjaye, Linus Blomqvist, Stewart Brand, Barry Brook, Ruth DeFries, Erle Ellis, Christopher Foreman et al., *An Ecomodernist Manifesto*, 2015, available at http://www.ecomodernism.org.
30 On the final page of *Vibrant Matter*, Bennett asserts that "ecohealth" will sometimes "call for grander, more dramatic and violent expenditures of human energy" (Bennett, *Vibrant Matter*, 122).
31 Bennett, *Vibrant Matter*, 120 and 116.
32 Although the category of "post-humanism" does not coincide perfectly with the material turn, there is considerable overlap.
33 Eduardo Kohn, *How Forests Think: Toward an Anthropology beyond the Human* (Berkeley: University of California Press, 2013), 7.
34 Kohn, *How Forests Think*, 9.
35 Kohn, *How Forests Think*, 40.
36 Kohn, *How Forests Think*, 91–2.
37 Leslie A. White, "The Symbol: The Origin and Basis of Human Behavior," *Philosophy of Science* 7, no. 4 (1940): 451–63.
38 Kohn, *How Forests Think*, 55.
39 Cary Wolfe, *What Is Posthumanism?* (Minneapolis: University of Minnesota Press, 2010), xii–xiii.
40 Donna J. Haraway, "A Cyborg Manifesto: Science, Technology, and Socialist Feminism in the Late Twentieth Century," in *Philosophy of Technology—The Technological Condition: An Anthology*, ed. Robert C. Scharff and Val Dusek (Oxford: Wiley Blackwell, 2014). In transcending the boundary between nature and artifice, the cyborg also transcends mortality. Meskell writes that the mummy is "the first cyborg," as transcending bodily death exemplifies the contemporary "desire for a cyborg future" (Meskell, "Objects in the Mirror," 59).
41 Donna J. Haraway, *Staying with the Trouble: Making Kin in the Chthulucene* (Durham: Duke University Press, 2016).
42 Alf Hornborg, "Dithering While the Planet Burns: Anthropologists' Approaches to the Anthropocene," *Reviews in Anthropology* 46, no. 2–3 (2017): 61–77.
43 Haraway, *Staying with the Trouble*, 29.
44 Don Ihde and Evan Selinger, ed., *Chasing Technoscience: Matrix for Materiality* (Bloomington: Indiana University Press, 2003).
45 Ihde and Evn Selinger, *Chasing Technoscience*, 47–8.
46 Bateson, *Steps to an Ecology of Mind*. For Bateson, however, such attempts at technologically replicating living systems did not justify a blurring of the boundary between technologies and organisms.
47 Wiebe E. Bijker, Thomas P. Hughes, and Trevor J. Pinch, ed., *The Social Construction of Technological Systems: New Directions in the Sociology and History of Technology* (Cambridge, MA: MIT Press, 1987).
48 Alf Hornborg, *Nature, Society, and Justice in the Anthropocene: Unraveling the Money-Energy-Technology Complex* (Cambridge: Cambridge University Press, 2019).

49 Andrew Pickering, "On Becoming: Imagination, Metaphysics, and the Mangle," in *Chasing Technoscience: Matrix for Materiality*, ed. Don Ihde and Evan Selinger (Bloomington: Indiana University Press, 2003).
50 Daniel Andersson, *Artificial Earth: On the Genealogy of Planetary Technicity*, Linköping Studies in Arts and Sciences No. 708 (Linköping: Linköping University, 2020). Heidegger's critique of the relentless globalization of technical instrumentalization is strikingly congruent with Marx's critique of the capitalist obsession with the endless growth of production for its own sake, which famously applied the concept of "fetishism" to political economy. For Heidegger, says Andersson, everything is "made *equivalent*, replaceable, and calculable in terms of uniform exchange value. Everything acquires a price, such that there is seemingly nothing that cannot be commodified and put up for sale" (Andersson, *Artificial Earth*, 64–5). Ihde writes that, for Heidegger, Technology (with a capital "T") is a way of seeing the world as "a kind of resource well […] in which all of nature becomes an energy resource for human instrumental use" (Don Ihde, *Philosophy of Technology: An Introduction* [New York: Paragon House, 1993], 41).
51 Regarding Gaia, Latour asks, "[W]hat difference is there, for a 'superorganism,' between the status of 'sentient being' and that of 'self-regulated system'?" (Latour, *Facing Gaia*, 95). This should be obvious to anyone who can distinguish between a living organism and a market or cybernetic machine. As Kohn reminds us, "Entities that exhibit self-organization, such as crystals, snowflakes, or whirlpools, are not alive. Nor, despite their name, do they involve a self" (Kohn, *How Forests Think*, 55).
52 Andersson, *Artificial Earth*.
53 David E. Nye, *Technology Matters: Questions to Live with* (Cambridge, MA: MIT Press, 2006), 210.
54 Martin Heidegger, "The Question Concerning Technology," in *Philosophy of Technology—The Technological Condition: An Anthology*, ed. Robert C. Scharff and Val Dusek (Oxford: Wiley Blackwell, 2014).
55 Ihde, *Philosophy of Technology: An Introduction*, 32–3.
56 Don Ihde, "Philosophy of Technology (and/or Technoscience?): 1996–2010," *Techné* 14, no. 1 (2010): 26–35, 29–30.
57 Andrew Feenberg, "Philosophy of Technology at the Crossroads: Critique of Heidegger and Borgmann," in *Philosophy of Technology—The Technological Condition: An Anthology*, ed. Robert C. Scharff and Val Dusek (Oxford: Wiley Blackwell, 2014), 362.
58 Feenberg, "Philosophy of Technology at the Crossroads," 362.
59 Karl Polanyi, *The Great Transformation: The Political and Economic Origins of Our Time* (Boston: Beacon, 1957); Anthony Giddens, *The Consequences of Modernity* (Cambridge: Polity, 1990); Zygmunt Bauman, *Liquid Modernity* (Cambridge: Polity, 2000).
60 These convergences are recognized in Tim Ingold's important insight that reflections on the emergence of a disembedded technology are cognate to those on the emergence of a disembedded economy. See Tim Ingold, "Eight Themes in the Anthropology of Technology," *Social Analysis: The International Journal of Social and Cultural Practice* 41, no. 1 (1997): 106–38, 108.
61 Latour, *Facing Gaia*, 69–70.
62 Latour, *On the Modern Cult*. To Latour, the very idea of fetishism is abhorrent: "To accuse something of being a fetish is the ultimate gratuitous, disrespectful, insane, and barbarous gesture" (Bruno Latour, "Why Has Critique Run Out of Steam? From Matters of Fact to Matters of Concern," *Critical Inquiry* 30 [2004]: 225–48, 243).

Cited Works

Allen, R. E. *The Concise Oxford Dictionary of Current English*. Eighth edition. Oxford: Clarendon Press, 1990.
Andersson, Daniel. *Artificial Earth: On the Genealogy of Planetary Technicity*. Linköping Studies in Arts and Sciences No. 708. Linköping University, 2020.
Asafu-Adjaye, John, Linus Blomqvist, Stewart Brand, Barry Brook, Ruth DeFries, Erle Ellis, and Christopher Foreman et al., *An Ecomodernist Manifesto*. 2015. Available at http://www.ecomodernism.org.
Bateson, Gregory. *Steps to an Ecology of Mind*. Frogmore: Paladin, 1972.
Bauman, Zygmunt. *Liquid Modernity*. Cambridge: Polity, 2000.
Bennett, Jane. *Vibrant Matter: A Political Ecology of Things*. Durham: Duke University Press, 2010.
Bijker, Wiebe E., Thomas P. Hughes, and Trevor J. Pinch, ed. *The Social Construction of Technological Systems: New Directions in the Sociology and History of Technology*. Cambridge, MA: MIT Press, 1987.
Danowski, Déborah and Eduardo Viveiros de Castro. *The Ends of the World*. Cambridge: Polity, 2017.
Feenberg, Andrew. "Philosophy of Technology at the Crossroads: Critique of Heidegger and Borgmann." In *Philosophy of Technology—The Technological Condition: An Anthology*, edited by Robert C. Scharff and Val Dusek, 362–74. Oxford: Wiley Blackwell, 2014.
Giddens, Anthony. *The Consequences of Modernity*. Cambridge: Polity, 1990.
Haraway, Donna J. "A Cyborg Manifesto: Science, Technology, and Socialist Feminism in the Late Twentieth Century." In: *Philosophy of Technology—The Technological Condition: An Anthology*, edited by Robert C. Scharff and Val Dusek, 610–30. Oxford: Wiley Blackwell, 2014.
Haraway, Donna J. *Staying with the Trouble: Making Kin in the Chthulucene*. Durham: Duke University Press, 2016.
Heidegger, Martin. "The Question Concerning Technology." In *Philosophy of Technology—The Technological Condition: An Anthology*, edited by Robert C. Scharff and Val Dusek, 305–17. Oxford: Wiley Blackwell, 2014.
Hornborg, Alf. "Artifacts Have Consequences, Not Agency." *European Journal of Social Theory* 20, no. 1 (2017): 95–110.
Hornborg, Alf. "Dithering While the Planet Burns: Anthropologists' Approaches to the Anthropocene." *Reviews in Anthropology* 46, no. 2–3 (2017): 61–77.
Hornborg, Alf. *Nature, Society, and Justice in the Anthropocene: Unraveling the Money-Energy-Technology Complex*. Cambridge: Cambridge University Press, 2019.
Ihde, Don. *Philosophy of Technology: An Introduction*. New York: Paragon House, 1993.
Ihde, Don. "Philosophy of Technology (and/or Technoscience?): 1996–2010." *Techné* 14, no. 1 (2010): 26–35.
Ihde, Don and Evan Selinger, ed. *Chasing Technoscience: Matrix for Materiality*. Bloomington: Indiana University Press, 2003.
Ingold, Tim. "Eight Themes in the Anthropology of Technology." *Social Analysis: The International Journal of Social and Cultural Practice* 41, no. 1 (1997): 106–38.
Kohn, Eduardo. *How Forests Think: Toward an Anthropology beyond the Human*. Berkeley: University of California Press, 2013.
Latour, Bruno. *We Have Never Been Modern*. Cambridge, MA: Harvard University Press, 1993.

Latour, Bruno. *Aramis or the Love of Technology*. Cambridge, MA: Harvard University Press, 1996.
Latour, Bruno. *Politics of Nature: How to Bring the Sciences into Democracy*. Cambridge, MA: Harvard University Press, 2004a.
Latour, Bruno. "Why Has Critique Run Out of Steam? From Matters of Fact to Matters of Concern." *Critical Inquiry* 30 (2004): 225–48.
Latour, Bruno. *Reassembling the Social: An Introduction to Actor-Network-Theory*. Oxford: Oxford University Press, 2005.
Latour, Bruno. *On the Modern Cult of the Factish Gods*. Durham, NC: Duke University Press, 2010.
Latour, Bruno. *Facing Gaia: Eight Lectures on the New Climatic Regime*. Cambridge: Polity, 2017.
Latour, Bruno. *Down to Earth: Politics in the New Climatic Regime*. Cambridge: Polity, 2018.
Meskell, Lynn. "Objects in the Mirror Appear Closer than They Are." In *Materiality*, edited by Daniel Miller, 51–71. Durham: Duke University Press, 2005.
Miller, Daniel. "Materiality: An Introduction." In *Materiality*, edited by Daniel Miller, 1–50. Durham: Duke University Press, 2005.
Mommersteeg, Geert. "Allah's Words as Amulet." *Etnofoor* 3, no. 1 (1990): 63–76.
Nye, David E. *Technology Matters: Questions to Live with*. Cambridge, MA: MIT Press, 2006.
Pickering, Andrew. "On Becoming: Imagination, Metaphysics, and the Mangle." In *Chasing Technoscience: Matrix for Materiality*, edited by Don Ihde and Evan Selinger, 96–116. Bloomington: Indiana University Press, 2003.
Polanyi, Karl. *The Great Transformation: The Political and Economic Origins of Our Time*. Boston: Beacon, 1957.
Strum, Shirley S. and Bruno Latour. "Redefining the Social Link: From Baboons to Humans." *Social Science Information* 26, no. 4 (1987): 783–802.
White, Leslie A. "The Symbol: The Origin and Basis of Human Behavior." *Philosophy of Science* 7, no. 4 (1940): 451–63.
Wolfe, Cary. *What Is Posthumanism?* Minneapolis: University of Minnesota Press, 2010.

Chapter 8

THE KANTIAN CATASTROPHE? ANTI-CORRELATIONISM AND THE ABSOLUTE

Lars Lodberg and Jacob Lautrup

Perhaps the most distinguishing feature of the various strands of ontologically ambitious thinking that have become associated with the much discussed and rarely adopted term "speculative realism" is the common opposition to the ostensibly anti-absolutist tendency in philosophy that Quentin Meillassoux has dubbed "correlationism." In *After Finitude*, Meillassoux identifies the rise of "correlationism" with Kant's transcendental turn[1]—the attempt to ground scientific knowledge by undermining the capacity of metaphysics to cognize supersensible truths independently of experience. For Meillassoux, this "Kantian catastrophe" involved the opposite of what was called for. Rather than de-centering subjectivity—which would have been a "true" Copernican revolution—Kant repositioned the objects of our experience as "mere" appearances, revolving around the cognizing subjectivity, hence depriving them of absolute independence of either thought or givenness and making for a "Ptolomaic counter-revolution" instead.[2]

We believe that Meillassoux's diagnosis is flawed in various ways that turn on the misidentification of Kant's transcendental turn as a traditionally ontological thesis rather than a methodological or epistemic thesis about the conditions of cognition. Thus, a central aim of this contribution is to present a corrective to Meillassoux's criticism of Kantian "correlationism." Though Meillassoux's diagnosis of so much contemporary thought as "correlationist" is instrumental in the sense of serving as the contrast to which his own ontology of contingency or *hyperchaos* is to be developed, we take Meillassoux's use of "correlationism" as a term of art to misrepresent not only Kant's own thought, but also the significance of transcendental philosophy in general. Thus, we take our defense of Kant to raise questions about the sustainability of Meillasoux's speculative realist project. Indeed, if anti-correlationism is poorly formulated, what potential remains of the striving to represent the absolute in a way that provides cognition rather than empty speculation?

However, we also find in Meillassoux's project a commitment to seek the absolute or unconditioned behind all mere appearances and a critique of speculative metaphysics that is very similar to Kant's own critique of dialectical reasoning. Indeed, it seems to us that Meillassoux's critique of what he calls *metaphysics* is surprisingly close to Kant's critique of what he called "speculative metaphysics."[3] Hence, where Meillassoux mainly differs from Kant cannot be in the affirmation of what Kant denies: the cognition of the absolute, because the absolute knowledge Kant denies turns out to be of the same kind of necessary existence that Meillassoux rejects in his attack on the principle of sufficient reason as the principle of metaphysics. Nevertheless, in *After Finitude* Meillassoux singles out Kant or "the Kant-event" in particular as the *correlationism* that is to be overcome by speculation.

We proceed in three steps. Firstly, we present in general terms the notion of correlationism and Meillassoux's attack on what we may call the *disappointment* of correlationism. Secondly, we turn to Meillassoux's criticism of Kant and our defense. Here we point to three problems in Meillassoux's attack on Kant in order to argue that Meillassoux is at best begging the question against Kantian transcendental idealism. Finally, we argue that calling Kant a correlationist is a misnomer and that some sort of speculative access to the absolute is permissible for Kant.

The Disappointment of Correlationism

Meillassoux gives us two versions of what the disappointment of correlationism consists in. The first—de-absolutizing—move is epistemic and historically manifested in the "Kantian catastrophe" or less hauntingly the "Kant-event": "We can never know being as it is in itself but only as it is *correlated* with thought."[4]

The second version is fully ontological but follows from the disappointment of the former. *Strong correlationism* holds, according to Meillassoux, that even *conceiving* being as noncorrelated with thought is nonsensical, and hence that "to be is to be a correlate."[5] This should be understood as the absolutization of the subject, positing absolutely everything as subjective.

Meillassoux's worry in *After Finitude* concerns not so much how we can know things as they are in themselves rather than merely how they appear, but rather how science can represent things that are the way they are independently of how we represent them or whether we have *access* to them. Since the advent of modern science gave us the capacity to represent objects and events in purely mathematized terms, we could allegedly subtract from these representations any relation to ourselves as contingently existing, cognizing animals. This indicated to us irrevocably that the world *could have been* the way it was[6] regardless of whether we had ever appeared, and that there can therefore be no *necessity* in the correlation between these mathematical properties of being and the existence of thinking beings such as ourselves. This reality "anterior to the emergence of the human species," or any form of life, Meillassoux calls *ancestrality*. According to him, such ancestrality is indicated to us by materials (be they actual fossils or decaying isotopes), which he calls *arche-fossils*.[7]

Now, as far as we can see, it is this fact of ancestrality that, according to Meillassoux, poses the biggest problem for the Kantian correlationist. Indeed,

8. The Kantian Catastrophe?   163

Meillassoux considers the very idea of the ancestral entity to be a problem for the would-be correlationist in virtue of its essential anteriority to givenness. The arche-fossil is supposed to have its independence in virtue of its temporal properties, which it therefore must have regardless of its relation to our cognitive faculties. This is intuitively appealing, if the relation of the object to our cognitive faculties is construed as fundamentally temporal and causal. It seems wholly intuitive that, for example, dinosaurs could not in any way depend upon the further fact that humans would eventually come to know of the formers' existence. However, it is clear to us that Kant's distinction between appearances and things in themselves does not imply this kind of dependence. Dinosaurs would qualify as belonging to the realm of appearances insofar as they are posited as existing (having existed) in virtue of having a causally necessary and discernable relation to fossil remnants, which we can experience and interpret. Any talk of "existent dinosaurs," which omitted this relation, would be as idle and noncognitive as a fairy tale about dragons.

While it is far from a settled question in Kant-scholarship, what the metaphysical implications of Kant's transcendental distinction between appearances and thing-in-themselves should be,[8] it seems strange that Meillassoux should prudently identify Kant's version of "correlationism" as an epistemic thesis ("we only have access to the 'correlation'") and yet present the anteriority of objects to humanity as the apparent proof of the failure of "correlationism" to account for what science and common sense can legitimately posit. Indeed it cannot on any account be taken for granted that objects or "being" temporally preceded the emergence of thinking subjects. Rather this can only be established on the basis of the very epistemic conditions Kant identified: forms of intuition and categories of thinking.

Thus, to understand better Meillassoux's criticism of Kant and the alleged "Kantian Catastrophe" we should introduce some definitions. For Meillassoux, the problem of ancestrality ultimately shows us that science is unfounded if we cannot show its mathematical essence to be absolute, i.e., unconditioned. This shows Meillassoux's commitment to what we might call an *absolute foundation thesis (AFT)*.

> *Absolute-foundation thesis* (AFT): Science is unfounded if it does not have an absolute foundation.

On Meillassoux's account AFT is connected to questions of metaphysics and speculation by involving reference to the "absolute." By metaphysics, Meillassoux understands

> *M-Metaphysics*: "every type of thinking that claims to be able to access some form of absolute being or access the absolute through the principle of sufficient reason."[9]

And by speculation

> *M-Speculation*: "every type of thinking that claims to be able to access some form of absolute"[10]

According to Meillassoux, the key to saving a notion of the absolute in a post-metaphysical world is defining the relationship between speculation and metaphysics in the right way. Thus he gives us

Relation Definition (Rel$_{def}$): All M-metaphysics is M-speculative, but not all M-speculation is M-metaphysical.[11]

Which lets us argue against the so called *de-absolutizing implication*:

De-absolutizing implication: if M-Metaphysics is obsolete so is any talk of the absolute

The Rel$_{def}$ allows us to see the possibility for M-speculation without M-metaphysics and thus talk of an absolute in philosophy without M-metaphysics.

Now, according to Meillassoux, Kant could not acknowledge this possibility because his position did not allow him to subscribe to Rel$_{def}$. So, Kantianism for Meillassoux amounts to

M-Kantianism: "weak correlationism," i.e., an anti-M-metaphysical position which does not acknowledge Rel$_{def}$ and thus subscribes to the (de-absolutizing implication)—making it anti-M-speculation.[12]

We take neither this characterisation of Kant's position nor the more general characterization *correlationism* to be a good fit. Before turning to the reasons why, we should note that the diagnosis of a "Kantian catastrophe" in the history of philosophy need not involve a commitment to a particular reading of Kant's philosophical works. As so many sweeping generalizations made across the history of philosophy, it might be that it should be taken as grounded merely in the historical efficacy of an idea and not in a reading of an actual philosophical position. Thus, Meillassoux could claim that no matter whether or not Kant himself was actually a correlationist, it was the introduction of transcendental idealism (the Kant-event) in the history of philosophy that paved the way for full-blown strong correlationism (or subjectalism). Whether or not this is true does not necessarily hinge on any claims about Kant's actual views. Therefore, our criticism of Meillassoux's reading of Kant and the Kantian Catastrophe does not extend to the historical thesis about the efficacy of Kant or Kantian ideas in the history of philosophy and science.

Nevertheless, as we shall see, Meillassoux's diagnosis of the "Kantian Catastrophe" involves claims about Kant's actual views, which are wrong in very instructive ways. Thus, in what follows, we shall defend Kant against the anti-correlationist charge on two counts. Firstly, we take up Meillassoux's most direct attack on the "transcendental philosopher" in *After Finitude*[13] and argue that Meillassoux at best begs the question against transcendental idealism and further misrepresents core tenets of transcendental idealism in order to get his argument going. Secondly, we criticize the very formulation of Kant's position as correlationism. Here we focus specifically on two points: the notion of access and Kant's understanding of the relation of <being> to <thought>. As we shall see, the fact that speculative thought, as Kant understands it, does not provide us with cognition of objects of possible experience—what Kant calls cognition of nature—does not (at least prima facie) exclude the possibility of M-speculation. Given a permissive interpretation of the access-relation, M-speculation seems permissible for Kant as long as thinking the absolute does not involve any contradictions. As we shall argue, however, for Kant interpreting the access-relation as the same type of access one has to objects of cognition in nature is to confuse two distinct levels or spheres of thought, namely the empirical and transcendental. Hence interpreting "access" in terms of empirical cognition of the absolute amounts to what Kant calls amphibolous reasoning.

Meillassoux's Attack on the "Kantian" Argument against Diachronicity

That we might charge his reasoning with an amphibolous confusion of the empirical and transcendental levels is addressed by Meillassoux. Indeed, as he points out, for the transcendental idealist, the idea of "a 'time of science', in which both bodies and the manifestation of bodies arose, is 'amphibolous'—it conflates the objective being of bodies [...] with the conditions for the objective knowledge of the objective being of bodies."[14] For him, however, the sharp distinction and separation between the two levels of thought are illegitimate simply because he takes the transcendental to be empirically conditioned.

According to Meillassoux, the Kantian argument at its core

> consists in immunizing the conditions of knowledge from any discourse bearing on the objects of science by arguing that a transcendental condition is not an object, and hence simply does not exist. The notion of condition allows one to "de-ontologize" the transcendental by putting it out of reach of any reflection about being.[15]

This is not a controversial statement about transcendental idealism. However, it is exactly what provides Meillassoux with the impetus to attack it. This de-ontologization, namely, is what, according to him, ultimately makes transcendental philosophy incapable of solving the task it sets out to solve: explaining the conditions of natural science. This is because the transcendental subject, and hence the carrier and instantiation of transcendental conditions of knowledge and science is itself empirically, materially conditioned by having a body. Thinking the material emergence of this body, however, is impossible for transcendental philosophy, since thinking this emergence is to think the emergence of the conditions for the *taking place* of the transcendental. However, the body is also a condition for science and hence transcendental philosophy cannot explain the conditions of science, which was its aim.

We should take a closer look at this argument. Meillassoux argues that the transcendental-idealist attempt to distinguish the transcendental conditions of cognition (and hence science) from the empirical conditions for the cognizing subject "is not likely to prevail"[16] because it falls into its own trap of confusing levels of conditions. In the first place this is ignoring the conditions for the transcendental subject. For, according to Meillassoux, though the transcendental itself does not exist as an object, the transcendental subject necessarily must. To show this, Meillassoux starts from the premise that there is some minimal sense in which the transcendental subject *is* (as opposed to *is not*). Hence, "nothing prevents us from reflecting [...] on the conditions under which there is a transcendental subject."[17] One such condition is that the transcendental subject *takes place*. By "taking place" Meillassoux means that "the transcendental, insofar as it refuses all metaphysical dogmatism, remains indissociable from the notion of a *point of view*."[18] The transcendental subject is finite, that is: it does not have cognitive access to the world as a totality, and this notion of finitude arises, Meillassoux claims, from the fact that the transcendental subject "is posited as a point of view on the world."[19] Were this not the case, the subject would not be bound by the forms of intuition and hence a subject not "taking place" *would* be able to cognize the world as a totality. Taking place in the world, however, should according to Meillasoux be understood quite literally as a positioning *in* the world, i.e., "localized among finite objects," which means that the transcendental subject "*remains indissociable from its incarnation in a body.*"[20] This means that the body is a necessary condition for the taking place of the transcendental. As Meillassoux puts it:

> That the transcendental subject has *this* or that body is an empirical matter, but that *it has* a body is a non-empirical condition of its taking place—the body, one could say, is the "retro-transcendental" condition for the subject of knowledge. [...] Objective bodies may not be a sufficient condition for the taking place of the transcendental, but they are certainly a necessary condition of it.[21]

Thus, Meillassoux thinks, the transcendental subject is "*instantiated* rather than *exemplified* by a thinking body."[22] Were there no bodies, there would be no transcendental subjects. Hence, according to Meillassoux, thinking the emergence of the body is thinking the emergence of a necessary condition for the takings place of the transcendental. This is important insofar as science as Meillassoux understands it thinks the emergence of the body, but does so specifically *in time*. But raising the question of the emergence of the body in time means to temporalize and spatialize the emergence of the conditions for the taking place of the transcendental. Science thus investigates a space-time anterior to the spatio-temporal forms of representation. This poses a problem for transcendental philosophy insofar as it cannot think a space-time independently of the forms of intuition. Transcendental philosophy, then, cannot think the emergence of the body. But the body, by being a necessary condition for the transcendental, is also a necessary condition for science even on the transcendental conception of it. Therefore, transcendental philosophy is not adequate to the task it has set itself, namely explaining the conditions for science, since it cannot explain the emergence of a body as one such condition.

In the end, then, it seems Meillassoux takes himself to have shown not only a problem for transcendental idealism but an inherent impossibility of the Kantian transcendental project. Any philosophy that posits the finitude of the cognizing subject as a way to explain the conditions of science is committed to admitting that it cannot explain the conditions for science.

As we see it, there are at least three problems with the above argument.

Problem 1: The first problem concerns the nature of the body as a condition for the "taking place of the transcendental." It seems that Meillassoux conflates having (human) senses with being bound by the forms of intuition. However, it is far from clear why we should think that a subject without a body could not be bound by the forms of intuition. Thus we could in principle conceive of incorporeal beings whose way of being receptive to the world was not through sensing it (since they were bereft of a body) but who nevertheless necessarily had to conceive of bodies in three-dimensional space and think of events as following each other according to an objective order of time. Such beings might have space and time as forms of intuition even without a body. Indeed, taking the expression literally, a body does not seem a necessary condition for having a *point* of view. All that seems to be required for that is having a location in space. But having a location (in space) does not entail having an extension (in space). Indeed a mathematical point has the former without the latter. That it is necessarily the case for human beings that our location comes with an extension follows from the ultimately contingent fact that we are embodied, not from the fact that we are finite cognizers, nor from the receptive nature of sensibility. Meillassoux thus ultimately conflates two different notions of "condition"; what Kant would call "real" or "empirical" conditions on the one hand and "necessary" or "transcendental" conditions on the other. Even if a point of view depends on having a body for human beings, it is not clear that having a body is anything other than a *real* condition for *receptivity* and thus *not* a necessary condition for being receptive in accordance with the forms of intuition in general.[23]

Problem 2: The above leads us to the next problem: it seems to us that Meillassoux confuses two different relations between conditions and necessity, namely being a necessary condition on the one hand and having a merely conditioned necessity on the other. Both apply to the transcendental subject; it is a necessary condition as well as having a conditioned necessity. However, those are two quite different notions. As a matter of definition, the transcendental subject is a set of necessary conditions on a specific type of cognition. That those necessary conditions apply to anything actual, and hence are *actually* necessary *for* anyone, is itself conditioned upon the instantiation of beings with that type of cognition. Hence, we need to distinguish between the transcendental conditions for knowledge and their "taking place," something Meillassoux fails to do adequately. Thereby he fails to recognize the status of the results of Kant's analysis of cognition in the *Critique*. Transcendental idealism, at least according to Kant, stems from an analysis of *our* form of cognition. That this is so, however, does *not* mean that Kant is committed to the view that this form of cognition is *exclusively* human. All Kant is committed to is the view that, if any being cognizes *like us*, it involves cognizing through synthesizing intuitional manifolds through concepts—that is, such beings must be discursive cognizers. Thus, all Kant is committed to saying is that the existence of (or "that there are") transcendental subjects *in their specifically human guise* is contingent upon their instantiation in a body. We should still say that the transcendental describes a set of atemporal, necessary conditions for cognition of objects, and add the caveat that such conditions only apply to a certain type of cognizer of which we humans are a token.

Even if we limit the argument to humans however it seems Meillassoux's argument still runs into trouble. For although instantiation by a body is a necessary condition for the taking place of the transcendental in humans and that this body must have emerged in time (and hence ultimately the conditions for the taking place of the transcendental must have emerged in time), this does not change the fact that the transcendental conditions for knowledge themselves are atemporal. They are not conditioned by time but rather include time as one of the conditions. The problem is that Meillassoux mixes up being a necessary condition and having a conditioned necessity. For any discursive cognizer, the forms of intuition as well as the categories are the necessary conditions of cognition. *That* they are such necessary conditions, however, is itself a conditioned necessity—it is conditioned upon our cognition being the way it is and not otherwise. Thus, the Kantian would say that whether or not the transcendental subject is *actually* instantiated in a human being, it remains the case that *if* a cognizer like us *were to* exist, it would necessarily cognize in the way described by the doctrines of transcendental idealism.

This leads us to the third and most serious problem.

Problem 3: Meillassoux mistakes the direction and methodology of the Kantian argument. Kant does not deduce the transcendental conditions of cognition by any appeal to a more fundamental principle or axiom. Rather he arrives at them through *analysis* of experience and then argues that we are *justified* in assuming them as conditions of experience afterwards.[24] Though it may seem like the *Critique of pure reason* starts by asserting the finitude of human cognition, it is not the methodological starting point. Rather, the *finitude* of human cognition is only given as a consequence of the *discursivity* of our intellect. Thus, Kant does not start by assuming a finite cognizer and from there retroactively constructing the conditions for such cognition. All Kant needs to assume, and indeed all he in fact assumes, is the fact that we have cognition. From the fact of cognition, Kant then proceeds to analyze the conditions of possibility of such cognition. The doctrine of such conditions Kant calls transcendental idealism. This doctrine includes centrally that human-like cognition requires both concepts and (sensible) intuitions. This latter claim—which Henry Allison has termed the "discursivity-thesis"—is what ultimately leads Kant to assert the finitude of the human cognizing subject. And, as Allison puts it, the discursitvity-thesis is key to understanding Kant's transcendental idealism exactly because it alone enables us to see how transcendental idealism is grounded in a reflection on the *a priori* conditions of human cognition (what I term "epistemic conditions") rather than, as in other forms of idealism (for example, Berkeley's), on the ontological status of what is known.[25]

However, Meillassoux has not argued against the discursivity-thesis. Instead, he seems to assume Kant's idealism as basically on par with Berkeley's, i.e., as grounded in the ontological status of what is known. As we shall see however, Kant does not conceive of being and thinking as inextricably connected. The correlation is not ontologically primary, only methodologically so. That is only insofar as the question we are asking is the question of the conditions of possibility on human(-like) cognition. If there is cognition of objects, then there is a certain correlation between the object and the cognizer.

Now, since Meillassoux has not successfully argued against the discursivity of the human intellect, he is still under the charge of amphibolous reasoning. On Kantian terms, he still makes the mistake of ontologizing the conditions of knowledge. He has shown that the transcendental project would be impossible if it dogmatically posited a finite subject as its point of departure, but that is not what Kant does. From the point of view of transcendental idealism, the finitude of human cognition is a result—*not* a point of departure. This bodes ill for Meillassoux's anti-correlationist project, since, if, as we argue, he has not shown the "objective being of bodies" to be a necessary condition for there being transcendental conditions on cognition, he is still at best begging the question against transcendental idealism. Indeed, by asserting the reality of ancestral space-time he is assuming transcendental realism in order to argue against transcendental idealism.

Taking stock, we do not deny that Meillassoux's critique of Kant gets traction from an explicative lacuna within transcendental idealism. Transcendental idealism, namely, cannot explain how it comes about that what is already transcendentally conditioned must be capable of giving rise to empirical beings whose thinking and behavior is guided by nonempirical conditions and rules. However, we do not see any speculative alternative faring much better. If we agree that the transcendental cannot be successfully reduced to empirically accessible features of objects, then speculative materialism would seem as ill equipped to make sense of the "transcendental taking place" as transcendental idealism. Indeed the speculative materialist seems bound to having to deny any meaningful role of the notion of "the transcendental." Once we have asserted the absolute independence of objects from cognition, we are still left with having to explain the *fact of cognition*. This may very well be done through common natural science in the case of sensory perception: we "cognise" by light waves impinging on rods and cones, and the visual cortex somehow produces an "accurate" image of "the object." However, it is far more difficult to explain a priori cognition, such as mathematics without somehow appealing to a nonempirical faculty. Kantian thought might leave us dissatisfied, since the capacity for cognition cannot itself be grounded in something more basic—like a Leibnizian principle of sufficient reason or a Cartesian God. Still, cognition is the fact with which we must begin.

Kant's Position: Questioning the Catastrophe

How then may we think of the way in which the Kantian "transcendental" can condition the empirical realm? Indeed, what shall we make of the relation between the "transcendental" in thought and the empirical object? In short, where does the above leave the characterization of Kant as a correlationist?

While we cannot answer these questions in full, we want to briefly provide a sketch of an answer that somewhat qualifies the distance between Kant and Meillassoux. Thus, we want to argue that Kant not only does not need to deny M-speculation—i.e., that thought has *access* to some form of absolute—but that labeling Kant a correlationist is a misnomer as is does not fit well with Kant's own understanding of the terms *being* and *thought*.

As we see it, whether or not Kant needs to deny M-speculation very much depends upon the interpretation of the access-relation of M-speculation. Indeed, Kant's denial of speculative cognition is heavily dependent upon his own definition of speculation. In fact, M-speculation seems prima facie permissible for Kant.

To see this, we should first note that for Kant, "thinking" is characterized as "cognition through concepts."[26] However, the requirements on the cognition involved in "mere" thought is not as demanding as the requirements on empirical cognition (which requires a combination of intuitions and concepts).[27] In fact, the requirements on what counts as thought for Kant seem to be quite loose, and indeed the only limiting principle on what counts as a mere *thought* is the principle of noncontradiction. In a footnote in the preface to the second edition of the *Critique of Pure Reason*, Kant tells us that

> I can think whatever I like, as long as I do not contradict myself, i.e., as long as my concept is a possible thought, even if I cannot give any assurance whether or not there is a corresponding object somewhere within the sum total of all possibilities.[28]

This means that the scope of thought for Kant is the domain of the logically possible.[29] The principle of noncontradiction, Kant says, counts as "the universal and completely sufficient principle of all analytic cognition."[30] Thus, "mere" thought provides us with analytic cognition, i.e., cognition of what is contained in the concepts of our thought. Such cognition does not suffice for cognition of objects since such cognition requires that we can show the *real possibility* of the object by exhibiting it in intuition. That said, there is nothing that hinders Kant in *thinking* some kind of absolute or even absolute entity as long as the concept of that absolute is internally consistent.

Indeed, it seems that even on Kant's own definition of speculation, the denial of speculative cognition for Kant—though it amounts to something very similar to the abandonment of M-metaphysics—does not necessarily force him to deny M-speculation. For Kant,

[a] theoretical cognition is speculative if it pertains to an object or concepts of an object to which one cannot attain in any experience.[31]

A cognition is theoretical, according to Kant, if it pertains to *what is* as opposed to *what ought be*.[32] Candidates for speculative cognition would thus be judgments that make claims about "what is," i.e., objects, where those objects are not part of possible experience—which for Kant means objects that cannot be part of *empirical* cognition. This means that the concepts involved in speculative thought lack what Kant calls *objective reality*, i.e., relation to a possible object and hence to anything empirical.[33] Thus, we must grant that for Kant there is nothing in the mere thought of an absolute, which would allow us to establish the existence of an object corresponding to our concept of it. That is to say, thought alone can give us analytic cognition, but for cognition of objects, synthetic cognition is required. Still, Kant allows us some form of (analytic cognitive) access to the absolute.

Interestingly, Meillassoux readily acknowledges the possibility for thinking the absolute for Kant, but does not seem to make the further inference to M-speculation.[34] This might be because this admittedly weak notion of access still seems unsatisfying to the speculative realist. In an attempt to weaken this dissatisfaction, we should briefly point out two things. Firstly, Kant's practical philosophy provides a stronger notion of access to the absolute. In Kant's practical philosophy, our capacity for action is identified as an *access* to the absolute in that it rests on no further conditions—least of all givenness. Thought here is capable of representing what is independent of thinking and of perception, but what is represented is not an existing object, but rather an absolute capacity of our own agency. It is for Kant a capacity that we would share with any rational being—even infinite beings—since it is inseparable from reason to seek the absolute. The Kant-event then should not be seen as disappointing, unless *the absolute* was already identified as something we could not possibly cognize. Secondly, Meillassoux's own notion of access cannot be interpreted in terms of object-cognition. As already noted, Meillassoux's own candidate for *the absolute* ultimately seems not to be things in themselves, despite his focus on the temporally ancestral. Rather it is "the necessity of contingency," an *absolute* at least as ideal and non-material as Kant's moral law. Thus, it is not clear to us that the speculative realist would want to define an access-relation so restrictively that the Kantian could not still have the relevant access to the absolute.

However, even if the anti-correlationist is not ready to grant the Kantian the possibility of M-speculation due to some more restrictive interpretation of the access-relation, calling Kant a correlationist would still be a misnomer. What Kant denies by denying speculative cognition is that mere thought should be able to provide us with cognition of *beings*, i.e., objects of possible experience.[35] *Being* (Dasein) for Kant is something attributed to entities only through their *positing*, i.e., their at least possible exhibition of the object in intuition. That is the cognition of the object "should also be possible *a posteriori*."[36] It is this understanding of the relation of thought and cognition to *being* that—at least on Kant's own terms—makes nonsense of calling him a correlationist.

While Meillassoux appeals readily to locutions like "thinking being" or "the correlation between thought and being"—this of course being a well-established type of expression in the philosophical tradition from Heidegger through to Badiou—we nowhere see Kant express the transcendental distinction between things in themselves and appearances in terms of a distinction between *thought* and *being*. Indeed the only legitimate use of the term "being" (Dasein) in Kant's theoretical philosophy is as a predicate of an otherwise determined concept of an object. As such *being* or *existence* may be used as a predicate, but only one that serves to tie the concept of something to sensory experience. To say of something that it exists is not equivalent to claiming that it is sensed, but the only legitimate use of being as a predicate is to establish a relation between our cognitive capacities (here sensation) and the thing we claim to exist or to have existed.

In this sense, we cannot merely *think* something as *being* for Kant. The thought of something cannot—as it were—contain its existence.[37] We can think whatever we will, under the law of non-contradiction, but we cannot add by mere thought *being* to the concept of the thing, which we represent.[38] This is the insight crystalized in the infamous statement by Kant that "existence is not a real predicate," which is pivotal to Kant's rejection of rationalist metaphysics insofar as the latter relied on the notion of an absolutely necessary being.

Now in one sense it may seem obvious that we can think of something as existing. I think of dinosaurs and dragons, and I have concepts of both dinosaurs and dragons. Yet I am also capable of judging dinosaurs to be (a former) part of actuality, whereas I judge dragons to be "merely" imagined—or conceived—entities. Importantly, however, my judgment that dinosaurs existed, whereas dragons never existed, cannot be *contained* in my concept of what dinosaurs and dragons are. We do however represent the temporal conditions for the existence of dinosaurs as independent of the temporal conditions for the emergence of *homo sapiens*. But Meillassoux cannot infer from this the absolute independence of dinosaurs from the condition of cognition in general.

Still, Meillassoux should not be entirely faulted for using the term "being" loosely in opposition to Kant. Indisputably, Kant does claim that we can only (properly) cognize what is also given to us—i.e., through some cognitive faculty. He also remains anti-totalizing in the sense that the characterization of *being* as a concept—not of an object—but of the object's relation to us, is not a definition of "being" but rather a prescription on how the concept of being may legitimately be employed.[39] We cannot cognize "being" in itself, but we can cognize something as *being*, existing—or: as actual—by establishing a connection to it through experience. According to Meillassoux, any correlationist position is viciously circular in thinking the in-itself, and in this way there is indeed a performative "circle" in Kant, but it is not a vicious one. Rather, the circularity is entirely at the level of appearances and hence also at the level of existence. In claiming that "x exists," I am *implicitly* claiming that x must have some relation to me. This is not because there are some entities, "thought" and "being," which can only be accessed in their "correlation." Rather it is because any representation of something as existing must necessarily carry with it the representation that it is I who represent it thus.

Concluding Remarks

In the above, we have defended Kant against the charge of correlationism. Negatively, we have argued that the attack on transcendental philosophy for being unable to provide an absolute foundation of itself in the advent of the material body is misplaced. Further, that this attack is founded in a misunderstanding of not only Kant's notion of "condition" but also more fundamentally the methodology of transcendental idealism. Positively, we have argued that not only is there a way in which Kant can provide speculative access to some kind of absolute, but further that framing his position in terms of a correlation of *thinking* and *being* is fundamentally at odds with his own understanding of those terms. For Kant, saying that we only have "access" to the "correlation of thinking and being" carries dubious presuppositions with it. Notably, it relies on an identity between "being" and "things in themselves," which Kant would and should not subscribe to. It further relies on a vague notion of "access", which, we have argued, Kant could plausibly accommodate—if not in his theoretical then in his practical philosophy.

Notes

1 In this chapter, we refer only to Kant's position in the *Critique of Pure Reason* (The Cambridge Edition of the Works of Immanuel Kant), ed. and trans. Paul Guyer and Allen Wood (Cambridge: Cambridge University Press, 1998). We follow the standard praxis and cite the pagination of the original first and second edition as (A pagination/B pagination). Unless otherwise noted all translations are taken from Kant 1998.
2 Quentin Meillassoux, *After Finitude. An Essay on the Contingency of Necessity* (London: Continuum, 2008), 118.
3 This is obscured by the difference in terminology. For Kant speculative metaphysics denotes the attempt by reason to arrive at cognitions of supersensible objects, notably "The immortal Soul," "God," and "The World." For Meillassoux, metaphysics concerns the establishing of some necessary feature of what there is, which sets it squarely against what he takes speculation to establish, namely that nothing is necessary save the necessary contingency of what there is.
4 In *After Finitude*, Meillassoux calls this epistemic disappointment *weak correlationism*. In a later paper, following various critiques, he prefers to reserve the term *correlationism* for this position. Cf. Quentin Meillassoux, "Iteration, Reiteration, Repetition: A Speculative Analysis of the Sign Devoid of Meaning," in *Genealogies of Speculation. Materialism and Subjectivity since Structuralism*, ed. Armen Avanessian and Suhail Malik (London: Bloomsbury, 2016).

5   Meillassoux has later abandoned the term *strong correlationism* in favor of the clearly metaphysical *Subjectalism*, cf. Meillassoux, "Iteration." Subjectalism is preferred by Meillasoux because of *subjectivism's* relativist connotations. Rather than being a relativist position, Subjectalism is thoroughly absolutist.
6   The past tense is obviously important here.
7   Meillassoux, *After Finitude*, 10.
8   Roughly put the scholarship has divided itself into three camps: (1) Those who think Kant is indeed making an ontological distinction between two kinds of objects and consequently think Kant is committed to an unfortunate dependence-relation between appearances and things in themselves, e.g., that things in themselves "cause" appearances (cf. e.g., Paul Guyer, *Kant and the Claims of Knowledge* [Cambridge: Cambridge University Press, 1987]; James van Cleve, *Problems from Kant* [Oxford: Oxford University Press, 1999]; Nicholas F. Stang, "The Non-Identity of Appearances and Things in Themselves," *Noûs* 48, no. 1 [2014]: 106–36; and Nicholas F. Stang, "Kant's Transcendental Idealism," *The Stanford Encyclopedia of Philosophy* [Winter 2018]). (2) Those who deny the ontological distinction but still think the distinction is metaphysically pregnant. Such positions, for example, spell out the relation between the appearance and the in itself as two "aspects" of what is ultimately the same object (cf. e.g., Rae Langton, *Kantian Humility* [Oxford: Oxford University Press, 1998]; Tobias Rosefeldt, "Dinge an sich und sekundäre Qualitäten," in *Kant in der Gegenwart*, ed. Jürgen Stolzenberg [Berlin/New York: de Gruyter, 2007]; Lucy Allais, *Manifest Reality* [Oxford: Oxford University Press, 2015]). Interestingly one of Allais's prime examples to spell out the relation of the aspects of the object is one between primary and secondary qualities—though for her this example can never amount to more than an analogy, see esp. 125ff). (3) Those who think that the distinction can never amount to more than an epistemic or even methodological distinction on Kant's part. In general, such positions agree that Kant is not committed to the existence of things in themselves but that such a concept springs from the mere recognition of the finitude of human cognition. Having set a limit, Kant merely recognizes the possibility of thinking something beyond that limit, but thinking this possibility could never amount to any more than the recognition of a logical possibility, never any hard metaphysical or ontological commitments (cf. e.g., Gerold Prauss, *Kant und das Problem der Dinge an sich* [Bonn: Bouvier, 1977]; Henry E. Allison, *Kant's Transcendental Idealism. An Interpretation and Defence* [New Haven: Yale University Press, 2004]; Graham Bird, *The Revolutionary Kant. A commentary on the Critique of Pure Reason* [La Salle: Open Court, 2006]). In this chapter, we are generally sympathetic to (3), since it does not leave Kant with the very problems Meillassoux finds in "correlationism."
9   Meillassoux, *After Finitude*, 34.
10 Meillassoux, *After Finitude*, 34.
11 Cf. Meillassoux, *After Finitude*, 34.
12 Cf. Meillassoux, *After Finitude*, 125.
13 See Meillassoux, *After Finitude*, 22–7.
14 Meillassoux, *After Finitude*, 23. This definition of amphiboly comes very close to Kant's own understanding of it as the *simultaneous* use (and hence conflation) of pure and empirical concepts in reflection, cf. Kant, *Critique of Pure Reason*, A260/B316ff. Indeed, an upshot of our argument in the following is that Meillassoux is still guilty

of transcendental amphiboly, "i.e. a confusion of the pure object of the understanding with the appearance" (Kant, *Critique of Pure Reason*, A270/B326).
15 Meillassoux, *After Finitude*, 24.
16 Meillassoux, *After Finitude*, 24.
17 Meillassoux, *After Finitude*, 24.
18 Meillassoux, *After Finitude*, 24.
19 Meillassoux, *After Finitude*, 24.
20 Meillassoux, *After Finitude*, 25.
21 Meillassoux, *After Finitude*, 25.
22 Meillassoux, *After Finitude*, 25.
23 It is simply a fact that our receptivity is sensory—i.e., it consists of both sensation and pure intuition. The Kantian move against Lockean dogmatism is to locate the spatiotemporal (primary qualities) in pure receptivity and the sensory (secondary qualities) in non-pure receptivity. Each is a form of representation rather than "the object in itself."
24 The direction and methodology of Kant's investigation of cognition are still a topic of discussion within Kant scholarship—in particular, when it comes to the famous deduction of the categories. Though there is widespread agreement that this deduction contains a regressive argument starting from the givenness of cognition and moving back to the conditions of its being given (cf. e.g., Dieter Henrich, "Kant's Notion of a Deduction and the Methodological Background of the First *Critique*," in *Kant's Transcendental Deductions. The Three Critiques and the Opus Postummum*, ed. Eckart Förster [Stanford: Stanford University Press, 1989]), some scholars suggest that this does not exclude the possibility that Kant intended the deduction to also include a progressive argument starting from the unity of consciousness and from there deriving the categories (cf. e.g., Dennis Schulting, *Kant's Deduction from Apperception. An Essay on the Transcendental Deduction of the Categories* [Berlin/Boston: de Gruyter, 2018]).
25 Allison, *Kant's Transcendental Idealism*, xv.
26 Kant, *Critique of Pure Reason*, A69/B94.
27 There is some interpretative scope her, as to whether Kant thought all theoretical cognition required intuitions as well as concepts, or whether mere conceptual representations, e.g., analytic judgments, could be said to be cognitive in themselves even while presupposing some intuited content. We can, for Kant, have cognition of nonexisting objects, e.g., perfect triangles; cognition is not "veridical" in the sense that cognition of X implies the existence of X.
28 Kant, *Critique of Pure Reason*, B XXVIIn.
29 In contrast, the scope of cognition (in the narrow sense) is the *really possible*.
30 Kant, *Critique of Pure Reason*, A151/B191.
31 Kant, *Critique of Pure Reason*, A635/B663.
32 Kant, *Critique of Pure Reason*, A633/B661.
33 cf. Kant, *Critique of Pure Reason*, A 109/B 137.
34 Meillassoux, *After Finitude*, 35.
35 This is of course incompatible with M-metaphysics, which Kant also at several places renounces. Indeed, it seems clear that the entirety of the latter part of the *Critique of Pure Reason* called *the transcendental dialectic* is meant as a refutation of M-metaphysics.
36 Kant, *Critique of Pure Reason*, A600/B628.

37 Cf. the famous example from the first *Critique* of the hundred dollars. Nothing further—real—is contained in the actual hundred dollars than in the concept of them (Kant, *Critique of Pure Reason*, A599/B629).
38 We can however, represent the relation between the object and our cognitive faculty, and thereby add to the concept of the object its *actuality*. This is the case, when we add to the concept of a prehistoric event—say the Cambrian Explosion—a relation to our cognition of it, namely the observation of fossilised remains of a multitude of species.
39 Kant, *Critique of Pure Reason*, A225/B272.

Cited Works

Allais, Lucy. *Manifest Reality*. Oxford: Oxford University Press, 2015.

Allison, Henry, E. *Kant's Transcendental Idealism. An Interpretation and Defence*. New Heaven: Yale University Press, 2004.

Bird, Graham. *The Revolutionary Kant. A commentary on the Critique of Pure Reason*. La Salle: Open Court, 2006.

Guyer, Paul. *Kant and the Claims of Knowledge*. Cambridge: Cambridge University Press, 1987.

Henrich, Dieter. "Kant's Notion of a Deduction and the Methodological Background of the First *Critique*." In *Kant's Transcendental Deductions. The Three* Critiques *and the Opus Postummum*, edited by Eckart Förster, 29-46. Stanford: Stanford University Press, 1989.

Kant, Immanuel. *Critique of Pure Reason* (The Cambridge Edition of the Works of Immanuel Kant). Edited and translated by Paul Guyer and Allen Wood. Cambridge: Cambridge University Press, 1998.

Langton, Rae. *Kantian Humility*. Oxford: Oxford University Press, 1998.

Meillassoux, Quentin. *After Finitude. An Essay on the Contingency of Necessity*. London: Continuum, 2008.

Meillassoux, Quentin. "Iteration, Reiteration, Repetition: A Speculative Analysis of the Sign Devoid of Meaning." In *Genealogies of Speculation. Materialism and Subjectivity since Structuralism*, edited by Armen Avanessian and Suhail Malik, 117-97. London: Bloomsbury, 2016.

Prauss, Gerold. *Kant und das Problem der Dinge an sich*. Bonn: Bouvier, 1977.

Rosefeldt, Tobias. "Dinge an sich und sekundäre Qualitäten." In *Kant in der Gegenwart*, edited by Jürgen Stolzenberg, 167-209. Berlin/New York: de Gruyter, 2007.

Schulting, Dennis. *Kant's Deduction from Apperception. An Essay on the Transcendental Deduction of the Categories*. Berlin/Boston: de Gruyter, 2018.

Stang, Nicholas F. "The Non-Identity of Appearances and Things in Themselves." *Noûs*, 48, no. 1 (2014): 106-36.

Stang, Nicholas F. "Kant's Transcendental Idealism." *The Stanford Encyclopedia of Philosophy* (Winter 2018).

Van Cleve, James. *Problems from Kant*. Oxford: Oxford University Press, 1999.

Chapter 9

NEW MATERIALISMS, NATURAL HISTORY, AND HUMAN HISTORY

Interview with Dipesh Chakrabarty by Benjamin Boysen & Jesper Lundsfryd Rasmussen

BB & JLR: In the introduction to the anthology *Historical Teleologies in the Modern World* you, together with your co-authors, suggest an intimate connection between history and nature.[1] Specifically, you trace the concept of teleology back to its origins in natural philosophy (Christian Wolff) and the endeavor to establish an adequate framework for understanding organic nature and matter. Predicated on these scientific debates, teleology was then transported into the modern discipline of history as a contestant for a mechanical or materialistic concept of time.

What were the imports of these discussions on the subject of history, and how do you see the role of teleology in our modern understanding of history as a scientific discipline today?

DC: As you know, and as we discussed in our Introduction to the volume you refer to, *Historical Teleologies in the Modern World*, the transfer of the idea of teleology from natural philosophy to history—at the same time as history emerged as an academic subject-cum-discipline in Europe—entailed various arguments and historiographical strategies about reconciling ideas about human "freedom" to the ends of history. These various ideas never came together to constitute any grand theory of history and human freedoms. However, through the nineteenth and twentieth centuries and thanks to both European justifications of their empires and the aspirations that drove anti-colonial and modernizing nationalisms of the educated classes in the colonies, two figures of freedom came to dominate thought about the goals of human history: (a) the freedom from oppression of one human by another and (b) freedom of humans from their supposed thralldom to nature, i.e., projects of mastery over the natural world. If the former became a defining element of the post-Enlightenment understanding of modernity, the latter became an essential element justifying all projects of modernization and underpinned Marxist historical debates on the so-called "capitalist transition." These two themes even dominated discussions of capitalist globalization in the last quarter of the twentieth century and into the twenty-first until the news of "global warming" and attendant planetary questions broke in the worlds of the social and human sciences.

Historians today—at least the thoughtful ones among them—are confronted with a dilemma: on the one hand, historians construct narratives and they know that narratives often take the shape of their arc from their endings—it is how a story ends that often determines how we construct its telling and its plot, but wouldn't the knowledge that our post-industrial and global capitalist civilization is careening toward a tipping point be too over-determining for historians' narratives, leaving little room for the play of necessity and freedom that characterize much modern historiography? Many of my colleagues are trying to find a way out of this dilemma by emphasizing more on the contingencies and accidents of history, the paths-not-taken accounts of the past, by trying to both acknowledge catastrophe we face and yet avoid the problem of "catastrophic" or "apocalyptic" or eschatological thinking in their narratives.

BB & JLR: Around 1800, we witness a prosperity in scientific and philosophical pursuits grappling with the concept of history. In disparate ways and in varying degrees thinkers such as Friedrich Schiller, Friedrich Wilhelm Joseph Schelling, and Georg Wilhelm Friedrich Hegel attempted to establish history as a scientific discipline by demarcating the realm of nature from that of humankind. What ultimately distinguishes natural from human processes is, according to these figures, the concept of freedom, which serves as an exclusively human category. Recently, this divide has been challenged from various angles. According to the theories of new materialism, the human being enjoys much less freedom, if any at all, than the modern period would normally concede, due to the human embeddedness in natural processes. For example, Timothy Morton argues that the human being is intertwined and absorbed as one insignificant object within inconceivable and all-embracing objects, the so-called *hyperobjects*, which defies any predictions.[2] According to Graham Harman, the human being and its freedom are largely determined by the capricious inner life of objects that incessantly determine the way we think and act. Another proponent of new materialism, Jane Bennett, proposes to distribute the capability of liable actions, so as to include things, which, consequently, share the moral responsibility of events such as blackouts. Hence, the modern notion of the great divide between the human being and nature is substantially blurred.

How do you generally assess these new trends in the humanities and social sciences?

DC: Yes, the question of "freedom," in various forms, has been central—since the Enlightenment—to defining and justifying worldly projects of many, many human groups, both on the side of oppressors and those oppressed. It is also true that this idea of "freedom"—the human capacity to construe reality in terms of different options and then to choose between or from them—has been predicated on the separation of the social from the natural or on a nature/culture distinction. This separation never had a basis except in the perceptions and hubris of humans, probably after the invention of agriculture, and strengthened with the coming of axial religions and later by the assumptions underpinning projects of modernization. The huge boost that economic growth, modern science, technology, medicine, public health measures, and personal hygiene gave to human flourishing probably reinforced the human sense of this distinction. Planetary environmental crises—the current pandemic related to human destruction of forests, climate change, scarcity of fresh water, warming and acidification of the seas, sea level rising, extreme weather events—are making us question this distinction. That we are connected to various other forms of life—not just in the history of evolution but in our everyday lives—is a realization that is slowly dawning in human consciousness. But that does not mean that we are fully given over this new consciousness yet. For the social, economic, and political elite in human societies still derive their elements of power and pleasure from their deep involvement with—and investment in—institutions founded on the assumption of there being a split or separation between humans and the natural world.

Latour, Herman, Morton, Bennett, Haraway, and many others have now written enough to convince us that this assumed separation of the human from the nonhuman is a piece of fiction. It is not how the world works. Humans are a form of life that is connected both to other forms of life and to nonhuman entities like minerals and gases (where are we without either oxygen or carbon dioxide?). Thing-theorists like Bill Brown have further advanced these lines of thinking. I also agree with object-oriented philosophers such as Herman that both human theories and practice operate with a reduced version of the world/earth, a point also made by the philosophers of the mind, Thomas Metzinger in his book, *The Ego Tunnel*.[3] This is also what Jane Bennett describes as the human preference for "thin" descriptions of the world. And, the problem is, human conceptions of the political are also based on such thin descriptions, which is why Bennett also acknowledges that posthumanism or new materialism cannot answer questions like slavery or racism.

I think the human sciences are at a crossroad. They want to take onboard the insights of speculative realism and other cognate areas while wanting to retain the deep interest in social justice that has shaped them since the 1960s. But new materialists are also aware of the problem and try to address them in their own ways, as in Latour's book on the *Politics of Nature*.[4] However, the reconciliation has not been successful yet.

BB & JLR: More specifically, what role do they play in your field, i.e., history as a scientific discipline?

DC: In my own field of history, there are creative attempts to produce narratives that give agency to the nonhuman, of both the living and the nonliving kinds. Timothy J. LeCain's book, *The Matter of History: How Things Create the Past*, is one example.[5] Slow but definite changes are taking place at the level of the doctoral dissertation. One interesting problem that emerges from all this is a critical difference in how we understand historical actors. When we are focused on human beings, we delve into their motivations. But animals and other creatures do not give you that opportunity, so you make inferences by studying behavior. The same thing happens to humans, too, if we increase vastly either the number of humans being studied or the time over which you are studying them. You would then be studying behavioral patterns as you would with animals.

BB & JLR: The new materialisms are occasionally compared to the rise of the romantic movement in Europe around 1800. One decisive difference is the substantial belittling of subjectivity and human autonomy, which figures prominently among the shared convictions of new materialists. In one of its more radical forms, Harman's critique of modern philosophy culminates in a theory that seems to neglect human reflexivity and freedom. While new materialism certainly must be differentiated from scientism due to its insistence on re-enchantment, others have suggested to interpret this trend as a kind of naturalism.

Where would you situate the new materialisms?

DC: The origins of new materialism and its cognate fields are surely dispersed among many fields and subfields of inquiry. For some time now, developments in genetics, neurology, brain studies, studies of the human microbiome, etc., have seriously undermined Lockean ideas of personhood or the idea of the autonomous subject that are still operative in some areas of social sciences and the humanities. This has reinforced and/or renewed the debate on "the subject" that post-structuralism once initiated. But there is indeed a belittling of subjectivity and human autonomy that such moves entail. Here I can only repeat a point that I have already made, or maybe try to put it differently. "Human autonomy" and "subjectivity" may be fictions. But can one argue about "social responsibility," "culpability," "suffering" without those fictions? There is a gap between human experience of the world, everyday human perceptions of how the world works, and the way the world is constituted. For most of the time over which humans have written their own histories, this gap—of which humans have been aware for a long time—did not matter. It was not a matter of grave concern to social scientists that humans could not perceive infrared, ultraviolet light or electromagnetic waves even though they knew, intellectually, that they existed. Nor did being unable to hear ultra-sonic sound bother us. The role of carbon dioxide in the atmosphere did not matter to our everyday lives, for humans simply took the world, as they found it, as given. It is this givenness of the world that is now being challenged by global warming, pandemic, and other planetary environmental problems. We now have no alternative but to care about the amount of a trace gas, carbon dioxide, in the atmosphere. These are the reasons why various strands of new-materialistic thinking are assuming increasing importance and finding traction.

BB & JLR: To which extent do you consider it possible to engage in historical studies under the auspices of new materialism?

DC: I think I have answered this question already in part (see Q3 in particular). Many historians will take on board the proposition that the nonhuman is a co-actor in history. But whether the nonhuman is the same kind of actor as the human will remain a point of contention. But that the human is entangled with the nonhuman seems irrefutable today. The question is: where, in the historian's methods, do we make room for human experience of the world?

BB & JLR: According to the philosopher Odo Marquard, a theoretical position should ideally be understood as an answer to a preceding question. In their own opinion, new materialisms conceive themselves as a response to flawed and dangerous elements in modernity's self-understanding.

To what question do you think new materialisms provide an answer, and why do you think we currently witness such influential trends and premodern inclinations?

DC: Let me answer this with regards to my own field, history. Human history, as we have discussed, has been studied in separation from natural history as the latter was taken to be the background against which the human story unfolded. As humans become a planetary force impacting the seas, the mountains, the clouds, the air, this "inert" (in human terms) background becomes part of human history. It ceases to provide merely a backdrop. Once that happens, the society/nature distinction is shown up for what it is—a false though convenient fable. This is where new-materialist propositions become attractive as a corrective to the false assumptions of modernity. The appeal of premodern peasant or indigenous societies arises from the same situation. Indigenous societies, as Eduardo Viveiros de Castro, the late Deborah Bird Rose, and others have shown, never made a distinction between human and animals or between nature and culture. They show us that it is possible to form sustainable human societies without making these distinctions, whereas actions and institutions based on or embodying these distinctions produce societies that seem unsustainable.

BB & JLR: Today, we are facing a host of challenges, of which the relation between the human being and its environment seems to play a salient part. In your work on the Anthropocene, you also question the traditional divide between natural history and human history.

How do you think these challenges have shaped our self-understanding as modern, secular beings?

DC: They have surely underscored for many the limitations of modernization and called into question all imaginations of infinite economic growth on a finite planet. They have also made us realize how energy-intensive our ideas of the modern have been until now. Of course, the field is marked by debates. Some think that switching to renewable sources of energy is the main if not the only challenge. Others ask if we should de-grow and find less energy-intensive forms for practices that speak to our ideas of freedom or rights.

"Secular" is a more difficult term to place. The Pope's 2015 encyclical on Climate Change clearly arraigns contemporary forms of capitalism that, by replacing human labor by intelligent machines, appear to have forgotten that humans were put on earth by God to labor. To the Pope, such a capitalism is clearly too secular or un-Christian. If, however, by secular we mean the features of something like what Charles Taylor called "a secular age" where religion and God could be replaced by other means and objects of transcendental thought, then I would say that the climate crisis can still bring out the secular in us. In many texts on the Anthropocene, the geological sublime provides an object for transcendental thought.[6]

BB & JLR: To what extent does this call for a rethinking of our notion of history and a revision of the methodology of historical research?

DC: This we have discussed above. But let me just say this: the distinction between natural and human history has now collapsed calling for a profound review of the assumptions of history-writing. Historians are looking for ways to construct historical narratives that are not premised on this distinction. But these are still early days.

BB & JLR: Where do you see the main difference between the new materialisms and your own conception of historical processes?

DC: I am deeply indebted to various strands of new materialist or posthumanist positions. The influence of Bruno Latour, Jane Bennett, and Quentin Meillassoux on my book, *The Climate of History in a Planetary Age*, would be visible to any discerning reader.[7] Even the central category I introduce in the book—the planet—is a noncorrelationist construction. The main difference, however, is that correlationism also has a place in my work. I do not deny, for instance, the phenomenological understanding of the human capacity to experience the world. This capacity is flawed, no doubt. There is much about the world, even about our own bodies, that we do not experience. But this limited nature of what constitutes everyday human experience of space and time, I think, is fundamental to the way I track and understand human response to anthropogenic climate change. This "understanding" in my work is Diltheyan and follows Gadamer. This does not stop me from intellectually appreciating the arguments and propositions of new materialists and I largely find them acceptable on their own terms. Noncorrelationist thinking does not come easily to humans. I give many instances in the last chapter of the book to suggest that. And that fact is salutary for it molds human responses to global warming and its consequences. But post-humanism gives me little insight into human experience and human affective dispositions that directly influence human judgment and action. I suppose I have never divested from humanism. But I take the views of post-humanists very seriously.

BB & JLR: Recently, the new materialisms have received critical attention from a Marxist perspective. Eco-Marxists such as Andreas Malm have expressed deep dissatisfaction with the theoretical underpinnings of these theories as well as their normative consequences, deeming them unfit to come up with proper solutions to contemporary challenges, e.g., the climate crisis. Andrew Cole, another Marxian voice critical of the new materialisms, named new materialism the metaphysics of capitalism.

You have previously expressed hesitation about Marxian analyses of perspectives on climate issues. Would you also extend this scepsis to the broader Marxian objections of the new materialisms for being ahistorical and fetishizing matter?

DC: We have already discussed some possible criticisms of new materialisms. But the Marxist objections seem to misunderstand what, say, speculative realism is all about. After all, questions of norms follow from our understanding of human subjectivity. But someone who approaches new materialisms in search norms for humans or looking for the revolutionary subject is also asking questions that new materialisms were not designed to answer. The debate on correlationism is not about the "norms" that may be a part of a correlationist outlook on the world. New materialisms contribute to our understanding of the depth of the crisis that modern civilization faces in having to deal with the facts of human entanglement with various "actors"—in the Latourian sense—in the world. Marxist narratives are too humanocentric in their conception of agency and structure to be able to appreciate new-materialist critiques of anthropocentrist thinking. See below for further elaboration of this answer.

BB & JLR: In light of this, how do you see your own contribution to solving contemporary issues such as the climate crisis?

DC: As I say explicitly in my book, I am not trying to "solve" the climate crisis but rather attempting to understand what makes solving the crisis such a difficult problem for humans. It is to this end that I present my book as an exercise in developing a new philosophical anthropology. I see the crisis as a genuine predicament for modern humans and try to offer some perspectives on the human to suggest why this may be so. But it is all done in the hope that such perspectives eventually help in our collective efforts to address anthropogenic climate change in ways that take into account the realities of human entanglement with the nonhuman on this planet. It is in carrying out the latter part of this exercise that I find new materialism extremely helpful.

That said, however, it has to be acknowledged that the "solving" of the climate crisis has to be a political task for humans. The world currently faces an institutional deficit in handling problems that are genuinely planetary. The UN was not set up to deal with planetary problems that in principle require urgent and synchronized collective action of nations. The UN works more as a bargaining platform where parties involved assume that they have indefinite amount of time at their disposal. Or, to give another and regional example, the rivers issuing from the Himalayas serve several nations, stretching from Pakistan to Vietnam. But there are no multilateral agreements between nations to protect the health of these rivers or of the glaciers that feed them. Both rivers and glaciers are treated as national properties. Yet we clearly need regional, semi-global governance mechanisms for such areas that affect the climate situation profoundly. The need for global governance of human societies is also underlined by the current politics of information and vaccination that surround the pandemic.

The relationship of such possible global politics to new-materialist philosophies and inquiries is twofold. A possible, new global politics for the welfare of all humans will have to take on board the insights afforded by new materialist thinkers about the entangled existence of humans on this planet. Such politics will have to respect what some Earth System scientists call "planetary boundaries."

At the same time, we increasingly realize that the human conception of the political remains, at the end of the day, parochially and provincially human. It is a near-impossible exercise to extend the terms of human morality and justice to other forms of life. It is true that human actions such as cutting down of forests have actively contributed to the recent spread of zoonotic diseases among humans. It is due to our actions that our bodies have become new evolutionary pathways for the Corona virus. But what kind of kin-making or friendship can we practice with such a virus when all it wants to do is to kill us?

The eventual solution must be, as E. O. Wilson and others suggest, in a contraction of the human realm on the planet so that we never take the biosphere for granted and are ever mindful of our entanglement with the nonhuman, both living and nonliving. But, ideally, this contraction should come about through processes that are democratic, nonpatriarchal, and not anti-poor. This would also entail the installation of some processes and institutions to regulate the currently unbridled growth of capitalism and technology. This is the task of future politics. Human politics are currently nowhere near this target. We may even, at our own peril, end up taking too long to evolve such politics and the forms of global governance they require. But I don't see any other option that will meet the needs of justice and fairness between humans and be at the same time sensitive to all that we have learned from new materialisms or from Earth System Science for that matter. The ultimate task—whether we succeed at it or not—is political.

Notes

1 Henning Trüper, Dipesh Chakrabarty, and Sanjay Subrahmanyam, ed., *Historical Teleologies in the Modern World* (London: Bloomsbury, 2015).
2 Timothy Morton, *Hyperobjects: Philosophy and Ecology after the End of the World* (Minneapolis: University of Minnesota Press, 2013).
3 Thomas Metzinger, *The Ego Tunnel: The Science of the Mind and the Myth of the Self* (New York: Basic Books, 2010; 2009).
4 Bruno Latour, *Politics of Nature: How to Bring the Sciences into Democracy*, trans. Catherine Porter (Cambridge, MA: Harvard University Press, 2004).
5 Timothy J. LeCain, *The Matter of History: How Things Create the Past* (Cambridge: Cambridge University Press, 2017).

6   Charles Taylor, *A Secular Age* (Cambridge, MA: Harvard University Press, 2007).
7   Dipesh Chakrabarty, *The Climate of History in a Planetary Age* (Chicago: The University of Chicago Press, 2021).

Cited Works

Chakrabarty, Dipesh. *The Climate of History in a Planetary Age*. Chicago: The University of Chicago Press, 2021.

Latour, Bruno. *Politics of Nature: How to Bring the Sciences into Democracy*. Translated by Catherine Porter. Cambridge, MA: Harvard University Press, 2004.

LeCain, Timothy J. *The Matter of History: How Things Create the Past*. Cambridge: Cambridge University Press, 2017.

Metzinger, Thomas. *The Ego Tunnel: The Science of the Mind and the Myth of the Self*. New York: Basic Books, 2010; 2009.

Morton, Timothy. *Hyperobjects: Philosophy and Ecology after the End of the World*. Minneapolis: University of Minnesota Press, 2013.

Taylor, Charles. *A Secular Age*. Cambridge, MA: Harvard University Press, 2007.

Trüper, Henning, Dipesh Chakrabarty, and Sanjay Subrahmanyam, ed. *Historical Teleologies in the Modern World*. London: Bloomsbury, 2015.

Chapter 10

THE REAL KANT & HEGEL: A POSTSCRIPT ON THE CRITIQUE OF SPECULATIVE REALISM AND OBJECT-ORIENTED ONTOLOGY

Andrew Cole

Does the existentialist really think hell is other people?[1] Has he tried interacting with things? Because it seems that "les choses sont contre nous!" So avers the new creature called the resistentialist, who studies things behaving badly, the way objects seem animate in their refusal to cooperate with us, their insistence on resistance— "the rug that quietly curls up so it can snag your toe, the sock gone AWOL from the dryer, the slippery piece of toast that always hits the floor jelly side down." Of course, resistentialism has a long history, going well beyond Emerson's observation that "[t]hings are in the saddle,/ And ride mankind."[2] For example, Augustine, in his *Confessions*, exclaims that things outright assault him: "As I gazed at them, they attacked me in massive heaps. As I thought about them, the very images of physical objects formed an obstacle to my return [to spiritual inwardness], as if saying 'Where are you going to, unworthy, soiled man?'"[3] Augustine is attempting to do what Plotinus instructs his initiates to perform, a phenomenological bracketing of your surroundings, and all its alluring and resistant objects, and proceed through a series of mental "separations" until you are left with the soul as "the image of the Divine Intellect."[4] But Augustine confesses to the impossibility of such bracketing, the real trouble with suspending our intentions toward things. Which is to say, things resist us even as we try to escape them; they pull at us as we try to dip away from them. So rooted in your mind are things that they tap into your body and, as Spinoza says, change you from within.[5] Kant, too, partakes of this tradition of expositing on the peskiness of things in his third critique, the *Critique of Judgement*, where he speaks of "the faculty of aesthetic judging," which can include "a feeling of displeasure at an object" and a distinct idea that the object itself is "purposive." To say it in our contemporary idiom, you feel the agency and purpose of the object when "violence is [...] wrought on the subject."[6] And just because the object frustrates your own plans doesn't mean that its entire purpose (*Zweck*) involves resisting you.

The problem is, fundamentally, what kind of philosophy do you develop out of complaints like these—or what kind of complaints you parlay into a philosophy—all those experiences when things or objects seem incorrigible and resistant to our schemes not only to use them but to know them, their essences, properties, and inner dynamics we perceive as agency. It's a question asked for millennia up to the present day, which now affords us the opportunity to study Kant and Hegel, two very significant thinkers within these traditions, with renewed focus in light of recent attempts not only to think the real but to reject the insights of these very philosophers who—like it or not—anticipate strategies of such fields as speculative realism and object-oriented ontology. Let's get real, then, with both of these philosophers.

The Real Kant

Perhaps the most interesting idea in the work of Quentin Meillassoux, whose short and highly readable *After Finitude* inspired "speculative realism" in the aughts, concerns "ancestrality" and the related question of the "arche-fossil." Both terms pertain to an experiment in thinking the real. For Meillassoux, "ancestrality" concerns "reality anterior to the emergence of the human species," and the "arche-fossil" accordingly indicates "the existence of an ancestral reality or event; one that is anterior to terrestrial life."[7] Because there are aquatic and microbial fossils for us to study, and in that we have scientific knowledge about the ancient earth that we hold to be certain, we do indeed think realities that we had not experienced ourselves. While this insight may strike the reader as just a garden variety realism, for him, the strength of this claim—and accordingly what he defends as an "*irremediable* realism*"*[8]—is that we are thinking realities before human consciousness itself ever existed, realities that assuredly never depended on a human mind to subsist. More loftily or perhaps profoundly, such a thought experiment involving "ancestrality" definitively severs the longstanding link between "being" and "thought," ontology and epistemology, freeing both to flourish on their own. Meillassoux finds a benefit here for philosophy in the delinking of "being" and "thought"—namely, that philosophy can finally operate outside of the "correlationist" circle, which—in its modern form—is a Kantian problem.

Here, then, is Meillassoux's full claim about Kant, correlationism, the problem of "being and thought," and the role of a "naïve realism" within philosophical inquiry:

> [T]he central notion of modern philosophy since Kant seems to be that of *correlation*. By "correlation" we mean the idea according to which we only ever have access to the correlation between thinking and being, and never to either term considered apart from the other. We will henceforth call *correlationism* any current of thought which maintains the unsurpassable character of the correlation so defined. Consequently, it becomes possible to say that every philosophy which disavows naïve realism has become a variant of correlationism.[9]

Readers will enjoy the essay in this volume by Jacob Lautrup and Lars Lodberg who challenge Meillassoux's use of 'correlationism' as a term of art to misrepresent not only Kant's own thought, but also the significance of transcendental philosophy in general.[10] My mutual interest here, as well as my critique of the forgoing formulation, is in asking whether Meillassoux elides the fact that Kant had already offered the resources for this kind of "access" to thought and being "apart from the other" (and—in due course—I'll discuss what Hegel had to say about "*irremediable* realism" when it devolves into an object-obsessed ontology with a similar desideratum to that expressed here).

Our approach to this problem of "thinking" the real outside our direct experience of it should bear in mind some crucially helpful distinctions Kant had offered in his critical philosophy—distinctions that I find are always missed in conversations about speculative realism (as well as object-oriented ontology).[11] That is, in the *Critique of Pure Reason*, Kant poses "knowing" and "thinking" as distinct activities, especially when it comes to what is, for him, the problem of "reality" outside of our minds—that is, the question of "things in themselves." Kant, in this regard, makes a signal distinction:

> But our further contention must also be duly borne in mind, namely, that though we cannot *know* [erkennen] these objects [Gegenstände] as things in themselves [Dinge an sich selbst], we must yet be in a position at least to *think* [denken] them as things in themselves; otherwise we should be landed in the absurd conclusion that there can be appearance without anything that appears.[12]

This distinction between knowing—rather, "experiencing"—things in themselves and "thinking" them is extremely crucial and would continuously fascinate Kant.

Indeed, in the *Critique of Judgement*, what's called the "third critique," Kant pursues even farther the dynamic between "knowing" and "thinking," which demonstrates quite how he became increasingly interested in the capacity for thinking what lies beyond in the supersensible realm. In this text, "knowing" or "cognizing" describes the insights about "experience" found in the first critique, which now stands as the default-setting epistemology against which the "analytic of the sublime" is conducted.[13] And, naturally, "thinking" describes the thought of what cannot be experienced, a "thinking" beyond the limit of knowing that enables reflection on the noumena, which may in some fashion be thought through the idea of the supersensible.

Yet before we even enter into the possibilities for "thinking," it's important to remember that Kant asserts that there is something we can "know" (erkennen) that survives the transit from the noumenal to phenomenal realm:

> Given a multiplicity of the homogeneous together constituting one thing, and we may at once cognize [erkennen] from the thing itself [aus dem Dinge selbst] that it is a *magnitude* (*quantum*). No comparison with other things is required.[14]

We can know or "cognize" from the thing in itself that it has magnitude—and of course, so much else, like volume, extension, and other *quantitative* attributes. Kant is sure to say that—lacking a way to compare this pure magnitude to another (thing of) magnitude—we have no "absolute" knowledge in this instance of its exact size: "[W]e see that the computation of the magnitude of phenomena is, in all cases, utterly incapable of affording us any absolute concept [absoluten Begriff] of a magnitude, and can, instead, only afford one that is always based on comparison."[15] Apart from Kant lacking the resources of more recent geometries like conformal mapping for thinking the mathematical real (in a way not pursued by Meillasoux), he nonetheless offers us here an instructive passage. For on the one hand it lays out clearly just one of the dynamics between noumena and phenomena—what is fully given to appearances from the thing itself, and what is not—and on the other hand it opens the door to a kind of mental habit, called "thinking" that's different from "knowing" or "cognizing."

Farther in the *Critique of Judgement*, for example, Kant turns to the capacity of "thinking" the supersensible to elaborate on just what he means by this bold claim of thinking magnitude, *as it is*, in the noumenal domain:

> But the point of capital importance is that the mere ability even to think it as a *whole* indicates a faculty of mind transcending every standard of the senses. For the latter would entail a comprehension yielding as unit a standard bearing to the infinite a definite ratio expressible in numbers, which is impossible. Still the *mere ability even to think* [Das gegebene Unendliche aber dennoch ohne Widerspruch *auch nur denken zu können*] the given infinite without contradiction, is something that requires the presence in the human mind of a faculty that is itself supersensible [übersinnlich]. For it is only through this faculty and its idea of a noumenon [dessen Idee eines Noumenons], which latter, while not itself admitting of any intuition, is yet introduced as substrate underlying the intuition of the world as mere phenomenon, that the infinite of the sensible world, in the pure intellectual estimation of magnitude, is *completely* comprehended *under* a concept, although in the mathematical estimation *by means of numerical concepts* it can never be completely thought.[16]

You can see how "thinking" and "knowing" operate in tandem (the latter rendering experience seamless as a "synthesis"). Kant is self-aware here, as if to gesture to the skeptical Kantian reader of his own creation who will expect him to demean the "mere ability even to think," but he forges on to address this "mere ability" more favorably on the second pass. This "thinking" points to a "faculty that is itself supersensible," a faculty that presents the "idea of a noumenon"[17] (which, true, remains "unknown" [i.e., not intuited]) that—and this is the important point—underlies cognition and contributes to the completeness of comprehension itself. Thinking refines knowing.

For Kant, this "thinking" that subtends "cognition" isn't the stuff only of aesthetics generally—which some neo-realists today appropriate without engaging the *Critique of Judgement*—but also of the sublime generally, and its subtypes (mathematical and dynamical):

> [W]e have only to do with nature as phenomenon, and that this itself must be regarded as the mere presentation of a nature in itself (which exists in the idea

of reason). But this idea of the supersensible [Übersinnlichen], which no doubt we cannot further determine—so that we cannot *cognize* [erkennen] nature as its presentation, but only *think* [denken] it as such—is awakened in us by an object [Gegenstand] the aesthetic judging of which strains the imagination to its utmost, whether in respect of its extension (mathematical), or of its might over the mind (dynamical).[18]

And there again we have our distinction between "knowing" (or "cognizing") and "thinking," but a distinction that identifies their interaction, *which is necessary if there is to be an aesthetics at all*, not only an aesthetics in the broadest acceptation of the term (the apprehension of the sensuous) but to the formation of a thought *discipline* called philosophy.[19]

Perhaps, however, Kant begins to think too expansively and starts to talk fast and loose, letting slip into this discourse about art such key terms like "the thing in itself." Letting it rip, he talks about speech and gesticulation this way:

> The justification […] of bringing formative art (by analogy) under a common head with gesture in a speech, lies in the fact that through these figures the spirit of the artist furnishes a bodily expression for the substance and character of his thought, and makes the thing itself speak, as it were, in mimic language [die Sache selbst gleichsam mimisch sprechen macht]—a very common play of our fantasy that attributes to lifeless things a spirit suitable to their form, and that uses them as its mouthpiece.[20]

What? The thing itself speaks, the ancient and medieval trope of the "call" of things?[21] An epistemological bridge too far, Kant, no? Perhaps he gets a pass here in not using the signal term, "Ding an sich," but that may not make a difference to our reading, because elsewhere he describes "die Sache selbst" as exactly the thing outside of its conceptualization, i.e., outside of experience (and the latter is a phrase Hegel himself picks up and develops).[22]

Yet Kant can be forgiven for the symptomatic slip in a rare moment of excitement, insofar as it only elevates the capacity of art, philosophy, and language to help with the apprehension of the supersensible, which he can describe effectively and more precisely in his remarks about what words are useful for thinking the real, the noumenal, in the manner of *indirection*:

> In language we have many such indirect presentations modelled upon an analogy enabling the expression in question to contain, not the proper schema for the concept, but merely a symbol for reflection. Thus the words *ground* (support, basis), *to depend* (to be held up from above), to *flow* from (instead of to follow), *substance* (as Locke puts it: the support of accidents), and numberless others, are not schematic, but rather symbolic hypotyposes, and express concepts without employing a direct intuition for the purpose, but only drawing upon an analogy with one, i.e. transferring the reflection upon an object of intuition to quite

a new concept, and one with which perhaps no intuition could ever directly correspond [nie eine Anschauung direkt korrespondieren kann].[23]

Catch that? There is no "direct correspondence" here, and so no "correlationism." Again, language, analogy, ideas, and *indirection*: we have our own philosophical terms that assist in "thinking" the realities of things in themselves, even if such linguistic aides are not the a priori forms of experience that help us "know." Such linguistic helps are not (constitutive) concepts that synthesize experience in a way that feels spontaneous to us, but rather terms that can *indirectly* pick something out about the real without knowing and do so as a (regulative) concept that is useful in our thinking, in our philosophy, even if no intuition can "directly correspond" to what's thought. One warning, however: whoever goes too far in this exercise and believes that her thinking is knowing, or that his regulative concept is a constitutive concept, then there begins the problem of projecting oneself into the noumenal realm—the philosopher who consequently "falls into anthropomorphism [gerät in den Anthropomorphism], just as, if he abandons every intuitive element, he falls into Deism [in den Deism] which furnishes no knowledge whatsoever—not even from a practical point of view."[24]

As the papers in this volume of essays show, the problems of anthropomorphism, animisms that amount to deism or mysticism, are what saddle neo-realisms, both speculative realism and object-oriented ontology, as well as the vitalism that goes by the name of "new materialism." Would that all these inventions that hang everything on the ability to "think" the real, even if we cannot know or experience it, began with a close reading of Kant who developed these strategies centuries beforehand. What's crucial to the story of Kant is his strengthening the capacity of aesthetics itself and modes of indirection and analogy to think things in themselves, to bolster, in other words, thinking the idea of the supersensible. With Kant's claims above about "indirection" as a way to think the supersensible, suddenly even the "weird realism" proposed by Graham Harman seems redundant: "The inability to make the things-in-themselves directly present does not forbid us from have *indirect* access to them."[25] Astonishingly, Harman intends this statement as a critique Kant, as well as the invention of some new philosophy. So much for that. And there will be no trophy for trying either, because this is a general problem in the neo-speculative philosophies, which operate as if Kant never wrote about any of these problems and never kicked the door open for thinking what cannot be experienced—let alone ignoring, in Meillassoux's case, that Kant was a first in the thinking the conditions of deep time millions of years ago, such as what the idea of the "arche-fossil" enables (as a part of the so-called "necessity of contingency" that puts "a primary absolute"—"Chaos"—into the ancestral order of things).[26] There's plenty in Kant to work with, in other words, for those whose game is neo-realism. As it stands, in any case, the signature move of these "philosophies" is to simplify Kant, call him a "correlationist," and get on with the project of thinking, as Meillassoux puts it, "the object in itself" and "subject in itself."[27] The "subject in itself?" Let's turn to the subject, now. It's time for Hegel.

The Real Hegel

With good reason Markus Gabriel points out in this volume of essays that an epistemologically somewhat indeterminate field of philosophical conflict.[28] There's still lots to ask about correlationism. For example, much has been made of the *object pole* of the "naïve realism" that Meillassoux proposes as the alternative to "correlationism." That is to say, the conversations are almost always about objects (the "being" side of the opposition of "thought and being"). But there are mostly crickets from this peculiar realism about the *subject pole*, quite how the realist's "access" to objects is not only achieved but described.[29] In their tour-de-force Introduction, the editors Benjamin Boysen and Jesper Lundsfryd Rasmussen make an important critique of these new materialisms and neo-object philosophies in showing how each displays a "radical realist commitment" to "put human subjectivity under erasure."[30] On top of this insight, I think it's fair to add that there still remains a kind of subject within these novel fields. In speculative realism, for example, the subject "is" speculation and calculation itself—"thinking"-strategies and thought experiments about the arche-fossil, above all; the writing of *mathemes*, a close second (oddly and ironically, there are no "equations"). *That* is the subject of realism, in short, who is apparently capable of apprehending the world more objectively, more objectly, than any other subject, all failures of correlationism. Quite honestly, though: a subject who toys with epistemological completeness and speaks about cognitive access just short of omniscience is, in fact, the most *centered* human subject ever proposed. We can't let neo-speculative philosophies off the hook in the assertion that they erase the subject.

Hegel could easily guess that no matter how speculative, new, weird, or wacky the realism becomes, it'll always have a corresponding subject, which is to say—on this topic of correspondence—that the subject is always adequate to the world it projects or pieces apart until, that is, it is not a subject at all, falling into disadequation and noncorrespondence, which is the movement opposite to that of the famous passage from substance to subject identified by Hegel (and associated with Spinoza). This is, more straightforwardly, the movement of dialectics—that whole array of Auflösungen, of dissolutions followed by resolutions that are themselves dissolutions once more, that render the subject always noncorrespondent and inadequate to whatever it posits or perceives.

In other words, there is no correlationism in Hegel because Hegel is always dialectical and never realist. Here springs his critique of the realist modes of perception. Accordingly, in the *Phenomenology of Spirit*, he names this inadequate or, better, *disadequated* subject "Consciousness" and explores all the ways in which it pursues "thinking" its way around, and within, things. At first glance, his chapter title feels like a misnomer because the exposition seems to be about objects—everything from houses and trees, tables and salt, to entities like things-in-themselves in the supersensible beyond. And true to form, this arguably deceptive titling carries over to the three sections within the chapter itself: "Sense-certainty," "Perception," and "Force and Understanding." It would seem that Hegel names these only to say that they don't work so well. The psychological faculty or subjective phenomenon named in the title to each section knows the object world in neither any "correlated" way or for that matter noncorrelated way, even as they all attempt various realisms that range from the commonsensical to the speculative. In sense certainty, for example, Hegel first asks "whether in sense-certainty itself the object is in fact the kind of essence that sense-certainty proclaims it to be; whether this notion of it as the essence corresponds [entspricht] to the way it is present in sense-certainty."[31] Then he runs through ways of gathering meaning from objects through various language strategies (literal, descriptive, and indexical language, for example). Finally, he concludes: "Hence [in sense certainty] it comes to pass for consciousness that what it previously took to be the in-itself is not an in-itself, or that it was only an in-itself *for consciousness*."[32] Similar results are gained in the sections "Perception" and "Force and Understanding": the "truth of perception is its dissolution [Auflösung]"; and "the Understanding experiences only itself" and not the noumenal world.[33] "Sense certainty" is anything but that; "Perception" is misperception; and "Understanding" misunderstands: Hegel is pursuing an object-focused inquiry so intensely that he diminishes the corresponding subject altogether, despite illustrating how such a subject might think a world designed, in advance, for it. Of course, the consequence is that we must quit "Consciousness" altogether, or rather behold Hegel redesign it via a sublation (i.e., "cancelling and raising") to give us "Self Consciousness" in the very next chapter.[34]

Yet as with all things Hegel, the point isn't the beginning or the end, neither the "proposition" nor "conclusion." Rather, it's about the journey:

> For the real issue [die Sache] is not exhausted by stating it as an aim, but by carrying it out, nor is the result the actual whole, but rather the result together with the process through which it came about [...] This concern with aim or results, with differentiating and passing judgement on various thinkers is therefore an easier task than it might seem. For instead of getting involved in the real issue [der Sache], this kind of activity is always away beyond it; instead of tarrying with it, and losing itself in it [statt in ihr zu verweilen und sich in ihr zu vergessen], this kind of knowing is forever grasping at something new; it remains essentially preoccupied with itself instead of being preoccupied with the real issue [der Sache] and surrendering to it. To judge a thing that has substance and solid worth is quite easy, to comprehend it is much harder, and to blend judgement and comprehension in a definitive description [Darstellung] is the hardest thing of all.[35]

As philosophical readers, we have to get real about the thing, *die Sache*: we must not rush to the *telos* but rather "tarry" and linger in the moment. Even so, Hegel fancies the many possibilities of the subject-in-realism, without his taking a snippy Kantian tone about it; because in so doing, he offers formulations close to what would later be called "speculative realism" or "object-oriented ontology" in terms of the problems of "correlationism" they seek to identify in everyone with a "comprehension" and "judgement" declared to be questionable.

Because the two sections, "Perception" and "Force and Understanding," within the chapter on "Consciousness" are crazily detailed and exhaustingly nuanced in the micro-positioning of the phenomenological observer—as if Hegel is constantly adjusting your head as would a hair stylist—I shall focus on them, leaving "sense-certainty" for the reader to enjoy further as a critique of "common sense" realism—that is, a homespun empiricism that morphs into a conscientious nigh academic realism in its talk of universals perhaps capturing the real or for that matter in themselves real.[36]

Perception: Or the Thing and Deception

The section fully entitled "Perception: Or the Thing and Deception" really has the goods because it moves from sense-certainty as a "receptive subject"[37] position to "Perception" as an *action* or indeed very active phenomenology, but with similar realist object lessons at hand: "the object […] is the essence regardless of whether it is perceived or not; but the *act of perceiving* […] is the unessential moment, the unstable factor."[38] This object needs no mind perceiving it to be an essence, and so strong is this point that the titular "perception" is said to be unessential, literally nothing. There are many such statements in this section, which contains the most relevant insights related to talk of speculative realism and especially object-oriented ontology (as a realism) insofar as Hegel exhaustively arranges the relations and nonrelations between thinking and being; and equally, he delineates almost every kind of autonomy possible for objects and their properties and goes well beyond Kant in this manner to anticipate formulations within object-oriented ontology today.

Hegel first presents objects whose properties are not related to other properties but which simply reside within the object "without ever coming into contact with one another" and are more or less "free from the others."[39] One property does not affect the other, just as the "whiteness [of salt] does not affect the cubical shape, and neither affects the tart taste."[40] Hegel calls this unusual object "thinghood" [Dingheit], suggesting that every property is autonomous.[41] Then he explains how this "thinghood" emerges as a "Thing" in its own right. This is a complex object: it is not the "medium" that simply "unites" all the properties into a "One," as if to compress properties together to make them relate to one another. Rather, the "Thing" is a "unity with negation": it is both the aforementioned properties and not the aforementioned properties. It is the properties if the properties belong to it in its sensuous particularity, and it is not the properties if the properties are strictly universals existing also outside of it (as a realism would hold). What this Thing is, is both. Hegel expands this construction to say that what goes for the Thing in its own right goes for the Thing in relation to other Things: "[T]he determinate properties do not only exist on account of other things and *for* other things, but in the Thing itself [sondern an ihm selbst]."[42] Which means that the Thing is given to appearances, "*for* other things," but also withdrawn into itself, whereby the properties are for it alone, as the Thing itself. Here there is no transcendental idealism, where appearances you perceive aren't necessarily the appearances objects give off to you, or to an insect, or indeed another object. Rather, realism is at issue here, for what the thing gives you is what it gives out to all other objects and, as such, things relate to other objects without a mind around to assimilate them into human relation: "Things are therefore in and for themselves determinate; they have properties by which they distinguish themselves from others."[43] Thus the ontological claim: "the Thing [...] *possesses intrinsic being*; and what is in it, is there as the Thing's essence, and not on account of other things." And the properties themselves "exist in and for themselves."[44]

Things relating to other things without a mind around to do the relating for them? That sounds suspiciously like an anti-correlationist position. So let's look at it. Of course, Hegel speaks of the "I" and "consciousness" abundantly in the chapter on "Perception." How can he not? But there's a point where he speaks of "truthful perceiving [Nehmen des Wahren],"[45] which is an interesting if not curious phrase, insofar as it's assigning a strong capability to a kind of "Consciousness" that can even observe objects in their workings with such detail to the point that its own observational activities can recede from view, and where instead the objects themselves can take the stage. The term "truthful" (Wahren) means not the opposite of "deceitful" or "wrong" but rather denotes the sheer facticity of exteriority, an empirical fact that there are things at all, minds be damned. And so as Hegel proceeds in speaking about consciousness in these sections (§122 and §123), he eventually stops doing so in the final third of §123. He peels away from consciousness to describe what's "outside of consciousness" altogether, offering a transparent, or in narrative terms "realist" or omniscient, point of view on object relations with other objects.

Here are the major movements of Hegel's exposition of his, let's call it, phenomenology of the thing *from the point of view of thing*—which I ask you to read as a narrative told from the object's point of view, and worry less on the first reading (at least) of the "what" of the story. Simply follow the thing doing its thing:

> In and for itself the Thing is self-identical, but this unity with itself is disturbed by other Things. Thus the unity of the Thing is preserved and at the same time the otherness is preserved outside of the Thing as well as outside of consciousness [so ist die Einheit des Dings erhalten, und zugleich das Anderssein außer ihm, so wie außer dem Bewußtsein].[46]

> in so far as the Thing through its *absolute difference* [absoluten Unterschied] comes into a state of opposition [Entgegensetzung], it is opposed to another Thing outside of it [hat es sie gegen ein anderes Ding außer ihm]. Of course, the further manifoldness is necessarily present in the Thing too, so that it cannot be left out; but it is the unessential [unwesenlich] aspect of the Thing.[47]

> the Thing is thereby in opposition to other Things [Gegensatze mit andern], but is supposed to preserve its independence in this opposition. But it is only a *Thing*, or a One that exists on its own account, in so far as it does not stand in this relation [Beziehung] to others; for this relation [Beziehung] establishes

rather its continuity with others, and for it to be connected with others is to cease its being-for-itself [und Zusammenhang mit anderem ist das Aufhören des für sich Seins].[48]

Hegel means a kind of "relation" that is not human, in other words not "perceived" (not yet at least), and is certainly not the relation of the Kantian a priori form of experience—"relation," as we know, being one of the major headings in Kant's "table of categories," "Of Relation [*Der Relation*]."[49] Hegel is, in other words, experimenting with pure object relations irrespective of minds, objects relating to objects against their tendencies to withdraw from one another into absolute difference. This is definitionally an object-oriented ontology, if it weren't clear already.[50] Indeed, it's not for nothing that in 2002 Robert Stern described this entire chapter on "Consciousness" as "object-orientated."[51]

But where Hegel embroiders most richly this world of objects relating to objects in speaking about their "*absolute difference*"[52] or, now, "absolute character"— "absolute" being (as above) that Kantian term for what pertains to "things in themselves" apart from minds—is right where the whole project collapses under its own weight, and his vocabulary begins to shift, accordingly, signaling a transition to a new moment:

It is just through the absolute character of the Thing [absoluten Charakter] and its opposition [*Entgegensetzung*] that it *relates* itself to *others* [verhältes sich zu andern], and is essentially only this relating [dies Verhalten]. The relation [das Verhältnis], however, is the negation of its self-subsistence [Selbstständigkeit], and it is really the essential property of the Thing that is its undoing [und das Ding geht vielmehr durch seine wesentliche Eigenschaft zu Grunde].[53]

As the object mode is clearly captivating for Hegel, who expends a good deal of writerly energy to objective description in all its minutiae, he can tarry no longer and thus welcomes back the subject, which is a change signaled by the different terms he uses for "relation"—object relations and subject/object relations respectively: namely, Beziehung (as above) and Verhältnis (here), the latter being the more usual term in his dialectical expositions. It's only after the objects get their due, perform how they must, does consciousness come back on the scene and is named as such, which is the moment Hegel offers a "summary," there for the convenience of the phenomenological observer or reader in speaking of what consciousness (Bewußtsein) experiences as necessity.[54]

As Hegel wraps up his section on "Perception," he bemoans the "sound common sense [gesunde Menschenverstand]" that is "Perception."[55] He says that such common sense "takes itself to be a solid, realistic consciousness [gediegne reale Bewußtsein]"[56] but "is, in the perceptual process, only the play of these *abstractions*; generally, it is always at its poorest where it fancies itself to be the richest."[57] A "realistic consciousness"? Why this phrasing? Because it's a prompt to appreciate his staging of all these "perceptions" in the section on "Perception" is an exercise in realism, in what is an almost exhaustive demonstration of how we can think about things, from the correlationist approach to the anti-correlationist perspective, from taking "thinking" and "being" as inseparable to delinking them altogether in the philosophical exposition, as seen above. You can find in Hegel's section on "Perception" variations on philosophical approaches to thinking objects, like what's known as the "bundle theory" or the "substratum theory" about objects in relation to their properties. Everything is asked in "Consciousness": What constitutes an object? Its properties? Its substrate? Its relation, or lack thereof, to other objects? Its perception? Its sensuousness? How can we perceive objects objectively? What kind of subject is necessary to do so? What does writing about objects apart from subjects even look like (and here Hegel delivers)? It's all there, because there was enough already in the history of philosophy up to Hegel's writing to supply virtually all the options for thinking things within and "without consciousness." And proleptically, he asks, in this section alone, most all of what's celebrated as novel in speculative realism as well object-oriented ontology—specifically, their supposed discovery that "relation" isn't just for human subjects anymore, but for objects, too, that (who?) relate to one another out of our view. He also vitiates avant la lettre the ersatz discovery that you can think the inner dynamics of objects outside of our experience; that objects withdraw not only from us but from each other; and that objects cannot be reduced to their properties.[58]

Force and Understanding

Hegel's not done, however, engaging with kinds of realism, in his day or in our own. In this the third and final section, "Force and Understanding [Kraft und Verstand]," he takes this whole inquiry to another, or rather deeper, level, with such daring claims as Force "must be completely set free from thought."[59] To the extent that this section is a foray into *Naturphilosophie*—and indeed it is in its talk of electricity, magnetism, and so forth—there is a question as to what kind of subject is required here to interpret that which is thoroughly nonsubjective—i.e., nature. Of course, we already can read that the subject will be represented by the faculty of the "Understanding" (Verstand), billed in the title. But to be clear about the difficulties here in constructing a subject at all in a natural philosophy, we recall what Hegel says in this *Philosophy of Nature*: "Nature confronts us as a riddle and a problem, whose solution both attracts and repels us: attracts us, because Spirit is presaged in Nature; repels us, because Nature seems an alien existence, in which Spirit does not find itself."[60] And as he would remark in the *Science of Logic*, there is no "subjective form" here.[61] The natural world doesn't reciprocate in "thinking you back," doesn't welcome you in, and doesn't pulsate with an archesentience that is analogous to our own self-awareness (which is about as opposite to "romantic conceptions of nature" in literature and philosophy as you can get), however much one tries to pressgang such notions into the service of romanticism).[62]

So we have no choice but to work with the "Understanding" as our own "subjective form"—largely because (after Kant, I suspect), Hegel knows that this faculty can engage in "thinking" the real in the absence of knowing or experiencing it and thus may have some success in that thought experiment, while in the process perhaps "knowing" the real anew.[63] And what of "Force"? It's defined as various "matters [Materien]" that happen to "mutually interpenetrate, but without coming into contact with one another [sie durchdringen sich gegenseitig, ohne aber sich zu berühren]." At best, these material nonrelations can be described as "porous [Porosität]"—but the nonsubjective oscillation of these matters between unity and independence, porosity as One and particularity as Many, constitutes the "movement" that is "Force."[64] Let's just say that the "Understanding" has its hands full, and that Force represents a quite impossible, nonsubjective domain that is nature and the supersensible.

So, in "Force and Understanding," we read from the perspective of the "Understanding," which is, again, according to Hegel, your best chance at knowing the real. Enter "realism"—a specific realism where the world "appears" as it really is, where things in themselves and all that falls under the "supersensible" are known through appearances after all:

> The inner world, or supersensible beyond [Das Innere oder das übersinnliche Jenseits], has, however, *come into being*: it *comes* from the world of appearance [Erscheinung] which has mediated it; in other words, appearance is its essence and, in fact, its realization [Erfüllung]. The supersensible is the sensuous and the perceived posited as it is in *truth*; but the *truth* of the sensuous and the perceived is to be *appearance*. The supersensible is therefore *appearance qua appearance*. We completely misunderstand this if we think that the supersensible world is *therefore* the sensuous world, or the world as it exists for immediate sense-certainty and perception; for the world of appearance is, on the contrary, not the world of sense-knowledge and perception as a world that positively *is*, but this world posited as superseded, or as in truth an *inner world*. It is often said that the supersensible world is not appearance; but what is here understood by appearance is *not* appearance, but rather the *sensuous* world as itself, the really actual [reelle Wirklichkeit].[65]

The "really actual," the "reelle Wirklichkeit": before "realisms" emerged (later in the century on into the twentieth century) in opposition to idealism itself, Hegel, owing to his place in time, had no choice but to describe the philosophical habit of thinking the real without the "ism" we know today. So, lacking the same point of view on intellectual history we enjoy now, he can only approach a "description [Darstellung]"[66] of a certain kind of realism and does so, as we'll now see, within the Kantian frame. So here he describes what's involved in *understanding* "the really actual," and he tarries there. "Inner world" is another term for "thing in itself" in the "supersensible beyond"; and that "inner" and hitherto inaccessible world Kant talked about in his transcendental idealism is now suddenly knowable and thinkable—more specifically, "understandable" by a *transcendental realism* Hegel resuscitates (but here does not name), which is the view that appearances are things in themselves,[67] and thus—on his reading—the supersensible is at this moment accessible and knowable, to say nothing of "thinkable."

There's nothing fancy about this viewpoint, even if the phrase, transcendental realism, is. It is simply an elaborate philosophy and empirical science built on, again, common sense or the aforementioned Menschenverstand, and is thus still very much an everyday realism in acid wash jeans. (In fact, Kant describes transcendental realism as a "common prejudice" to take "appearances as beings in themselves."[68]) The fate of this perspective is clear: throw your lot in with "understanding," and you're going to start thinking that the supersensible world is *so accessible* that you can even dwell in it.

> It is manifest that behind the so-called curtain which is supposed to conceal the inner world, there is nothing to be seen unless *we* go behind it ourselves, as much in order that we may see, as that there may be something behind there which can be seen. But at the same time it is evident that we cannot without more ado go straightway behind appearance.[69]

Hegel ends "Force and Understanding" with that declaration, which is also a joke, as if to say, Sure, be a realist, understand anything you like on the other side of knowing, but let's see you go there; let's see you report on your experience in the desert of the real. What's it like cruising "in the void [where] nothing is known," that "inner world"? How is it with those things in themselves—"determined as the beyond of consciousness"?[70] There are no dispatches from such a place, nor of course can there be, which is why these kinds of realism fall back almost exclusively to the subject pole and become a philosophy about philosophy, or rather, a philosophy about itself: hence Hegel's "the Understanding experiences only itself."[71] This is Hegel's version of the Kantian—and now contemporary—critique of realism as anthropomorphism.

Of course, in his definition of realism, Harman, the contemporary weird realist, has an anticipatory defense against this very charge that there can be no reports from the land of the real: "Realism does not mean that we are able to state correct propositions about the real world." Well, then what *does* it mean? The very next sentence yields an answer right from the textbook of Kant 101, if not Plato for Dummies: "Instead, it means that reality is too real to be translated without remainder into any sentence, perception, practical action, or anything else."[72] So *that* is the great new discovery? Behold the reinvented Kantian wheel.

Essays in this volume touch on this very problem of the realist subject from several angles with quite a range of significances. In Diana Khamis's contribution, there is the failure of the subject that is Meillassoux himself to think through his own theses to counter correlationism with all the resources of correlationism (and I'd add, Kant was able to do precisely that). Or in Benjamin Boysen's piece, there is Hans Gumbrecht's desideratum to self-annihilate as the experience of presence and immediacy, existing as a life form that would simply occupy space without doing much else—as close to the admission of mysticism as one could ever find.[73] In Jesper Lundsfryd Rasmussen's chapter, there is Bruno Latour's attempt to break from the enclosed world of modernity in a "never-been-modern" way that happens to be, well, distinctly modern after all, in that Latour applies a modern conception of freedom—drawn from Hobbes's notion of the human subject—to the "much more real" quasi-objects said to be unimpeded in their actant capacities.[74] Zahi Zalloua's exposition of the central problem of object-oriented ontology expresses— intentionally satirically—a certain paradox, where subtracting the subject in fact adds a subject of another sort, the passionate, febrile subject-in-realism: desire for more reality (and less humanity) takes the form of a passion for objects or "object fever," with "enjoyment" as its primary affect.[75] And so intense is this "enjoyment" to decenter the subject that Alf Hornborg's pithy claim could not ring truer: "[T]he ambition to abandon anthropocentrism risks leading to anthropomorphism and fetishism," whereby every object becomes a itself subject—animate and sentient.[76] Hans Ruin, above all, hits the nail on the head in describing the problem at hand, arguing that it "takes little effort to say that one has access to the *real* world as opposed to only a mediated/interpreted world [...]. But stating this obvious fact does not in itself lead closer to its implied reality"[77]—the "claim to access the real over and against its interpretation and mediation, simply in virtue of its claim to do so."[78]

There isn't, in short, a philosophical *demonstration*, as the classic phrase goes in Aquinas, Scotus, and countless others, all of whom take this term from the Greek—all of whom write on subjects about which *they admittedly cannot know*, cannot experience, and thus never really demonstrate. The late medieval version of this problem resonates well in the way—on the one hand, there was university-centered philosophy and theology seeking to *describe* what makes experience coherent, or what makes certain divine ideas real, or what the beatific vision might be like. And on the other hand, there were the mystics falling down and *experiencing* these things and recording them for posterity by their own hand or through their amanuenses. It is no wonder that the medieval philosopher-theologians would accuse these mystics of heresy, time and again—with Marguerite Porete being a case in point—and it's also perhaps an explanation for why "heresy" happens to be a motive category for related speculative fields like nonphilosophy, after François Laruelle,[79] to say nothing—again—of mysticism that at base informs the twenty-first-century speculative philosophies of the real. Hegel, for his part, offers some of his most numinously cultic passages in his tarrying with realisms—talk of the "Eleusinian Mysteries" or the "holy of holies" [das *Helige*]—knowing that there's something about realism and mysticism that needs working out[80]: "[W]e can tell those who assert the truth and certainty of the reality of sense-objects [Realität der sinnlichen Gegenstände] that they should go back to the [...] ancient Eleusinian Mysteries of Ceres and Bacchus."[81] In many respects, all these neo-speculative philosophies have gone back to these premodern modes and came back with a distinctly logocentric and self-centered approach to the world.[82]

Bildung

Jean Hyppolite once said that "one cannot over emphasize Hegel's realism."[83] Yet from none of this should it be decided that Hegel is a realist, even if he writes in the realist mode for several pages as matter of curiosity if not sheer fun. He's quite made up his mind about that particular philosophical "ism," after all, despite the fact that it barely had a name by 1806: again, it had yet to emerge in refutation of idealism in the way it would do with a vengeance decades later. Which is probably why Hegel is usually omitted in the critiques of realism, but like so much of what he writes, he's ahead of his moment and always relevant to our own. And if it weren't obvious enough already, Hegel abandons these realist lines of inquiry and their corresponding consciousness or subject, and proceeds instead to a proper idea of the subject in the next section on "Self Consciousness," centered on survival (let's call it, not dying), desire, labor, the material problem of possession, sociality, struggle, and proper dialectics of identity-in-difference.[84] This move is instructive for several reasons—the first being, more mundanely, that Hegel empties out the subject in that final section on "Understanding" only to return to the subject in the very next chapter in such full force as to speak of "Self-Consciousness" and its patently *intersubjective* features. What a contrast! Second, "Self Consciousness" is significant in the way continental philosophy after Hegel builds on this particular section in the *Phenomenology of Spirit*—especially Marxism, existentialism, and Lacanian psychoanalysis, all with powerful models of the subject in the object world. Third, we can see what Hegel leaves behind and, therefore, encourages us to reject: realism. For him, there is more to the world, indeed more to life, than philosophizing about objects and banging on about your own personal realism—with the implication that recent speculative realisms and object ontologies find themselves rather stuck in a moment, constant repetition of the same idea as if it's still the naughts and you're checking your flip phone at the Wilco show. But in their defense, speculative realisms and especially object ontologies do have a place in Hegel's *Phenomenology of Spirit* as necessary beginnings, as first steps, in the way diapers, pacifiers, mobiles, bulb syringes, bibs, boppies, sippy cups, mashed peas, potty seats, rubber swim britches, abecedaria, stair gates, teddy bears, and training wheels are necessary to one's *Bildung*. You need them but abandon them when you're no longer a baby.

Problems remain yet in respect to what really matters. The pseudo-split between the subject and object, the failure of the subject to know the object completely, the difficulty of the subject to give itself over to objects and become one itself, the undelivered promise of realism—all these tensions and impossibilities run up the rungs to where the greatest problem lies, at the planetary scale of global capitalism and climate catastrophe for humans and animals evolved to the current yet fast changing conditions. It's why Dipesh Chakrabarty for all his interest in speculative realism and flat ontologies stresses here the importance of politics, in the last instance: "The ultimate task—whether we succeed at it or not—is political."[85] In his words, "the reconciliation"—between "social justice" and speculative realism, Latour, object-oriented philosophies, and the rest—"has not been successful yet," which one can either read as a hope that they will be successful one day after so much trying or interpret as an admission that they will never advance beyond failure to truth and praxis.

Notes

1. Jean-Paul Sartre, *Huis Clos*, ed. Keith Gore (London: Routledge, 1992), 95: "l'enfer, c'est les Autres."
2. Charles Harrington Elster, "The Way We Live Now: On Language," *The New York Times*, Sept. 21 (2003), section 6, page 20.
3. Augustine, *Confessions*, trans. Henry Chadwick (New York: Oxford University Press, 1991), 120; see 183.
4. "One certain way to this knowledge is to separate first, the man from the body—yourself, that is, from your body; next to put aside that Soul which moulded the body, and, very earnestly, the system of sense with desires and impulses and every such futility, all setting definitely towards the mortal: what is left is the phase of the Soul which we have declared to be an image of the Divine Intellect" (Plotinus, *The Enneads*, trans. Stephen MacKenna, abridged with an introduction and notes by John Dillon [New York: Penguin, 1991], 374).
5. As Spinoza knew: "this remains to be noted about love: very often it happens that while we are enjoying a thing we wanted, the body acquires from this enjoyment a new constitution, by which it is differently determined, and other images of things aroused in it; and at the same time the mind begins to imagine other things and desire other things" (Benedict de Spinoza, *Ethics*, ed. and trans. Edwin Curley [New York: Penguin Books, 1996], 103 [P59, Scholium]).
6. Immanuel Kant, *Critique of Judgement*, trans. James Creed Meredith; ed. Nicholas Walker (New York: Oxford University Press, 2007), 89/259.
7. Quentin Meillassoux, *After Finitude: An Essay on the Necessity of Contingency*, trans. Ray Brassier (New York: Continuum, 2008), 10.
8. Meillassoux, *After Finitude*, 17.
9. Meillassoux, *After Finitude*, 5.
10. Lautrup and Lodberg, *intra* 161.
11. This is a central point in Andrew Cole, "Those Obscure Objects of Desire," *Artforum* summer (2015): 317–23.
12. Immanuel Kant, *Critique of Pure Reason*, trans. Norman Kemp Smith (New York: St. Martin's Press, 1965), 27 [B.xxvi]; cf. 173 [B165]; *Kritik der reinen Vernunft*, ed. Jens Timmermann (Hamburg: Felix Meiner, 1998), 28. Note that Kant adds this distinction in his second preface to the *Critique of Pure Reason*. It's not in his first preface, i.e. Likewise, in the chapter on "Phenomena and Noumena," Kant cuts some material from the first edition that could lead to confusion (e.g., 263–4 [A245–6]), and all in all offers many new paragraphs—the paragraphs marked as "B"—that elaborate on this (new) point: see 267–70 [B307] and his discussion of "intellectual" intuition (as opposed to "sensible" intuition).
13. See Kant, *Critique of Judgement*, 115 [285], 117 [288], 172 [344–5].
14. Kant, *Critique of Judgement*, 79 [248]; *Kritik der Urteilskraft*, ed. Heiner F. Klemme (Hamburg: Felix Meiner, 2006), 110.
15. Kant, *Critique of Judgement*, 79 [248]; *Kritik der Urteilskraft*, 110. I note here that Kant uses various phases that loosely translate as, or can be understood to denote, a "thing in itself" or "things in themselves," most notably "Ding an sich, "Ding an sich selbst," "die Sache an sich selbst," "Dinge an sich selbst," and "Ding selbst" (as here). To begin with, the following quotation makes clear that Kant doesn't always hew closely to the precise phrasing of "Ding an sich" when he speaks of the "thing in itself." For example,

he changes his phrasing even when precisely speaking about the central insights of his critical philosophy: "This situation yields, however, just the very experiment by which, indirectly, we are enabled to prove the truth of this first estimate of our *a priori* knowledge of reason, namely, that such knowledge has to do only with appearances, and must leave the thing in itself as indeed real *per se*, but as not known by us. For what necessarily forces us to transcend the limits of experience and of all appearances is the *unconditioned*, which reason, by necessity and by right, demands in things in themselves [Aber hierin liegt eben das Experiment einer Gegenprobe der Wahrheit des Resultats jener ersten Würdigung unserer Vernunfterkenntnis a priori, daß sie nämlich nur auf Erscheinungen gehe, die Sache an sich selbst dagegen zwar als für sich wirklich, aber von uns unerkannt, liegen lasse. Denn das, was uns notwendig über die Grenze der Erfahrung und aller Erscheinungen hinaus zu gehen treibt, ist das *Unbedingte*, welches die Vernunft in den Dingen an sich selbst notwendig und mit allem Recht zu allem Bedingten]" (B.xix-xx [*Critique of Pure Reason*, 24; *Kritik der reinen Vernunft*, 23–4]; cf. Rasmussen's salutary caution in this volume concerning the plural form of this phrase in question; Rasmussen, *intra* nn. 9 and 52). Furthermore, as Gerold Prauss shows with statistical stamina, the most precise Kantian wording would be "Ding an sich selbst," which we should read as "Dinge—an sich selbst betrachtet" or "things considered in themselves." See his *Kant und das Problem der Dinge an Sich* (Bonn: Grundman, 1974). Prauss's suggestion here gets at the double problem or, you could say, "reality," of such things as at once phenomena and real objects; or as transcendental objects and noumena. See, for instance, Kant, *Critique of Pure Reason*, 80; *Kritik der reinen Vernunft*, 113 (A38/B55). It's never, in other words, only a metaphysical problem of a "thing" lurking behind appearances but rather one in which we must "consider" the "two sides [zwei Seiten]" (*Critique of Pure Reason*, 80; *Kritik der reinen Vernunft*, 113 [A38/B55]) of appearance—the side of our experience and the side of the object, whatever it really is and however we may "think" it. That second "consideration" is the topic of my treatment of Kant, as well as that, in part, by Lautrup and Lodberg in this volume. For my purposes, when Kant is speaking about the magnitude of a thing (itself), he is attempting to propose a property that traverses the noumenal and phenomenal divide. Though the moment the knowing subject cannot compare one magnitude to the other is when the limit in cognition is reached, this only means that the measure of magnitude is unknown within the *human* frame of reference and doesn't negate the fact that there remains a thing of magnitude among things of magnitude.
16 Kant, *Critique of Judgement*, 85 (254–5); *Kritik der Urteilskraft*, 119.
17 It should be borne in mind that for Kant an "idea" is a "concept of reason," and it serves a "regulative" (rather than "constitutive") function. In fact, his usage of "idea" in this passage from the *Critique of Judgement* is very consistent with the following statement from the *Critique of Pure Reason*, which says that thinking an "idea" basically provides a guidance or even a boost to "cognition" and underlies it in some crucial fashion:

> Although we must say of the transcendental concepts of reason that *they are only ideas* [sie sind nur Ideen], this is not by any means to be taken as signifying that they are superfluous and void. For even if they cannot determine any object, they may yet, in a fundamental and unobserved [Grunde und unbemerkt] fashion, be of service to the understanding [Verstande] as a canon for its extended and consistent employment. The

understanding does not thereby obtain more knowledge of any object than it would have by means of its own concepts, but for the acquiring of such knowledge [in dieser Erkenntnis] it receives better and more extensive guidance (Kant, *Critique of Pure Reason*, 319–20; *Kritik der reinen Vernunft*, 433 [A329/B386]).

And as when (below) Kant warns about "anthropomorphism" when thinking the supersensible, he offers this caution about ideas: "If, however, we overlook the restriction of the idea to a merely regulative use, reason is led away into mistaken paths. For it then leaves the ground of experience, which alone can contain the signs that mark out its proper course, and ventures out beyond it to the incomprehensible and unsearchable [Unbegreiflichen und Unerforschlichen], rising to dizzy heights where it finds itself entirely cut off from all possible action in conformity with experience" (Kant, *Critique of Pure Reason*, 561; *Kritik der reinen Vernunft*, 745 [A689/B717]). Finally, it's worth observing that Kant calls his whole "architectonic" that is the first critique—which aspires to a certain completeness—an "idea": "No one attempts to establish a science unless he has an idea upon which to base it [Niemand versucht es, eine Wissenschaft zu Stande zu bringen, ohne daß ihm eine Idee zum Grunde liege]" (Kant, *Critique of Pure Reason*, 654; *Kritik der reinen Vernunft*, 862 [A834/B862]); "philosophy is a mere idea of a possible science" [Auf diese Weise ist Philosophie eine bloße Idee von einer möglichen Wissenschaft]" (Kant, *Critique of Pure* Reason, 657; *Kritik der reinen Vernunft*, 865 [A838/B806]).

18 Kant, *Critique of Judgement*, 98 [268]; emphasis original; *Kritik der Urteilskraft*, 138–9.
19 A bit later in the *Critique of Judgement* Kant says more about this interaction between "knowing" and "thinking" in the way an "idea of the supersensible" seems somehow to attach to an "intellectual concept":

[E]ven an intellectual concept may serve, conversely, as attribute for a representation of the senses, and so enliven the latter with the idea of the supersensible; but only by the aesthetic aspect subjectively attaching to the consciousness of the supersensible being employed for the purpose. So, for example, a certain poet says in his description of a beautiful morning: "The sun arose, as out of virtue rises peace." The consciousness of virtue, even where we put ourselves only in thought in the position of a virtuous man, diffuses in the mind a multitude of sublime and comforting feelings, and gives a boundless outlook into a happy future, such as no expression within the compass of a definite concept completely attains. (Kant, *Critique of Judgement*, 145 [316])

20 Kant, *Critique of Judgement*, 152 [324]; *Kritik der Urteilskraft*, 216.
21 See Andrew Cole, "The Call of Things: A Critique of Object-Oriented Ontologies." *The Minnesota Review: A Journal of Creative and Critical Writing* 80 (2013): 106–18.
22 "Nun beruht aber alle unsere Unterscheidung des bloß Möglichen vom Wirklichen darauf, daß sas erstere nur die Position der Vorstellung eines Dinges respectiv auf

unseren Begriff und überhaupt das Vermögen zu denken, das letztere aber die Setzung *des Dinges an sich selbst (außer diesem Begriffe)* bedeutet" (Kant, *Kritik der Urteilskraft*, 315–6; my emphasis; see Kant, *Critique of Judgement*, 229 [402]).
23 Kant, *Critique of Judgement*, 180 [352–3]; *Kritik der Urteilskraft*, 255.
24 Kant, *Critique of Judgement*, 180 [353]; *Kritik der Urteilskraft*, 255.
25 Graham Harman, *Weird Realism: Lovecraft and Philosophy* (Winchester, UK: Zero Books, 2012), 17, original emphasis.
26 See Immanuel Kant, "Universal Natural History and Theory of the Heavens," in *Natural Science*, ed. Eric Watkins (Cambridge: Cambridge University Press, 2012), 189–308. And Meillassoux, *After Finitude*, 64–71.
27 Meillassoux, *After Finitude*, 5. Meillassoux's critique of Kantian epistemology—i.e., that the transcendental subject presupposes having a body (25)—was anticipated by Maurice Merleau-Ponty in his text of 1944, *Phenomenology of Perception*, trans. Donald A. Landes (New York: Routledge, 2012), 107–8, 149, 317. It always struck me too that Jean Baudrillard thinks the capacity of "ancestrality" to decenter human subjectivity before Meillassoux's formulation: "The very idea of the millions and hundreds of millions of years that were needed peacefully to ravage the surface of the earth here is a perverse one, since it brings with it an awareness of signs originating, long before man appeared, in a sort of pact of wear and erosion struck between the elements […]. What is man if the signs that predate him have such power?" (*America*, trans. Chris Turner [New York: Verso, 1988; 1986, 3]).
28 Gabriel, *intra* 74.
29 Literary realism was as much a genre of subjectivity, pertaining to consciousness rather than character, as much as it was objectal, ekphrastic, or rotely "realist" in the vulgar acceptation. On this question of the subject, there is the following essay collection that is a true companion volume to this one: *Subject Lessons: Hegel, Lacan, and the Future of Materialism*, ed. Russell Sbriglia and Slavoj Žižek (Evanston, IL: Northwestern University Press, 2020).
30 Boysen and Rasmussen, *intra* n. 30.
31 Georg Wilhelm Friedrich Hegel, *Phenomenology of Spirit*, trans. A. V. Miller (Oxford: Oxford University Press, 1977), 59/§94; *Phänomenologie des Geistes*, ed. Hans-Friedrich Wessels and Heinrich Clairmont (Hamburg: Felix Meiner, 1988), 70.
32 Hegel, *Phenomenology of Spirit*, 54/§85.
33 Hegel, *Phenomenology of Spirit*, 71/§118 [*Phänomenologie des Geistes*, 84]; 82/§136; 103/§165.
34 Though Hegel does this rather abruptly in the transition from one chapter to the next, from—that is—"Consciousness" to "Self Consciousness."
35 Hegel *Phenomenology of Spirit*, 2–3/§3; *Phänomenologie des Geistes*, 4; 5.
36 John Niemeyer Findlay, who supplies an "analysis" in the most used English edition of this text, is rightly prompted to speak of realism when interpreting the section on "sense-certainty," stating that "[r]ealism is thus not an imposed theory but part and parcel of our most elementary experiences" (Hegel, *Phenomenology of Spirit*, 508).
37 Hegel, *Phenomenology of Spirit*, 58/§90.
38 Hegel, *Phenomenology of Spirit*, 67/§112; emphasis original.
39 Hegel, *Phenomenology of Spirit*, 68/§113.
40 Hegel, *Phenomenology of Spirit*, 68–9.
41 Hegel, *Phenomenology of Spirit*, 69; *Phänomenologie des Geistes*, 81.
42 Hegel, *Phenomenology of Spirit*, 73/§120; *Phänomenologie des Geistes*, 85.
43 Hegel, *Phenomenology of Spirit*, 73/§120.

44 Hegel, *Phenomenology of Spirit*, 73/§120.
45 "Consciousness thus finds [...] that not only *its* truthful perceiving [...] contains the *distinct moments of apprehension and withdrawal into itself*, but rather that the truth itself, the Thing, reveals itself in this twofold way" (Hegel, *Phenomenology of Spirit*, 74/§122; *Phänomenologie des Geistes*, 86).
46 Hegel, *Phenomenology of Spirit*, 75/§123; *Phänomenologie des Geistes*, 87.
47 Hegel, *Phenomenology of Spirit*, 75/§124; *Phänomenologie des Geistes*, 88.
48 Hegel, *Phenomenology of Spirit*, 75/§125; trans. modified; *Phänomenologie des Geistes*, 88.
49 Kant, *Critique of Pure Reason*, 113 [A80/B106]; *Kritik der reinen Vernunft*, 156.
50 "The more important principle is to put object-object relations on exactly the same footing as subject-object relations. Only in this way can we reverse Kant's Copernican Revolution" (Graham Harman, *The Quadruple Object* [Winchester, UK: Zero Books, 2011], 140).
51 Robert Stern, *Hegel and the Phenomenology of Spirit* (New York: Routledge, 2002), 68. In the same year, Harman released *Tool-Being: Heidegger and the Metaphysics of Objects* (Chicago: Open Court, 2002), in which his "object-oriented philosophy" is first articulated in print (as far as I know); see 219–96.
52 This phrase cannot be described as just another kind of dialectical "difference"—not with the term "absolute" there.
53 Hegel, *Phenomenology of Spirit*, 75–76/§125.
54 Hegel, *Phenomenology of Spirit*, 76/§125: "Die Notwendigkeit der Erfahrung für das Bewußtsein, daß das Ding eben durch die Bestimmtheit, welche sein Wesen und sein für sich Sein ausmacht, zu Grunde geht, kann kurz dem einfachen Begriffe nach so betrachtet warden" (Hegel, *Phänomenologie des Geistes*, 88).
55 Hegel, *Phänomenologie des Geistes*, 90.
56 Hegel, *Phänomenologie des Geistes*, 90.
57 Hegel, *Phenomenology of Spirit*, 77/§131. Notice that Hegel is making a parallel here between kinds of knowing. At the outset of the portion on "sense certainty," he remarks that "sense-certainty immediately appears as the *richest* kind of knowledge" (Hegel, *Phenomenology of Spirit*, 58/§91) insofar as it concerns what's in front of your face, what we observe spontaneously as a "receptive subject," a "pure I," a "natural consciousness" susceptible to what "just happens to us" (Hegel, *Phenomenology of Spirit*, 58/§90, 58/§91, 64/§109, 67/§111). Now, as he wraps up "Perception," which concerns the "*act of perceiving*" (*Phenomenology of Spirit*, 67/§111; original emphasis), he finds this activity to be as limited as sense certainty, even if the former is more agile in its thinking about things.
58 Some readers may know Harman's criticism of philosophies that engage in the "undermining" and/or "overmining" of objects, which I mention not only because Harman contrasts his version of object "realism" against these old methods of defining objects, but because Hegel likewise offers these methods up in order to reject them, in order to experiment with object-oriented philosophy in this chapter on "Consciousness." See Harman, *Quadruple Object*, 8, 10; 60–8.
59 Hegel, *Phenomenology of Spirit*, 82/§136.
60 Georg Wilhelm Friedrich Hegel, *Philosophy of Nature: Part Two of the Encyclopedia of the Philosophical Sciences*, trans. A. V. Miller (New York: Oxford University Press, 1970), 3.
61 Georg Wilhelm Friedrich Hegel, *The Science of Logic*, ed. and trans. George Di Giovanni (Cambridge: Cambridge University Press, 2010), 740.

62　For a rigorous in-depth treatment of nature and spirit, see Adrian Johnston's mighty *Prolegomena to Any Future Materialism: A Weak Nature Alone* (Evanston, IL: Northwestern University Press, 2018).

63　This passage from Kant comes to mind: "For if understanding [au: 'Verstand,' at line 20] thinks [denkt] it—let it think [denken] it how it will—then the thing is represented merely as possible. If it is conscious of it as given in intuition, then it is actual, and no thought of any possibility enters into the case" (Kant, *Critique of Judgement*, 230 [402]; *Kritik der Urteilskraft*, 316).

64　Hegel, *Phenomenology of Spirit*, 81/§136; *Phänomenologie des Geistes*, 95.

65　Hegel, *Phenomenology of Spirit*, 89/§147; *Phänomenologie des Geistes*, 103; trans. modified.

66　Hegel, *Phänomenologie des Geistes*, 5.

67　Kant distinguishes between transcendental idealism and transcendental realism: "The transcendental realist thus interprets outer appearances (their reality being taken for granted) as things-in-themselves, which exist independently of us and of our sensibility, and which are therefore outside us—the phrase 'outside us' being interpreted in conformity with the pure concepts of the understanding [Verstandesbegriffen]. It is, in fact, this transcendental realist who afterwards plays the part of the empirical idealist. After wrongly supposing the objects of the senses, if they are to be external, must have an existence by themselves, and independently of the senses, he finds that, judged from this point of view, all our sensuous representations are inadequate to establish their reality" (Kant, *Critique of Pure Reason*, 346; more generally, see on 345-6 [A369]; *Kritik der reinen Vernunft*, 485).

68　Kant, *Critique of Pure Reason*, 594 [A740/B678].

69　Hegel, *Phenomenology of Spirit*, 103/§165. Incidentally, Hegel's closing passage here motivates Jean Hyppolite to say that the "realism of naïve consciousness leads to transcendental idealism," but that's wrong: it leads to transcendental realism (*Genesis and Structure of Hegel's "Phenomenology of Spirit,"* trans. Samuel Cherniak and John Heckman [Evanston, IL: Northwestern University Press, 1974], 67).

70　Hegel, *Phenomenology of Spirit*, 88-9/§146 is extremely relevant here and deserves analysis.

71　Hegel, *Phenomenology of Spirit*, 103/§165.

72　Harman, *Weird Realism*, 16.

73　Boysen quoting Gumbrecht, *intra* 104.

74　Rasmussen quoting Latour, *intra* 131.

75　Zalloua, *intra* 43f.

76　Hornborg, *intra* 143.

77　Ruin, *intra* 120.

78　Ruin, *intra* 120.

79　See François Laruelle, *Le Christ futur: Une leçon d'hérésie* (Paris: Exils, 2002); *Future Christ: A Lesson in Heresy*, trans. Anthony Paul Smith (New York: Continuum, 2010).

80　Hegel, *Phenomenology of Spirit*, 65/§109; 89/§146; *Phänomenologie des Geistes*, 103.

81　Hegel, *Phänomenologie des Geistes*, 77.

82　See Cole, "The Call of Things: A Critique of Object-Oriented Ontologies."

83　Jean Hyppolite, *Studies on Marx and Hegel*, trans. John O'Neill (New York: Basic Books, 1969), 107; here, though, by "realism" he means Hegel's interest in contemporary history and current events: "To read the newspaper is […] the modern man's morning-prayer: it enables us to find our bearings in the historical world."

84 See Andrew Cole, "The Lord and the Bondsman," in *The Birth of Theory* (Chicago: University of Chicago Press, 2014), 65–85.
85 Chakrabarty, *intra* 185.

Cited Works

Augustine. *Confessions*. Translated by Henry Chadwick. New York: Oxford University Press, 1991.
Baudrillard, Jean. *America*. Translated by Chris Turner. New York: Verso, 1988; 1986.
Cole, Andrew. "The Call of Things: A Critique of Object-Oriented Ontologies." *The Minnesota Review: A Journal of Creative and Critical Writing* 80 (2013): 106–18.
Cole, Andrew. *The Birth of Theory*. Chicago: University of Chicago Press, 2014.
Cole, Andrew. "Those Obscure Objects of Desire." *Artforum* summer (2015): 317–23.
Elster, Charles Harrington. "The Way We Live Now: On Language." *The New York Times*, Sept. 21 (2003), section 6, page 20.
Harman, Graham. *Tool-Being: Heidegger and the Metaphysics of Objects*. Chicago: Open Court, 2002.
Harman, Graham. *The Quadruple Object*. Winchester, UK: Zero Books, 2011.
Harman, Graham. *Weird Realism: Lovecraft and Philosophy*. Winchester, UK: Zero Books, 2012.
Hegel, Georg Wilhelm Friedrich. *Phenomenology of Spirit*. Translated by A. V. Miller. Oxford: Oxford University Press, 1977.
Hegel, Georg Wilhelm Friedrich. *Phänomenologie des Geistes*, edited by Hans-Friedrich Wessels and Heinrich Clairmont. Hamburg: Felix Meiner, 1988.
Hegel, Georg Wilhelm Friedrich. *Philosophy of Nature: Part Two of the Encyclopedia of the Philosophical Sciences*. Translated by A. V. Miller. New York: Oxford University Press, 1970.
Hegel, Georg Wilhelm Friedrich. *The Science of Logic*. Edited and translated by George Di Giovanni. Cambridge: Cambridge University Press, 2010.
Hyppolite, Jean. *Studies on Marx and Hegel*. Translated by John O'Neill. New York: Basic Books, 1969.
Hyppolite, Jean. *Genesis and Structure of Hegel's "Phenomenology of Spirit."* Translated by Samuel Cherniak and John Heckman. Evanston, IL: Northwestern University Press, 1974.
Johnston, Adrian. *Prolegomena to Any Future Materialism: A Weak Nature Alone*. Evanston, IL: Northwestern University Press, 2018.
Kant, Immanuel. *Critique of Pure Reason*. Translated by Norman Kemp Smith. New York: St. Martin's Press, 1965.
Kant, Immanuel. *Kritik der reinen Vernunft*, edited by Jens Timmermann. Hamburg: Felix Meiner, 1998.
Kant, Immanuel. *Kritik der Urteilskraft*, edited by Heiner F. Klemme. Hamburg: Felix Meiner, 2006.
Kant, Immanuel. *Critique of Judgement*. Translated by James Creed Meredith; ed. Nicholas Walker. New York: Oxford University Press, 2007.
Kant, Immanuel. "Universal Natural History and Theory of the Heavens." In *Immanuel Kant, Natural Science*, edited by Eric Watkins. Cambridge: Cambridge University Press, 2012.

Laruelle, François. *Le Christ future: Une leçon d'hérésie*. Paris: Exils, 2002.
Laruelle, François. *Future Christ: A Lesson in Heresy*. Translated by Anthony Paul Smith. New York: Continuum, 2010.
Meillassoux, Quentin. *After Finitude: An Essay on the Necessity of Contingency*. Translated by Ray Brassier. New York: Continuum, 2008.
Merleau-Ponty, Maurice. *Phenomenology of Perception*. Translated by Donald A. Landes. New York: Routledge, 2012.
Plotinus. *The Enneads*. Translated by Stephen MacKenna, abridged with an introduction and notes by John Dillon. New York: Penguin, 1991.
Prauss, Gerold. *Kant und das Problem der Dinge an Sich*. Bonn: Grundman, 1974.
Sartre, Jean-Paul. *Huis Clos*, edited by Keith Gore. London: Routledge, 1992.
Sbriglia, Russell and Slavoj Žižek, ed. *Subject Lessons: Hegel, Lacan, and the Future of Materialism*. Evanston, IL: Northwestern University Press, 2020.
Spinoza, Benedict de. *Ethics*. Edited and translated by Edwin Curley. New York: Penguin Books, 1996.
Stern, Robert. *Hegel and the Phenomenology of Spirit*. New York: Routledge, 2002.

LIST OF CONTRIBUTORS

Zahi Zalloua is the Cushing Eells Professor of Philosophy and Literature and director of Indigeneity, Race, and Ethnicity Studies at Whitman College and Editor of *The Comparatist*. He is the co-author, with Ilan Kapoor, of *Universal Politics* (2021), and the author of *Solidarity and the Palestinian Cause: Indigeneity, Blackness, and the Promise of Universality* (2023), *Being Posthuman: Ontologies of the Future* (2021), *Žižek on Race: Toward an Anti-Racist Future* (2020), *Theory's Autoimmunity: Skepticism, Literature, and Philosophy* (2018), *Continental Philosophy and the Palestinian Question: Beyond the Jew and the Greek* (2017), *Reading Unruly: Interpretation and Its Ethical Demands* (2014), and *Montaigne and the Ethics of Skepticism* (2005).

Diana Khamis received her PhD in philosophy from the University of Bonn. Her research focused on Schelling's late Naturphilosophie and its relation to contemporary speculative thought. Since then, she no longer practices philosophy professionally and is now studying to be a medical doctor at the Radboud University in Nijmegen.

Markus Gabriel holds the chair for Epistemology, Modern and Contemporary Philosophy and is director of the International Centre for Philosophy and director of the Center for Science and thought at the University of Bonn. His most recent books include *The Meaning of Thought* (2020), *The Power of Art* (2020), *Neo-Existentialism* (2018), and *Fields of Sense: A New Realist Ontology* (2015).

Benjamin Boysen is author of *Nothingness, Negativity, and Nominalism in Shakespeare and Petrarch* (2020), *Poetry and Philosophy in Plato* (2020, in Danish), and *The Ethics of Love: An Essay on James Joyce* (2013). He is currently completing a monograph, *The Embarrassment of Being Human: A Critical Essay on the New Materialisms and Modernity in an Age of Crisis*.

Hans Ruin is professor of philosophy at Södertörn University (Stockholm). He is the co-editor of Nietzsche's *Collected Works* in Swedish. Most recent books include *In the Shadow of Reason. Essays on Nietzsche* (in Swedish, 2021), *Reduction and Reflection, Introduction to Husserl's Philosophy* (in Swedish, 2020), and *Being with the Dead. Burial, Ancestral Politics, and the Roots of Historical Consciousness* (2019).

Jesper Lundsfryd Rasmussen is Carlsberg Reintegration Fellow at the University of Copenhagen, *History of Nature: Henrik Steffens and the Foundation of the Modern Earth Sciences*. He is participant and postdoc in the DFF Explorative Network

Transformative Transmissions: German-Scandinavian Intellectual Communities 1790–1860, University of Copenhagen. Rasmussen is the author of *Mythos und Konstruktion. Zu Schellings System des Wissens (1800) und dem Bedürfnis einer neuen Mythologie* (forthcoming 2023).

Alf Hornborg is an anthropologist and Professor Emeritus of Human Ecology, Lund University, Sweden. He is the author of *The Power of the Machine* (2001), *Global Ecology and Unequal Exchange* (2011), *Global Magic* (2016), *Nature, Society, and Justice in the Anthropocene* (2019), and *The Magic of Technology* (2023).

Jacob Lautrup Kristensen is teaching associate professor at Centre for Applied Philosophy, University of Aalborg.

Lars Lodberg obtained his PhD in philosophy from Aarhus University in 2022. His research focuses mainly on Kantian epistemology and its relevance to contemporary systematic philosophy in particular centered on the notion of reflection.

Dipesh Chakrabarty is the Lawrence A. Kimpton Distinguished Service Professor of History, South Asian Languages and Civilizations, and the College at the University of Chicago. Most recent books include *The Climate of History in a Planetary Age* (2021), *The Crises of Civilization: Exploring Global and Planetary Histories* (2018), and *The Calling of History: Sir Jadunath Sarkar and His Empire of Truth* (2015).

Andrew Cole is the Woodrow Wilson Professor of Literature in the Department of English and Director of the Gauss Seminars in Criticism at Princeton University. His recent work focuses on the built environment, architecture, and the dialectic of space in thinkers ranging from Hegel to Fanon. His next book is *Being and Space*.

INDEX

Abrahamsson, Christian 27
Adorno, Theodor Wiesengrund 113
al-Ash'ari, Abu al-Hasan 11
al-Ghazali 11
Allais, Lucy 174 n.8
Allison, Henry 168
Andersen, Hans Christian 2
Andersson, Daniel 152, 158 n.50
Aquinas, Thomas 133–4, 201
Archimedes 132
Arendt, Hannah 104
Aristotle 92, 116, 152
Ashby, William Ross 151
Augustine 187

Badiou, Alain 54 n.4, 79, 172
Barad, Karen 5, 12–13, 19, 20–1, 125, 136 n.3
Bateson, Gregory 151, 156 n.20, 157 n.46
Baudrillard, Jean 206 n.27
Bennett, Jane 4–7, 10–12, 15, 19–24, 27, 29, 33 n.62, 46, 125, 148–9, 155, 157 n.30, 178–9, 182
Benoist, Jocelyn 110–11, 119
Berkeley, George 169
Berlusconi, Silvio 112, 120
Borgmann, Albert 153
Boscagli, Maurizia 25
Boyle, Robert 126, 128–30, 132–5, 138 n.26, 138 n.41, 139 n.55, 140
Boysen, Benjamin 193, 200
Braidotti, Rosi 21, 32 n.30
Bramhall, John 134
Braque, George 79
Brassier, Ray 79, 81, 84, 110
Brown, Bill 31 n.9, 179
Bruno, Latour 8, 11–12, 46, 125–6, 138, 144, 155, 182, 200
Bryant, Levi 22

Cairo, Alberto 26
Chakrabarty, Dipesh 202
Cole, Alyson 28
Cole, Andrew 10–11, 28, 183
Coole, Diana 4, 12, 18, 32

D'Angelo, Diego 110
de Castro, Eduardo Viveiros 181
DeLanda, Manuel 10, 32 n.30, 109
Deleuze, Gilles 109, 114–15, 148–9, 151
Derrida, Jacques 114
Descartes, René 7, 13, 45, 69, 91, 93, 139 n.53, 140 n.62
Diderot, Denis 17
Dilthey, Wilhelm 116, 182
Dolphijn, Rick 13
Durkheim, Émile 30, 153

Edelman, Lee 56 n.70
Ellenzweig, Sarah 27, 137 n.10
Elliot, George 94
Ellul, Jacques 153
Emerson, Ralph Waldo 187

Feenberg, Andrew 153
Felski, Rita 12, 13
Ferraris, Maurizio 79, 85, 109, 111–16, 120, 121 n.3
Figal, Günther 110, 112–13, 116, 120
Findlay, John Niemeyer 206 n.36
Foucault, Michel 114–15
Freud, Sigmund 13, 16
Frost, Samantha 4, 12, 18, 32

Gabriel, Markus 109, 121 n.3, 193
Gadamer, Hans-Georg 113–14, 182
Galloway, Alexander R. 28
Gayk, Shannon 10
Giddens, Anthony 153
Gumbrecht, Hans Ulrich 3, 7, 12, 91–105, 200

Haraway, Donna 136 n.3, 150–2, 155, 179
Harman, Graham 3–4, 6–7, 136 n.9,
    10–12, 15, 21, 33 n.62, 43–50, 53, 55
    n.33, 55 n.44, 55 n.52, 67–8, 79, 81, 84,
    109–10, 121 n.2, 125–6, 136 n.9, 137
    n.9, 178, 180, 192, 200, 207 n.58
Hegel, Georg Wilhelm Friedrich 17, 49,
    79, 85, 112, 178, 188–9, 191–202, 206
    n.34, 207 n.57, 207 n.58, 208 n.69,
    208 n.83
Heidegger, Martin 14–17, 44–5, 55 n.52,
    74, 79, 91, 95, 98, 99–104, 109–14, 116,
    120–1, 152–3, 158 n.50, 172
Hobbes, Thomas 8, 126, 128–130, 133–5,
    138 n.26, 138 n.28, 138 n.41, 139 n.55,
    140, 201
Hollier, Denis 52
Horkheimer, Max 113
Hornborg, Alf 201
Houellebecq, Michel 23
Hume, David 95
Husserl, Edmund 74, 109–110, 120
Hyppolite, Jean 201, 208 n.83

Ihde, Don 150, 152, 158 n.50
Ingold, Tim 158 n.60

Kant, Immanuel 3, 7, 12–15, 18, 20, 43, 59,
    60, 61–3, 69, 71 n.71, 72 n.27, 75–7,
    84–5, 104, 109, 126, 136 n.9, 137 n.9,
    139 n.52, 161–5, 167–73, 173 n.3,
    174 n.8, 174 n.14, 175 n.24, 175 n.27,
    175 n.35, 187–92, 194–5, 197–200,
    203 n.12, 203 n.15, 204 n.15, 204 n.17,
    205 n.17, 205 n.19, 207 n.50, 208 n.63,
    208 n.67
Khamis, Diana 200
Knausgård, Karl Ove 2, 29, 31 n.10
Kohn, Eduardo 149, 158 n.51
Krause, Sharon 24–5

Lacan, Jacques 43–4, 48–9, 202
Latour, Bruno 8, 10–12, 15, 21–2, 28, 33
    n.62, 46, 84, 125–35, 136 n.3, 137 n.10,
    137 n.21, 138 n.26, 138 n.28, 138 n.41,
    139 n.50, 139 n.52, 139 n.53, 139 n.55,
    140 n.60, 140 n.61, 140 n.64, 144–52,
    154–5, 156 n.22, 158 n.51, 158 n.62,
    179, 182–3, 200, 202

Lautrup, Jacob 139, 188, 204 n.15
Leak, Andy 51
LeCain, Timothy J. 179
Lester, Anne E. 10–11
Levinas, Emmanuel 43–5, 55 n.33
Lévy, Bernaard-Henri 23
Lewis, David 87 n.36
Little, Katherine C. 10–11
Locke, John 95, 136 n.9, 137 n.9, 175, 180,
    191
Lodberg, Lars 139, 188, 204 n.15
Lovecraft, Howard Phillips 47, 53, 55 n.44
Lovelock, James 152, 156 n.22
Lukács, György 113–14
Lyotard, Jean-François 1

Malebranche, Nicolas 11
Malo, Robyn 10
Malm, Andreas 137 n.14, 182
Mann, Thomas 113–14
Marcuse, Herbert 153
Marquard, Odo 181
Marx, Karl 13, 28–30, 48, 158 n.50
Meillassoux, Quentin 3, 33, 43, 59–70,
    71 n.17, 71 n.25, 72 n.27, 74–81, 84,
    126, 161–72, 173 n.3, 173 n.4, 174 n.5,
    174 n.14, 182, 188–9, 192–3, 200,
    206 n.27
Merkel, Angela 79
Merleau-Ponty, Maurice 74, 206 n.27
Meskell, Lynn 155 n.4, 156, 157 n.40
Mesmer, Franz Anton 7
Metzinger, Thomas 179
Miller, Daniel 156 n.4
Mircovic, Nicola 110
Moi, Toril 13
Morton, Timothy 6, 7, 21, 33 n.62, 48,
    178–9
Munitz, Milton 82

Nietzsche, Friedrich 13, 111–21
Novalis (Friedrich von Hardenberg) 14
Nye, David 152

Peirce, Charles Sanders 149
Pessoa, Fernando 26
Plato 84, 116–18, 144, 200
Plotinus 187
Porete, Marguerite 201

Rasmussen, Jesper Lundsfryd 193, 200, 204
Rawls, John 26
Rekret, Paul 12, 28
Ricœur, Paul 13, 114
Rilke, Rainer Maria 30
Robbins, Bruce 28
Robertson, Kellie 10
Rose, Deborah Bird 181
Rousseau, Jean-Jacques 17–18, 25
Ruin, Hans 201

Salomé, Lou 115
Sartre, Jean-Paul 44, 49, 51, 53, 54 n.8
Saussure, Ferdinand de 93–4
Schaffer, Simon 128–9, 138 n.26
Schelling, Friedrich Wilhelm Joseph 60–1, 79, 85, 152, 155, 178
Schiller, Friedrich 7, 178
Schopenhauer, Arthur 115
Scotus, John Duns 201
Sellars, Wilfred 79
Shapin, Steven 128–9, 138 n.26
Shields, David 3
Simmel, Georg 30, 153

Spinoza, Benedict de 117, 148, 187, 193, 203 n.5
Stern, Robert 197
Suárez, Francisco 134

Taylor, Charles 9–11, 182
Tokarczuk, Olga 1–2, 8
Tönnies, Ferdinand 153
Trump, Donald 112, 120
Tuin, Iris van der 13

Washick, Bonnie 28
Weber, Max 9, 30, 97, 106, 153
White, Leslie 149
Wingrove, Elizabeth 28
Wittgenstein, Ludwig 13, 120
Wolfe, Cary 150
Wolfendale, Peter 26
Wyk, Alan R. van 6

Zahavi, Dan 74–5, 110
Zalloua, Zahi 201
Zammito, John 27, 137 n.10, 139
Žižek, Slavoj 5, 11, 26, 31 n.9, 49, 53, 54 n. 4
Zupančič, Alenka 48

www.ingramcontent.com/pod-product-compliance
Lightning Source LLC
Chambersburg PA
CBHW052110300426
44116CB00010B/1608